redemption.

A VERSE BY VERSE
WALK THROUGH HEBREWS

JULI CAMARIN

ISBN-13: 978-0615862293
ISBN-10: 0615862292
ASIN: B00J6G2UK2

Except where otherwise indicated, Scripture quotations in this book are taken from THE HOLY BIBLE, NEW INTERNATIONAL VERSION®, NIV® Copyright © 1973, 1978, 1984, 2011 by Biblica, Inc.™ Used by permission. All rights reserved worldwide.

Verses marked AMP are taken from the Amplified Bible. Scripture quotations taken from the Amplified® Bible, Copyright © 1954, 1958, 1962, 1964, 1965, 1987 by The Lockman Foundation. Used by permission. (www.Lockman.org)

Verses marked KJV are taken from the King James Version of the Bible.

Verses marked The Message are taken from the The Message Bible. Scripture taken from The Message. Copyright © 1993, 1994, 1995, 1996, 2000, 2001, 2002. Used by permission of NavPress Publishing Group.

Project Editors: Dave Seawel, Sue Bussey

Cover Art by Juli Camarin.

To My Husband Hector,
Your love & support gives me strength.
Thank you for the freedom to study & write.

To My Cheerleaders, Megan, Gina & Scott,
The Lord knew I needed you!

& Especially to My Friends & Editors,
Dave Seawel & Sue Bussey,
Thank you for your hard work & dedication.
Without you, this would not have been possible!

Contents

introduction

Several years ago, my husband and I were walking back to our car after a concert. We had parked on a hilltop two miles away because of the large number of people in attendance. As we returned to our vehicle we came by a small creek which meandered through the countryside. Because of heavy rainfall, the creek had become a fast torrent of high water.

Some brave souls tried to jump the creek falling short and into the water. Some tried to climb down the water carved earth to walk through to the other side. Some like us looked for a bridge to safely cross over.

The book of Hebrews is like this; it is the bridge that believers must understand in order to safely navigate life. This bridge is the connection piece between the Old and the New Testaments; the bridge is Jesus. Unless you understand the role of Jesus and the better, more perfect covenant He offers, you will be like the people who tried to jump across the creek winding up wet and frustrated.

Jesus Changed Everything!

Jesus came to earth with the goal of redeeming humanity. His short time on this earth changed the course of history forever. His entrance into humanity was the pinnacle of the ages. He came to show us God in a living and breathing way; way we had not previously understood. God's entire nature was made manifest and revealed in the person of Jesus Christ.

Understanding the book of Hebrews, God's marvelous story of redemption, will change your perspective in so many ways. It will solve some of the big questions about God that Christians ask. It will reconcile the differences in the covenants and give you a clear picture of God and what it means to be redeemed.

This book is a verse by verse look at the book of Hebrews with the hope of helping believers gain a deeper revelation of Jesus. Hebrews has been one of my favorite books since I first read it so many years ago. It is one to reread regularly to remind us of the amazing redemption provided in Jesus' sacrificial death and resurrection and the boldness we now have in approaching Him because of His position as our eternal High Priest.

Thank you for joining me on this amazing journey of discovery.

Juli Camarin

historical
OVERIVEW OF
HEBREWS

Author: Unknown; although suggested authors have included, Paul, Barnabas, Silas, Apollos, Priscilla or Aquila.

Date Written: 63-69 A.D.

Recipients: Jewish believers

Major Themes: Jesus' Superiority. God's provision for the perfect high priest and sacrifice in Christ. Believers direct access to God through faith in Christ Jesus.

Background & Setting: This generation of Hebrew believers were familiar with the Levitical sacrificial system. At the time this letter was written, the community of Hebrew believers were facing intense persecution. This letter claims Jesus' superiority over angels and the Law of Moses. Then compares and contrasts the repeated sacrifices of the Levitical system with Christ's one and only sacrifice. This letters explains how Jesus redeemed humanity and how He forever holds that redemption in place by His position as Lord and the Covenant He established with us.

hebrews 1.

THE SUPERIORITY

OF CHRIST

Jesus is the Expression of God's Love Toward Us

"In the past God spoke to our forefathers through the prophets at many times and in various ways, but in these last days he has spoken to us by his Son, whom he appointed heir of all things, and through whom he made the universe" (Hebrews 1:1-2)

I was watching a documentary about the sea. Scientists were studying the life that existed at incredible depths. Most of the creatures that inhabited the deepest points of the ocean still surfaced occasionally to eat plankton and various particles that were produced from the natural flow of life on this planet.

However as they explored these incredible depths, they soon discovered life forms living far beyond the reach of our sun. Until this time, science operated under the assumption that all life on this planet was sustained by the sun and photosynthesis. Needless to say this discovery baffled the deep sea scientists.

Finding these creatures disproved the theory that life is supported by our sun, showing rather that life is sustained by the Son. Jesus is the one who created the universe and who holds it in place by His powerful word. *"He is the image of the invisible God, the firstborn over all creation. For by him all things were created: things in heaven and on earth, visible and invisible, whether thrones or powers or rulers or authorities; all things were created by him and for him. He is before all things, and in him all things hold together"* (Colossians 1:15-17). By these life forms found in the deep sea, science has opened a door for others to understand what believers have long understood: Jesus created the universe, Jesus holds it together, and Jesus sustains life on this planet.

The apostle John told us, *"Through him all things were made; without him nothing was made that has been made. In him was life, and that life was the light of men" (John 1:3-4).* Understanding who Jesus is, is the beginning of life. Not just physically but completely and eternally. Jesus himself told us, *"I have come that they may have life, and have it to the full" (John 10:10b).*

Jesus Helps Us to Understand God's Nature

The Old Testament only gave partial revelation of God's nature, but Jesus gives us the clear and perfect image. Jesus is the expression of God's love toward us. *"In the past God spoke to our forefathers through the prophets at many times and in various ways, but in these last days he has spoken to us by his Son, whom he appointed heir of all things, and through whom he made the universe" (Hebrews 1:1-2).* God has always tried to communicate with us. He sent messengers, prophets and kings to show us His intentions. Each one gave a portion of the truth. But we could not fully understand God's character by the limited revelation they conveyed, so God sent Jesus to communicate His full nature to us. *"No one has ever seen God, but God the One and Only, who is at the Father's side, has made him known" (John 1:18).*

Jesus, the very same person who created the universe, who holds it together by His word, who sustains life on this planet, was sent to reveal God's love to us. Everything Jesus is, shows us the Father in a complete way so we can know and understand Him. I John 4:8 tells us that *"God is love".* Love is not an attribute of God; it is the essence of God. John went on to explain, *"This is how God showed his love among us: He sent his one and only Son into the world that we might live through him. This is love: not that we loved God, but that he loved us and sent his Son as an atoning sacrifice for our sins" (I John 4:9-10).*

The Word Became Flesh

Jesus came to communicate God's message of love. To do this, He entered into humanity and became flesh. The apostle John records, *"The Word became flesh and made his dwelling among us. We have seen his glory, the glory of the One and Only, who came from the Father, full of grace and truth" (John 1:14).*

He came to the world He created with a simple and glorious message, that God loves us and has provided the way for reconciliation through the Son. Jesus came to proclaim the good news that God was not holding mankind's sins against them and He would provide the way to the Father. The messengers that God previously sent forecasted these events and longed to see them transpire. As Luke records, *"For I tell you that many prophets and kings wanted to see what you see but did not see it, and to hear what you hear but did not hear it." (Luke 10:24).* What they longed to see was Jesus, the expression of God's love in the flesh!

Even in the deepest parts of the sea, the creatures that live there draw life from the Son. They testify to this incredible message of God's love in the person of Jesus Christ. He is the author of all things and He willingly offers eternal life to all who call upon His name. *"Now this is eternal life: that they may know you, the only true God, and Jesus Christ, whom you have sent" (John 17:3).* The message of Jesus is clear, He came to show us the Father and to reconcile the world to Himself (II Corinthians 5:18-19). We are forgiven, accepted and loved. Jesus has perfectly communicated God's true nature and character. By knowing Jesus, we know the Father.

Jesus is the Perfect Imprint of God's Nature

"The Son is the radiance of God's glory and the exact representation of his being, sustaining all things by his powerful word. After he had provided purification for sins, he sat down at the right hand of the Majesty in heaven" (Hebrews 1:3)

When you think of God, do you picture him sitting on a cloud with a lightning bolt in hand ready to strike? Many people do. Many are waiting for the day that God will punish them for their mistakes, sins and messes. Thinking it is just a matter of time before it all catches up with them.

Perhaps this imagery is propelled by the notion that God is angry with mankind because of their sins. We look at them, see our failures, where we struggle and assume that God feels the same way. However, these ideas are not the picture of God which is painted in the Bible. We can understand God by looking at Jesus.

Jesus Has Revealed God to Us

A few days before His death, Jesus was giving last minute instructions to his disciples. He told them, *"I am the way and the truth and the life. No one comes to the Father except through me. If you really knew me, you would know my Father as well. From now on, you do know him and have seen him."* (John 14:6-7).

Throughout His ministry Jesus said these types of things. He told people that He was God's son, He only did what He saw God doing and they've seen God by seeing Him. These statements fueled hatred toward Him on many occasions, but He was clear in communicating that He came to reveal God to mankind in a way that had not been understood in the past.

"No one has ever seen God, but God the One and Only, who is at the Father's side, has made him known" (John 1:18).

Jesus is the perfect imprint of God's nature manifest in the flesh. *"The Son is the radiance of God's glory and the exact representation of his being" (Hebrews 1:3a).* Jesus is the visible demonstration of the divine. He is the outpouring of God's radiance and glory. To understand God's full nature, we must look at, understand and know who Jesus is and know what part He had to play in history.

Mankind Grew Out of God's Desire for a Family

God was never lonely. He did not create mankind because something was missing in His life. Perfect love abounded in the trinity from eternity past. God the Father, God the Son and God the Holy Spirit existed in a triune of divine equality and incredible love for one another. Each one completely God and yet one in unity. Their desire to create mankind grew from a longing for a family to share this love with.

God is love and being perfected in love, He created humans with free will. He chose us and in His love He gave us the right to choose or reject Him. God in His foreknowledge was aware it would not take long for sin to creep in and destroy what He wanted to create but chose to do it anyway. The fall of mankind did not catch God off guard. Jesus wasn't an afterthought. He was not the backup plan when sin corrupted God's creation. Jesus was the solution to the problem long before it existed. *"He [Jesus] was chosen before the creation of the world, but was revealed in these last times for your sake" (I Peter 1:20).*

Since Jesus was the solution, the lamb slain before the foundation of the world (Revelation 13:8), God went forward with His plans for a family by speaking the world into existence. The word He spoke was Jesus. *"In the beginning was the Word, and the Word was with God, and the Word was God. He was with God in the beginning. Through him all things were made; without him nothing was made that has been made" (John 1:1-3).*

↳ We have life all because of Jesus -John 14:6

Creation was complete in seven days, and then God rested. *"By the seventh day God had finished the work he had been doing; so on the seventh day he rested from all his work. And God blessed the seventh day and made it holy, because on it he rested from all the work of creating that he had done" (Genesis 2:2-3).*

He didn't rest because He was tired from creating, He rested because it was finished and there was nothing left to make. Jesus created everything with the ability to reproduce itself so that when it was finished He would never have to create anything again.

In the same fashion as creation, it is Jesus who holds the universe in place by His word. *"The Son is the radiance of God's glory and the exact representation of his being, sustaining all things by his powerful word. After he had provided purification for sins, he sat down at the right hand of the Majesty in heaven"* *(Hebrews 1:3)*. Jesus built the world and Jesus upholds, maintains and propels it by His word. Jesus illustrated God's nature to us in creating the world out of His desire for a family, then letting us choose Him.

God Desired to Reconcile the World to Himself

The paradise of the garden didn't last long. Sin crept in and corrupted it while deadening our ability to fellowship with God as He created us to do. God knew this would happen and this is why Jesus was chosen before the foundation of the world to be our sin substitute. (I Peter 1:19-20).

Jesus, true to God's nature, entered humanity to bridge the gap between mankind and God. *"For God so loved the world that he gave his one and only Son, that whoever believes in him shall not perish but have eternal life. For God did not send his Son into the world to condemn the world, but to save the world through him"* *(John 3:16-17)*. These verses should remove the notion that God is angry at mankind because of sin. Because of God's love, He sent Jesus to save the world, not condemn it.

Our Sins are Completely and Eternally Forgiven

As humans we still sin. We struggle with it and feel guilty because of it. As such, we rationalize that our sin is an issue with God. This perspective is what fuels this notion that God is upset with us because of sin. Many feel that God is waiting for an excuse to strike them down. Even believers are sin-conscious before God, but this should not be.

The truth is Jesus has paid for the sins of the entire world. *"He is the atoning sacrifice for our sins, and not only for ours but also for the sins of the whole world"* *(I John 2:2)*. If sin was atoned for then by Jesus' blood we are forgiven by God. Even people that reject Jesus have been forgiven of all of their sin. We know this because Jesus only made one sacrifice, for sin, for all times. *"And where these have been forgiven, there is no longer any sacrifice for sin" (Hebrews 10:18).* Sin is not the issue; the issue is our non-Biblical perspective of it and its effect on our relationship with God.

Jesus, the one who created the Universe and holds it together with His powerful word, is the same one who provided purification for our sins. Purification is both an action and its result. This means that Jesus took away our sins as well as cleansed us from the guilt associated with it. Just as God rested after creation was finished because there was nothing left to create, Jesus sat down at the right hand of the Father because our redemption was completely and eternally finished! The same Word that upholds the universe upholds our purification before God, it is a done deal. *"For God was pleased to have all his fullness dwell in him, and through him to reconcile to himself all things, whether things on earth or things in heaven, by making peace through his blood, shed on the cross. Once you were alienated from God and were enemies in your minds because of your evil behavior. But now he has reconciled you by Christ's physical body through death to present you holy in his sight, without blemish and free from accusation" (Colossians 1:19-22).*

If we are forgiven and free from accusation then the only thing that keeps us from approaching God with confidence is our sin-consciousness. But our purification was twofold; we were forgiven of sin and cleansed from its guilt, therefore we must let forgiveness and mercy overcome any accusation sin has on us. *"How much more, then, will the blood of Christ, who through the eternal Spirit offered himself unblemished to God, cleanse our consciences from acts that lead to death, so that we may serve the living God!" (Hebrews 9:14).*

This is an important truth! Jesus took care of the sin problem. Sin is not an issue with God. This is a radical statement, but one that will change your perspective in approaching God. Knowing that you are forgiven gives you confidence to approach Him by faith. Faith placed in what Jesus did to restore your relationship with God. *"Let us then approach the throne of grace with confidence, so that we may receive mercy and find grace to help us in our time of need" (Hebrews 4:16).*

Relationship with God is the result of knowing that you are forever forgiven. Past sins and guilt should not keep you in chains. This knowledge of God's forgiveness will keep you moving forward in life. *"For if you possess these qualities in increasing measure, they will keep you from being ineffective and unproductive in your knowledge of our Lord Jesus Christ. But if anyone does not have them, he is nearsighted and blind, and has forgotten that he has been cleansed from his past sins" (II Peter 1:8-9).* We are to be God-conscious not sin-conscious.

Jesus is the perfect imprint of God's nature and shows us God's goodness, love and mercy in an incredible way. Since Jesus is seated at the right hand of the Father we know our redemption and forgiveness is secure and eternal.

Knowing the truth about God will take Him off of the judgment cloud with lightning bolt in hand and elevate Him to where He belongs. He is a loving father that tasked His Son with creating paradise, and then redeemed it so that He could have the family He desired. He has done everything possible to bring you into this family, but the choice is still yours. What you do with Jesus is the deciding factor. Jesus is life!

"To him who loves us and has freed us from our sins by his blood, and has made us to be a kingdom and priests to serve his God and Father—to him be glory and power forever and ever! Amen" (Revelation 1:5b-6).

Jesus Holds the Name Above Every Name

"So he became as much superior to the angels as the name he has inherited is superior to theirs" (Hebrews 1:4)

When we think of Jesus, most of the time we think of Him as He walked and talked on this earth. While this is a true and wonderful picture of our Savior, now we can look at Jesus in an entirely different way. With His resurrection, redemption was complete, so He sat down at the right hand of the Father. Now Jesus is both resurrected and glorified in heaven and this position has changed everything including the name which He now owns. God was so pleased with what Jesus did that He has given Him a name far above any other name in existence.

The Name, The Title, The Rank

A name is an important identifier. A name means something. When Jesus was born into this world the angel instructed Joseph to give him the name of Jesus, *"She will give birth to a son, and you are to give him the name Jesus, because he will save his people from their sins" (Matthew 1:21).* The name Jesus is a transliteration of the Hebrew word for Joshua, *'Jehovah is salvation',* or *'is the savior'.* This name was given to the incarnate Son of God as His personal name to show us what He would be and what He would do.

After Jesus reconciled the entire world back to God with His death on the cross (II Corinthians 5:18-19) His name took on a whole new dimension. Look how this passage talks about the power and superiority of this wonderful name; *"And being found in appearance as a man, he humbled himself and became obedient to death— even death on a cross! Therefore God exalted him to the highest place and gave him the name that is above every name, that at the name of Jesus every knee should bow, in heaven and on earth and under the earth, and every tongue confess that Jesus Christ is Lord, to the glory of God the Father" (Philippians 2:8-11).* God was so pleased with Jesus, that His name was exalted far above every other name. This wonderful exalted name secured forever His eternal position, far superior than any other created thing, including angels.

With the resurrection Jesus also took on the title of Lord. He had always been identified with this title while on the earth, after all it was a customary title of respect and many naturally used it when addressing Him. But its association in the Old Testament signified *'Jehovah, Lord God Almighty'.* Jesus also accepted the nuance of the title while on earth tying it back to the Old Testament definition. What is interesting is the fact that after His resurrection, His followers, realizing His deity, never again use this word in the common way. Jesus changed forever the meaning of this word, so that whenever it is used in the rest of the New Testament, early Christian writers only used it to refer to, or address Jesus. The title Lord means *'having power or authority, supreme in power'.* It is a fitting title for our Savior and Lord Jesus Christ. His resurrection and position of authority in heaven is the proof that He now holds the title of Lord eternally.

How can we understand the awesomeness of Christ? Even His name is supreme over every other thing in existence. Paul understood this when he wrote, *"if you confess with your mouth, "Jesus is Lord," and believe in your heart that God raised him from the dead, you will be saved. For it is with your heart that you believe and are justified, and it is with your mouth that you confess and are saved. As the Scripture says, "Anyone who trusts in him will never be put to shame." (Romans 10:9-11).* Our faith and salvation rests in Jesus and His position as Savior of the world. Confessing your faith in both His name and title and what those hinge on is the only thing you need to do to have eternal life.

Jesus holds many names and titles, each one giving us revelation into who He is. The book of Revelation describes a few of the names that Jesus holds. These names are described in chapter 19 where we get a glimpse of the glorified, resurrected Jesus sitting on His white horse. All of these identifiers should encourage and excite us for the wonderful things that are to come with knowing the Lord Jesus and spending eternity with Him. Here is a summary of Jesus' many names and their meanings.

The Lord God Almighty

(Revelation 19:6). Supreme in authority. All ruling, absolute and universally sovereign. Omnipotent. The supreme deity. Exceedingly God. The One true God. Unoriginated in form, immutable, *eternal*, self-sustaining, infinite in knowledge and creative power. Holy, righteous, faithful, true. Full of love and mercy.

Lamb

(Revelation 19:7, 9). In the Old Testament, the sacrificial lamb is a foreshadow of Jesus. In the New Testament, Jesus is presented as the Lamb of God's appointment for the payment of sins. But in the Apocalypse an entirely different word is used than in other passages in both the Old and New, the word found in Revelation is *'arnion'*. We translate both words as lamb in our language. *Arnion* likewise presents Jesus on the ground of His sacrifice but, perhaps more importantly; it shows Him with His acquired majesty, dignity, honor, authority and power as the resurrected Lamb of God. It is a wonderful picture of Jesus and perhaps the best thought of all is that through God's grace our names can be written in the Lamb's book of Life, never erased, because Jesus is the Lamb keeping account.

Faithful and True

(Revelation 19:11). Jesus is called faithful. This means He is trustworthy, sure and true. We can believe the words He spoke to us as it is impossible for Him to lie (Hebrews 6:18). Jesus is also called true, which means He is the real deal, the genuine article and faithful to His Word. What wonderful names to have as they demonstrated Christ's eternal character. Our faith can rest in this as it is part of the glorious name and title Jesus inherited with His resurrection.

A Name Written on Him that No One Knows

(Revelation 19:12). What is this name? The arrangement of the Greek signifies that absolutely no one knows this but God himself. Or as the Amplified points out *"He has a title (name) inscribed which He alone knows or can understand" (Revelation 19:12b AMP)*. Perhaps this name is too awesome for our mortal minds to comprehend. However, the more we know Christ, the more the Holy Spirit will reveal to our spirit this name and its meaning. We can look forward to the day when we are before Jesus and the revelation of this name that no one knows or can understand is revealed in fullness. What a glorious day that will be!

Word of God

(Revelation 19:13). Perhaps this one is my favorite! Jesus is called the Word of God. This is important to grasp because the word used here is the word *'logos'* which means *'expression or thought'*. Jesus was the manifestation of God in the flesh. Full deity in human form. He was the expression of God to mankind. He was the radiance and glory of God in the flesh. Christ came in the fullness of God to show us God in a way that was not understood previously. He was everything that God is, His exact representation, nature and likeness. By knowing Jesus we know God.

King of Kings and Lord of Lords

(Revelation 19:16). On Jesus' robe and inscribed on His thigh is the title, *"King of Kings and Lord of Lords"*. He is the First and the Last, the beginning and the end, the Alpha and the Omega. Jesus will rule eternally as King and Lord. Everything in heaven, earth and under the earth will one day confess this before Him (Philippians 2:10-11). All of this because Jesus is the Savior of the world, He reconciled everything that sin corrupted with the fall of mankind back to God (II Corinthians 5:18-19; Colossians 1:20). Jesus holds the title of King and Lord forever because His work was so complete and perfect, that God the Father bestowed this honor on Him.

Believing in His Name

Taking all of these things into account we can see why Jesus is far superior to angels. Understanding His current position helps us comprehend the completeness of the redemption He provided for us. Now Jesus is in heaven guaranteeing the offer of eternal life made to us. This is the promise, *"Yet to all who received him, to those who believed in his name, he gave the right to become children of God — children born not of natural descent, nor of human decision or a husband's will, but born of God" (John 1:12-13).*

Jesus Came with the Full Blessing and Authority of God

"For to which of the angels did God ever say, "You are my Son; today I have become your Father"? Or again, "I will be his Father, and he will be my Son"? And again, when God brings his firstborn into the world, he says, "Let all God's angels worship him" (Hebrews 1:5-6)

Most are familiar with the 'Christmas Story', the biblical account of the birth of Jesus. How He was born to normal everyday people in the most humble of circumstances. Because there was no room for Him in the inn, He was born among animals in a stable carved out of the earth. As Christians we annually celebrate this story at Christmas time and the entire country enjoys the holiday that has been designated to remember Christ's birth.

We look at the Christmas story from the viewpoint of humanity, in other words from the humble beginnings of our Savior. But Jesus' birth was a celebrated occasion in heaven. He sent a host of angels to announce this monumental event.

"And there were shepherds living out in the fields nearby, keeping watch over their flocks at night. An angel of the Lord appeared to them, and the glory of the Lord shone around them, and they were terrified. But the angel said to them, "Do not be afraid. I bring you good news of great joy that will be for all the people. Today in the town of David a Savior has been born to you; he is Christ the Lord. This will be a sign to you: You will find a baby wrapped in cloths and lying in a manger." Suddenly a great company of the heavenly host appeared

with the angel, praising God and saying, "Glory to God in the highest, and on earth peace to men on whom his favor rests" (Luke 2:8-14).

As the shepherds were lying in the fields protecting their sheep, a host of angels appeared glorifying God for sending Jesus to mankind. The Amplified Bible describes this as the appearance of *"an army of the troops of heaven (a heavenly knighthood)"* (Luke 2:13 AMP). While we might see Jesus' birth as a humble beginning, the reality of it was that God pulled out all the stops to celebrate and glorify Jesus for entering into humanity as the Savior. The message was simple, because of Jesus' obedience; peace was extended toward mankind on behalf of God. He was not angry or upset with us because of sin. Instead He was providing the way to be reconciled once again, through Jesus.

Jesus Has God's Stamp of Approval

From Hebrews 1, we see the supremacy of Jesus. He is far superior to the angels, even the name He owns is much greater than theirs (Hebrews 1:4). In this passage we are reminded that God has called Jesus His Son. Now Jesus has always existed with the Father and the Holy Spirit. He always was, is and will be. He was with God in the beginning and created everything that we see, taste and touch (John 1:1-3). He is a part of the trinity which exists in divine equality. So the significance of Jesus becoming the only begotten Son is realized when we understand that Jesus came to earth with the full blessing and full authority of God. God put His stamp of approval on Jesus and everything Jesus said and did was initiated, backed up and approved by God. What a marvelous thing!

Many times throughout the gospels Jesus reminded the people that what He said He had heard first from the Father. He told them the things He did, was what He saw His Father doing. He expressed on several occasions that He was there to do the work that His Father gave Him to do. This intimate relationship in the Trinity is expressed to us in a way we can understand, the Father/Son relationship. Jesus was not God's servant because a servant does not know what the master is doing. Jesus is God's Son and the Son has the full rights, privileges, authority, knowledge and counsel of God. Everything Jesus heard from the Father, He has made known to us.

No wonder that God announced Jesus' birth with a host of heavenly angels; it was one of the most significant events in the history of humanity.

redemption.

Heaven celebrated this while mankind slept through the night. God has never placed such glory and honor on an angel but He has on Jesus because Jesus is the Savior. What He did for mankind far exceeds anything else ever done. What a wonderful truth to soak in. Jesus, the Savior, was sent by God and now resides at His right hand because His work is finished. Now He is both glorified and resurrected and offers hope and salvation to everyone that calls on His name.

Jesus' Kingdom is Signified by Righteousness

"In speaking of the angels he says, "He makes his angels winds, his servants flames of fire." But about the Son he says, "Your throne, O God, will last for ever and ever, and righteousness will be the scepter of your kingdom" (Hebrews 1:7-8)

I grew up on old movies. I remember my parents occasionally renting a VCR for the weekend from the movie store when we were very young. At that time, they would pick out a few movies to bring home. Most of the time they were old movies from the forties and fifties. Of course we wanted the newer ones but they had a love for the classics and so we grew up on all the greats.

The one thing I remember most about those old movies is the way the king was portrayed. You would never miss him because of his appearance. He was usually donned with a crown, a robe, a signet ring and a scepter. No other attire came close to resembling this picture of royalty. After all, those things are the objects of a king, possessing them speaks to ones position and authority.

This is the picture that Hebrews paints for us of Jesus. By looking at this passage of scripture one cannot miss the kinghood of Christ. The writer is showing Jesus' superiority to angels, mere servants in His kingdom. The contrast is great. On one hand we have the angels who serve the king and minister to Him. On the other hand we have the Lord Jesus seated on the throne at the right hand of God the Father, taking His rightful place of glory and honor. Just as in the old movies I watched, one cannot mistake the king. Jesus is far superior to the angels.

Righteousness Will Be the Scepter of His Kingdom

Not only is Jesus' throne an eternal and everlasting throne but righteousness is the scepter of His kingdom. A scepter is a symbolic ornamental staff held by the ruling monarch. On top is an ornament that signifies their rule. For instance the scepter of King Richard of England contained a cross and a dove, and Edward III had a bear on his. Sometimes the object represented the royal seal but in any case it was symbolic of both their kingship and what it was about.

How wonderful to know that Jesus' kingship is signified by righteousness. To understand and appreciate this fully we must look at its definition from the Vine's Dictionary. *"Righteousness (dikaiosune) is the character or quality of being right or just; it was formerly spelled 'rightwiseness,' which clearly expresses the meaning. It is used to denote an attribute of God. For example Romans 3:5, the context of which shows that "the righteousness of God" means essentially the same as His faithfulness, or truthfulness, that which is consistent with His own nature and promises: Romans 3:25, 26 speaks of His righteousness as exhibited in the Death of Christ, which is sufficient to show men that God is neither indifferent to sin nor regards it lightly. On the contrary, it demonstrates that quality of holiness in Him which must find expression in His condemnation of sin" (Vine's Expository Dictionary of New Testament Words).* All of that to say, Jesus values being true, right, holy, faithful and perfect. These attributes characterize the very essence of Jesus and His eternal rule.

Since Christ's kingdom is signified by righteousness, His subjects, in turn, must value and hold to this standard as well. Jesus told the people *"unless your righteousness surpasses that of the Pharisees and the teachers of the law, you will certainly not enter the kingdom of heaven" (Matthew 5:20).* What a shock this statement must have been seeing how they were the most religious, holy and devout people around. Isaiah put it best when he said that *"all our righteous acts are like filthy rags" (Isaiah 64:6b).* Both Jesus and Isaiah were talking about self-righteousness, the things we do to be right with God. They will never add up because God's righteous standard is far superior to what we are capable of attaining.

The good news is Jesus offers His righteousness to us as a gift. Romans says, *"But now a righteousness from God, apart from law, has been made known, to which the Law and the Prophets testify. This righteousness from God comes through faith in Jesus Christ to all who believe. There is no difference, for all have sinned and fall short of the glory of God, and are justified freely by his grace through the redemption that came by Christ Jesus" (Romans 3:21-24).* By believing in Jesus we are brought into right relationship with God (righteousness). This righteousness is unobtainable by obedience to the law or by our own merit. But if we trust in Christ we become the *'righteousness of God'* (II Corinthians 5:21). Through faith in Jesus we become everything that God requires mankind to be, but could never be on our own. What an amazing truth!

So righteousness is the scepter of Jesus' kingdom. We join this kingdom through faith in Christ and are given His righteousness in place of our sin (II Corinthians 5:21). And when we get to heaven, to the marriage supper of the Lamb, we will be given white robes to wear that signify this kingdom. *"Then I heard what sounded like a great multitude, like the roar of rushing waters and like loud peals of thunder, shouting: "Hallelujah! For our Lord God Almighty reigns. Let us rejoice and be glad and give him glory! For the wedding of the Lamb has come, and his bride has made herself ready. Fine linen, bright and clean, was given her to wear." (Fine linen stands for the righteous acts of the saints)" (Revelation 19:6-8).* How wonderful to know that we have been included in Christ's kingdom through faith, looking forward to the day when we see Him face to face reigning in righteousness forever and ever.

Jesus was Anointed With Joy Far Above His Companions

"You have loved righteousness and hated wickedness; therefore God, your God, has set you above your companions by anointing you with the oil of joy" (Hebrews 1:9)

When I was a young adult, several of the local churches in town got together to pass out the *'Jesus Film'*. They did fundraisers and church members sponsored the purchase of these videotapes. Then they spent a Saturday walking through neighborhoods delivering the movies; it was a small part of a larger operation that happened on a national level. I also remember coming home from work that day to find one of these movies on my own doorstep.

I eventually watched this movie and it was well done. It presented the gospel in a clear and accurate way. But the thing I remember most about this video and the many others like it that have been made, is that Jesus is always presented as somber, aloof, distant and unfriendly. He walks around teaching and healing the sick, but you never saw Him smile. The way He is portrayed makes Him seem unapproachable. To me, this is not an accurate picture of the Savior while on earth.

Scripture backs this up. Psalms 45:7 prophesied that Jesus would be anointed with the oil of joy beyond anyone else who ever lived. This is the passage that Hebrews is quoting about Jesus. He was anointed with joy. This means He was happy, glad, approachable, caring and let's face it, Jesus would have been a blast to be around. I feel sure He walked around with a smile continually on His face. He probably hugged and kissed His disciples every morning. I know He made them laugh, feel special and loved. He saw the crowds come to Him and had compassion on them. He would stand from morning to night teaching, healing and blessing them. Jesus drew people to Him because He was so full of life they had to find out what it was about. He was like no one they had ever seen before.

Why Jesus Was Anointed With Joy

It is not by chance that Jesus was full of joy; there is a reason for it. From the same passage of scripture that is quoted in Psalm 45, comes the answer, *"you love righteousness and hate wickedness; therefore God, your God, has set you above your companions by anointing you with the oil of joy" (Psalms 45:7).* Hebrews 1:9 makes it clear that this verse is about Jesus. The reason He was anointed with joy far above anyone else is because He loved righteousness and hated wickedness.

The Amplified Bible gives a great definition of righteousness versus wickedness; *"You have loved righteousness [You have delighted in integrity, virtue, and uprightness in purpose, thought, and action] and You have hated lawlessness (injustice and iniquity)" (Hebrews 1:9a AMP).* There is a stark contrast between these two extremes. However Jesus' love of righteousness went beyond possessing this viewpoint, it propelled Him to act. He knew we were hopeless without Him because sin had destroyed any chance we had of being reconciled to God. His love of righteousness compelled Him to destroy sin and lawlessness in one act on the cross. Then He freely offered this righteousness to mankind. *"God made him who had no sin to be sin for us, so that in him we might become the righteousness of God" (II Corinthians 5:21).* Now through Christ we are holy and blameless. *"For God was pleased to have all his fullness dwell in him, and through him to reconcile to himself all things, whether things on earth or things in heaven, by making peace through his blood, shed on the cross. Once you were alienated from God and were enemies in your minds because of your evil behavior. But now he has reconciled you by Christ's physical body through death to present you holy in his sight, without blemish and free from accusation" (Colossians 1:19-22).*

This is why Jesus was anointed with the oil of joy far above His companions, because His love of righteousness compelled Him to act on our behalf to remove sin, shame and its effects on mankind. His gift of grace was far superior than the effects of the fall. *"But the gift is not like the trespass. For if the many died by the trespass of the one man, how much more did God's grace and the gift that came by the grace of the one man, Jesus Christ, overflow to the many! Again, the gift of God is not like the result of the one man's sin: The judgment followed one sin and brought condemnation, but the gift followed many trespasses and brought justification"* (Romans 5:15-16). It was reconciling the world back to God that brought Jesus such joy. We are so valuable to Him that He gave up everything so we could be saved.

Jesus wasn't unapproachable, He wasn't unfriendly, and He wasn't somber. He was full of life. He was full of joy. He was full of love. Waking up every morning knowing He was one day closer to dying for us, conquering sin and destroying death. The anticipation of the cross gave Him joy, knowing we would be reconciled back to God.

Jesus Has Given Us His Joy!

"But the fruit of the Spirit is love, joy, peace, patience, kindness, goodness, faithfulness, gentleness and self-control. Against such things there is no law. Those who belong to Christ Jesus have crucified the sinful nature with its passions and desires. Since we live by the Spirit, let us keep in step with the Spirit" (Galatians 5:22-25). As believers the fruit of the Spirit has been deposited in our born again spirits. The fruit listed in Galatians 5 is Jesus' character and His nature. As believers our spirits are identical to Christ Jesus (I John 4:17). Therefore we have His joy the moment we believe. By living after the Spirit instead of the flesh, this joy will be evident in our lives. It will overtake us, it will overflow out of us and it will be apparent to everyone around us. We don't have to wake up dreading the day, instead we can wake up looking forward to life because Jesus lives inside us.

What a wonderful truth to know we have been made like Jesus. As He was anointed with joy for the task at hand, we too can experience this incredible joy every day, every moment of our lives. All we need to do is look at Jesus. *"Therefore, since we are surrounded by such a great cloud of witnesses, let us throw off everything that hinders and the sin that so easily entangles, and let us run with perseverance the race marked out for us. Let us fix our eyes on Jesus, the author and perfecter of our faith, who for the joy set before him endured the cross, scorning its shame, and sat down at the right hand of the throne of God. Consider him who endured such opposition from sinful men, so that you will not grow weary and lose heart"* (Hebrews 12:1-3).

Jesus is Eternal and His Rule Will Never End

"He also says, "In the beginning, O Lord, you laid the foundations of the earth, and the heavens are the work of your hands. They will perish, but you remain; they will all wear out like a garment. You will roll them up like a robe; like a garment they will be changed. But you remain the same, and your years will never end" (Hebrews 1:10-12)

This earthly world is the staging area for what is to come; eternity. It is hard to imagine that one day the world as we know it will come to an end. It won't happen by global warming or nuclear holocaust as the media has suggested. It will happen by fire as fulfillment of the scriptures in II Peter 3:7-13. This world and all material elements of the universe will be dissolved and done away with, melting in the intense heat. What will remain are the things that cannot be burned up.

The reason this earth will one day be destroyed is that it too was corrupted with the fall of mankind. In other words sin destroyed creation as God intended it to be. What we see has been ruined by the decay of sin. But this is not the final word, *"The creation waits in eager expectation for the sons of God to be revealed. For the creation was subjected to frustration, not by its own choice, but by the will of the one who subjected it, in hope that the creation itself will be liberated from its bondage to decay and brought into the glorious freedom of the children of God. We know that the whole creation has been groaning as in the pains of childbirth right up to the present time" (Romans 8:19-22).*

Jesus dealt permanently with the issue of sin, forgiving it and conquering it on the cross. And yet we are still waiting to see the physical reconciliation of the earth back to God, just as we are waiting for our physical bodies to be redeemed; although we currently possess the down payment, our born again spirit. In the same way, creation is waiting expectantly to be restored to its rightful place; a paradise created by Jesus. For this to happen, all traces of sin must be gone, which is why the earth will be destroyed and a new one created in its place.

The Things That Will Remain

Knowing destruction is the fate of the world, the question becomes what will remain after it is burned up? The first obvious answer is Jesus. He will remain. He is eternal, immortal and His rule will never end. He will not and cannot change. The Bible teaches us that *"Jesus Christ is the same yesterday and today and forever" (Hebrews 13:8)*. The book of Revelation, which is a revelation of Jesus, says this about Him, *"I am the Alpha and the Omega," says the Lord God, "who is, and who was, and who is to come, the Almighty" (Revelation 1:8)*. His years will never come to an end. He will reign in glory eternally.

Since everything physical will be burned up and destroyed the only things that can remain are spiritual and eternal in nature. This is one of the reasons we are given a new spirit when we are born again. It is a nature free from sin (Romans 6:6) and it cannot be destroyed by fire. *"And you also were included in Christ when you heard the word of truth, the gospel of your salvation. Having believed, you were marked in him with a seal, the promised Holy Spirit, who is a deposit guaranteeing our inheritance until the redemption of those who are God's possession—to the praise of his glory" (Ephesians 1:13-14)*. If you possess God's spirit then you are one of His. This born again spirit is your down payment guaranteeing the promises of God and a future in heaven with Him.

The next thing that will remain is good deeds. That is not to say, the things you do to earn salvation. For the Bible clearly teaches that salvation is a gift. Nor is it the things you do to win favor with God. Those things are meaningless in comparison to what Jesus did for you. The fruit that you bear by existing and dwelling in the vine of Christ, will remain and last forever. These things are also eternal and will not pass away. The contrast is huge; *"If any man builds on this foundation using gold, silver, costly stones, wood, hay or straw, his work will be shown for what it is, because the Day will bring it to light. It will be revealed with fire, and the fire will test the quality of each man's work. If what he has built survives, he will receive his reward. If it is burned up, he will suffer loss; he himself will be saved, but only as one escaping through the flames" (I Corinthians 3:12-15)*. So the results of abiding in Christ are the fruit of good works brought about by faith. They will last eternally and the reward will be great. The difference in these works is a matter of the heart.

Jesus' Years Will Never End

"He is the image of the invisible God, the firstborn over all creation. For by him all things were created: things in heaven and on earth, visible and invisible, whether thrones or powers or rulers or authorities; all things were created by him and for him. He is before all things, and in him all things hold together. And he is the head of the body, the church; he is the beginning and the firstborn from among the dead, so that in everything he might have the supremacy" (Colossians 1:15-18).

What a wonderful truth to know that Jesus will reign forever, even though the world as we know it will eventually end. How awesome it will be to spend eternity with Him in heaven, a place free from evil, sin, sickness and death. To our mortal brains, eternity is hard to conceive. But knowing we will be with Jesus, I cannot wait to experience every single day of it. Each time I ponder living forever with my savior, I am reminded of the words in the last verse of Amazing Grace, *"When we've been there ten thousand years, bright shining as the sun. We've no less days to sing God's praise, than when we'd first begun."*

I am thankful that Peter's prophecy, of how the earth is destroyed, does not end only with fire but also with a pledge, *"in keeping with his promise we are looking forward to a new heaven and a new earth, the home of righteousness"* (II Peter 3:13). This is where the King will live and all of His royal subjects, forever and ever!

Jesus is Lord

"To which of the angels did God ever say, "Sit at my right
hand until I make your enemies a footstool for your feet"?
Are not all angels ministering spirits sent to serve those
who will inherit salvation?" (Hebrews 1:13-14)

The entire first chapter of Hebrews compares the greatness and superiority of Jesus with the angels. We gain understanding into the glory and majesty of Christ when we use this comparison, because everything about Him is superior. His name, His title, His rank and His position as Son. The work that He has done, speaks for itself. His creative power and His redemptive work have earned Him the preeminent spot in the Universe. In fact the angels are there to worship and serve Him.

Everyone Confesses Christ as Lord

A time will come when everyone will confess Christ's lordship to His face. Currently, He is seated at the right hand of the Father waiting for that day. The day when His enemies will be made a footstool for His feet. No one will escape this confession after looking upon Jesus. His awesomeness will be unmistakable.

This confession will be demanded because of the glory due Him as Savior of the world. *"And being found in appearance as a man, he humbled himself and became obedient to death— even death on a cross! Therefore God exalted him to the highest place and gave him the name that is above every name, that at the name of Jesus every knee should bow, in heaven and on earth and under the earth, and every tongue confess that Jesus Christ is Lord, to the glory of God the Father" (Philippians 2:8-11).* This confession will bring glory to God as He is pleased with Jesus and the work He has done.

The amazing thing about this is that because of His grace we have the opportunity to confess His Lordship now. As believers, this is what we do when we call on His name for salvation. *"If you confess with your mouth, "Jesus is Lord," and believe in your heart that God raised him from the dead, you will be saved. For it is with your heart that you believe and are justified, and it is with your mouth that you confess and are saved. As the Scripture says, "Anyone who trusts in him will never be put to shame" (Romans 10:9-11).* We have been given a choice. We can confess His Lordship now and escape the coming wrath of rejecting Jesus and gain the eternal life He offers. Or we can wait until it is too late and receive the punishment for refusing the Savior and His gift of grace and gain an eternity without Him.

By His position of authority at the right hand of the Father and the confession that will be made by everyone, it proves Jesus' supremacy.

The Believers Position is Also Higher than the Angels

An amazing truth from God's word is that the believer has also been elevated to a position that is far superior to the angels. At the time of salvation we were raised and seated with the Lord Jesus in Heaven. *"And God raised us up with Christ and seated us with him in the heavenly realms in Christ Jesus, in order that in the coming ages he might show the incomparable riches of his grace, expressed in his kindness to us in Christ Jesus" (Ephesians 2:6-7).* This is a past tense event. We are raised and seated with Him in Heaven. Our citizenship is in heaven, this is where we are and where we belong. Many of us look to the time when our physical bodies will be reunited, but the reality is that our spirits are united already and we are seated in heaven with Christ Jesus.

"Since, then, you have been raised with Christ, set your hearts on things above, where Christ is seated at the right hand of God. Set your minds on things above, not on earthly things. For you died, and your life is now hidden with Christ in God. When Christ, who is your life, appears, then you also will appear with him in glory" (Colossians 3:1-4). These verses give us wonderful insight to living the Christian life. We live like who we are: co-heirs with Christ raised and seated with Him, focused on heavenly things.

In light of these truths we see that the believer also has a position of authority superior to angels. In fact, this passage in Hebrews shows one of their purposes. *"Are not all angels ministering spirits sent to serve those who will inherit salvation?" (Hebrews 1:14).* Angels are sent by God to render service to believers. Meaning they are available to us to help us when needed. God uses them in a variety of ways, and seeing how they are sent to serve and help us, shows us our importance in God's eyes.

Jesus Will Hand Over the Kingdom to God

"Then the end will come, when he hands over the kingdom to God the Father after he has destroyed all dominion, authority and power. For he must reign until he has put all his enemies under his feet. The last enemy to be destroyed is death. For he "has put everything under his feet." Now when it says that "everything" has been put under him, it is clear that this does not include God himself, who put everything under Christ. When he has done this, then the Son himself will be made subject to him who put everything under him, so that God may be all in all" (I Corinthians 15:24-28).

Christ was chosen before the foundation of the world to be its Savior (I Peter 1:20). In the end He will hand it all back over to God, packaged, restored and redeemed. What a wonderful and awesome truth. The take away is to evaluate whether or not you have confessed Christ as Lord. His superiority is evident in everything He is and has done. The time is short to make this confession and reap the benefits of it. We have this lifetime on earth to understand this amazing truth of God's grace and accept His free offer of life. Not only does this offer benefit us in the next life, but it makes this one worth living as well.

hebrews 2.

IN SALVATION

Paying Attention to the Message of Jesus

"We must pay more careful attention, therefore, to what we have heard, so that we do not drift away" (Hebrews 2:1)

Jesus came to earth with an important message. The message of God's love and forgiveness. He has shown us the Father in a way that had not been previously disclosed or understood. The book of Hebrews opens with this amazing truth, *"In the past God spoke to our forefathers through the prophets at many times and in various ways, but in these last days he has spoken to us by his Son, whom he appointed heir of all things, and through whom he made the universe" (Hebrews 1:1-2).* Once again, we are reminded to pay close attention to the Son's message so that we do not become complacent and forget what we have heard.

Jesus is both the author and subject of the Bible. We see Him woven throughout the entire scriptures. In fact everything the law and the prophets testified to was about Jesus (Matthew 17:3; Luke 24:25-27; John 1:17; Hebrews 1:1-2). On the mount of transfiguration, Jesus was transformed right before Peter, James and John. His face shone like the sun and He took on His glorified heavenly state while they looked on. What is interesting about this event is that Jesus appeared with Moses and Elijah. Moses represents the Law and Elijah represents the prophets. Both standing there with Jesus testifying that He was who He said He was, God's son. Then the voice of God came out of the cloud that enveloped them and said, *"This is my Son, whom I love; with him I am well pleased. Listen to him!" (Matthew 17:5b).* If Moses, Elijah and God took the time to tell the disciples the importance of the message Jesus came to share, then it is extremely important for us to listen to it as well.

God's Message of Grace

John chapter 3 summarizes the message of God's grace that Jesus came to share in its simplest form. *"For God so loved the world that he gave his one and only Son, that whoever believes in him shall not perish but have eternal life. For God did not send his Son into the world to condemn the world, but to save the world through him. Whoever believes in him is not condemned, but whoever does not believe stands condemned already because he has not believed in the name of God's one and only Son." (John 3:16-18).* This simple truth is so profound. God loves us so much that He gave Jesus to die in our place. He has forgiven every sin ever committed and cancelled the debt that opposed and accused mankind. Sin cannot keep you from God. Jesus bridged that gap two thousand years ago. The only thing that will send you to hell is rejecting Jesus. The only thing that will keep you from spending eternity in hell without God, is accepting Jesus. The gift is free, the choice is yours.

Which choice will you make? Fortunately, God has already given us the answer. *"This day I call heaven and earth as witnesses against you that I have set before you life and death, blessings and curses. Now choose life, so that you and your children may live" (Deuteronomy 30:19).* The answer is Jesus! God has given us the answer He desires us to make. He wants us to choose Him and live.

This is the message to which the writer of Hebrews reminds us to pay close attention. He doesn't want us to miss it or become complacent about it. The message is what Jesus came to share. God loves us. God desires a relationship with us. God wants us to know Him in a deep and intimate way.

How Shall We Escape
if We Ignore Such
a Great Salvation

"For if the message spoken by angels was binding, and every
violation and disobedience received its just punishment,
how shall we escape if we ignore such a great salvation?
This salvation, which was first announced by the Lord, was
confirmed to us by those who heard him" (Hebrews 2:2-3)

I was five years old when I asked Jesus into my heart. I remember sitting
in my bedroom with my mom, my brothers and sister as she explained the
gospel to me in a simple way. I invited Him in to be my Savior that day,
surrounded by my family. We all celebrated together, happy to know that
each one of us belonged to God.

When I was thirteen this truth became real in my life as I started to
understand what Jesus did for me. As I grew, so did my understanding.
Beyond just simply believing in Jesus, as I did when I heard the gospel
message in my bedroom, I began to comprehend it with more than my
head. There was an awakening inside and I knew that this message of grace
was true.

This was because the gospel is confirmed by the Holy Spirit. When we hear
it, He witnesses with our spirit this amazing truth and validates it. Jesus
came to introduce us to this message of God's unconditional love and now
He has sent the Holy Spirit into the world to confirm it. This is why the
message is so prevailing; it comes with the full power of God. Paul reminds
us in Romans, *"I am not ashamed of the gospel, because it is the power of God
for the salvation of everyone who believes: first for the Jew, then for the Gentile"*
(Romans 1:16).

The Salvation Message is Confirmed by the Holy Spirit

Since we have the witness of the Holy Spirit to confirm the gospel to us, there is no excuse for rejecting the message of Jesus. His purpose in our lives before salvation is to lead and draw us to Christ (John 6:44). He works on our heart and brings people into our paths that will show us God's love. So when the gospel is presented to us we are ready to hear and accept it. Then he confirms it by His witness in our spirit so we know it is real and true.

This is truly a great salvation! God's unconditional love and His mercy expressed in the person of Jesus Christ, who came to earth to die in our place, to take on the punishment for our sins so that we could be forgiven and free from its accusation. Now Jesus offers us eternal life by believing in His name and trusting in Him to save us. This is the gospel message that was *"announced by the Lord, was confirmed to us by those who heard him"* *(Hebrews 2:3b).*

A Lesson from the Law

"Anyone who rejected the law of Moses died without mercy on the testimony of two or three witnesses. How much more severely do you think a man deserves to be punished who has trampled the Son of God under foot, who has treated as an unholy thing the blood of the covenant that sanctified him, and who has insulted the Spirit of grace?" (Hebrews 10:28-29).

When the law was given, it was put into effect and ratified by the angels (Acts 7:38, 53; Galatians 3:19; Hebrews 2:2). It proved authentic and every act of disobedience against it was judged and received swift punishment. In fact one of the first offenses after the law was given was a man who was stoned to death because he was picking up sticks on the Sabbath Day, which was forbidden (Numbers 15:32-36). This went against the law and he received the punishment of the law, death. This is an extreme example but the point I am making is that the law, which was put in place by angels, carried weight with God. So that each violation and disobedience received the prescribed punishment, how much more do you think you will be punished if you reject Jesus, the sole expression of God's glory? Hebrews reminds us, *"It is a dreadful thing to fall into the hands of the living God"* *(Hebrews 10:31).*

This is why God sends the Holy Spirit to confirm with our spirit the gospel message. He doesn't want us to miss it! He wants us to accept Jesus, to accept His forgiveness, to accept His payment for our sins, and to accept His invitation to live eternally with Him. He loves us and did absolutely everything to bring us into relationship with Him, but He still gives us the choice. He has made our options very clear, Jesus is the only way. We can choose Him and live, or we can reject Him and suffer the result of that decision.

This verse is a powerful reminder of this choice, *"For if the message spoken by angels was binding, and every violation and disobedience received its just punishment, how shall we escape if we ignore such a great salvation?" (Hebrews 2:2-3a).* Jesus is the only way to the Father. His gift of grace is free. And the offer is open to everyone. The gospel message is brilliant, I pray that you understand it, trusting solely in Jesus to save you.

Jesus; Endorsed by God, Approved by Signs and Wonders

"God also testified to it by signs, wonders and various miracles, and gifts of the Holy Spirit distributed according to his will" (Hebrews 2:4)

In John 9, there is an account of Jesus healing a man born blind. As Jesus passed him, He was urged by compassion to stop and heal the man. He spat on the ground making mud with His salvia and put it on the man's eyes. After this, Jesus sent the man to wash in the Pool of Siloam. The man came home seeing. When asked by the Pharisees how he could see, he related the story to them. Most were amazed and questioned whether or not this was the same man born blind. No one had ever heard of such a thing happening before. They even brought his parents to testify that this was their son who had been born blind. They couldn't argue that he now could see, so they questioned whether he was blind in the first place.

As he related his story, an argument arose because the Pharisees said the man responsible for his healing couldn't be from God as He didn't keep the Sabbath Day. They questioned him about everything, and then tried to coerce the former blind man into condemning Jesus as a sinner. The man's response was amazing, even facing exile from the synagogue, his community and his family. *"Whether he is a sinner or not, I don't know. One thing I do know. I was blind but now I see!" (John 9:25).* This man truly received his sight that day.

Signs and Wonders Shall Follow

The blind man understood an important truth that the Pharisees, who knew the scriptures, missed. Anyone who is sent and approved by God has the power of God to endorse the message delivered. Even the former blind man understood this. The book of John recounts the man's response to the Pharisees this way; *"Now that is remarkable! You don't know where he comes from, yet he opened my eyes. We know that God does not listen to sinners. He listens to the godly man who does his will. Nobody has ever heard of opening the eyes of a man born blind. If this man were not from God, he could do nothing"* *(John 9:30-33)*. The former blind man took the evidence of this miracle and decided that Jesus was the Messiah because signs and wonders testified to this fact.

The Pharisees should have come to the same conclusion since they knew the scriptures. Isaiah prophesied that blind eyes would be opened by the Messiah, *"Then will the eyes of the blind be opened and the ears of the deaf unstopped. Then will the lame leap like a deer, and the mute tongue shout for joy"* *(Isaiah 35:5-6a)*. If you look through the gospels you will see that Jesus restored the sight of the blind, He opened deaf ears, and He healed the crippled, lame and freed the tongues of mutes. He fulfilled everything that scripture said the Messiah would do. This shows God's endorsement on His life.

Proof that Jesus is the Savior

"This salvation, which was first announced by the Lord, was confirmed to us by those who heard him. God also testified to it by signs, wonders and various miracles, and gifts of the Holy Spirit distributed according to his will" *(Hebrews 2:3b-4)*. Here are four key truths to understanding that Jesus was sent by God as the Savior of the world. First it was announced by angels. Then it was confirmed by the Holy Spirit quickening the message to those who heard it. Then it was supported by the signs and wonders. And now, as believers, we are given the gifts of the Holy Spirit.

"But to each one of us grace has been given as Christ apportioned it. This is why it says: 'When he ascended on high, he led captives in his train and gave gifts to men' *(Ephesians 4:7-8)*. These gifts are to show the world around us that we too are endorsed and approved by God.

"Now to each one the manifestation of the Spirit is given for the common good" (I Corinthians 12:7). When we put our faith in Jesus we become part of a large community of believers who have been given spiritual gifts to complement the body and bring fullness to it. Seeing the church operate in this capacity fulfills Jesus' final instructions to the church, *"Go into all the world and preach the good news to all creation. Whoever believes and is baptized will be saved, but whoever does not believe will be condemned. And these signs will accompany those who believe: In my name they will drive out demons; they will speak in new tongues; they will pick up snakes with their hands; and when they drink deadly poison, it will not hurt them at all; they will place their hands on sick people, and they will get well" (Mark 16:15-18).* The church is proof that Jesus is who He said He was. Now we are His ambassadors on earth, proclaiming the message of God's grace which Jesus revealed to us. We are His living, breathing legacy and we are fully equipped to carry unto completion the work of His kingdom!

At Present We Do Not See Everything Subject to Him

"It is not to angels that he has subjected the world to come, about which we are speaking. But there is a place where someone has testified: "What is man that you are mindful of him, the son of man that you care for him? You made him a little lower than the angels; you crowned him with glory and honor and put everything under his feet." In putting everything under him, God left nothing that is not subject to him. Yet at present we do not see everything subject to him" (Hebrews 2:5-8)

Have you ever wondered why there is so much suffering in the world? A common question that I hear both believers and nonbelievers ask is why does God allow it? Why is there pain and suffering? How can a loving God permit such things to happen? Or my personal favorite, why does God cause sickness, disease, natural disasters and tragedies in our lives?

Many wrongly assume that these things are sent from God or that He somehow approves of them. There is an underlying doctrinal teaching assumed in such questions, that God controls everything in our lives, whether good or bad. He lets the bad happen to teach us a lesson. Or He uses them to make us reliant on Him. Even some churches teach that He will put sickness on us so that we submit to Him and repent of the sin that got us punished in the first place. But none of these ideas are scriptural.

Complete Authority Was Given to Adam in the Garden

When we ask how God can allow such suffering to take place, we are blaming God for our mess. He's not at fault. In the garden God gave complete authority and control of creation to Adam.

"Then God said, "Let us make man in our image, in our likeness, and let them rule over the fish of the sea and the birds of the air, over the livestock, over all the earth, and over all the creatures that move along the ground." So God created man in his own image, in the image of God he created him; male and female he created them. God blessed them and said to them, "Be fruitful and increase in number; fill the earth and subdue it. Rule over the fish of the sea and the birds of the air and over every living creature that moves on the ground." Then God said, "I give you every seed-bearing plant on the face of the whole earth and every tree that has fruit with seed in it. They will be yours for food. And to all the beasts of the earth and all the birds of the air and all the creatures that move on the ground—everything that has the breath of life in it—I give every green plant for food." And it was so" (Genesis 1:26-30).

God created everything; and as soon as it was done, He turned the keys over to Adam as humankind's representative. Why else do you think that Adam had the power to plunge the entire world into sin? He had it, because it was given to him by God. This is also evident in the fact that God brought all the animals to Adam to name them. He did this because the animals fell under the authority of Adam, not God. *"Now the LORD God had formed out of the ground all the beasts of the field and all the birds of the air. He brought them to the man to see what he would name them; and whatever the man called each living creature, that was its name" (Genesis 2:19).* He turned over creation to mankind, lock, stock and barrel.

Authority and Dominion Was Transferred to Satan

It didn't take long before sin ruined paradise. Satan deceived Eve and Adam followed suit in disobeying the one command from God not to eat from the tree of the knowledge of good and evil. With that, Satan lawfully became the rightful owner on the lease of the world. He used the system that God set up to take dominion and authority from Adam. God being just and true to the system He ordained didn't take it back simply because mankind had failed.

Now, I must point out that God was completely merciful to Adam and Eve. First, because even though they knew right away the difference between good and evil, they never fully understood the gravity of their mistake. God could have given them full revelation of what the world would become because of sin, but He didn't. They knew they were naked, but they didn't know the pain and suffering that exists today because God was merciful and loving toward them, protecting them from fully understanding the consequences of their sin.

Secondly, even as He announced their punishment, He promised them Jesus. *"I will put enmity between you and the woman, and between your offspring and hers; he will crush your head, and you will strike his heel" (Genesis 3:15)*. In other words, God told them the redemption plan was already in place. Jesus was chosen before sin entered into the picture to crush the head of Satan (I Peter 1:19-20; Revelation 13:8). Eve must have breathed a sigh of relief knowing that the plan was already in place to regain full control and dominion of the earth and to reconcile mankind back to God. And what a marvelous loving God to promise that redemption through their offspring.

As His most important act of mercy on Adam and Eve, He banished them from the Garden of Eden. Not because He was angry and wanted to remove them from His sight. Instead if they stayed, they could eat of the tree of life and live forever in the condition of fallen man. Think of all the suffering and disease we have today, what if we couldn't die? What if a person with cancer had to live forever in that condition, imagine how horrible that would be. So in an act of mercy the Lord banished them from the garden. *"The LORD God made garments of skin for Adam and his wife and clothed them. And the LORD God said, "The man has now become like one of us, knowing good and evil. He must not be allowed to reach out his hand and take also from the tree of life and eat, and live forever." So the LORD God banished him from the Garden of Eden to work the ground from which he had been taken. After he drove the man out, he placed on the east side of the Garden of Eden cherubim and a flaming sword flashing back and forth to guard the way to the tree of life" (Genesis 3:21-24)*. In mercy, He banished them from the Garden so that He could send Jesus to restore mankind back to the sinless condition we were in before the fall. Now that this has been done, when we get to heaven, God will once again invite us to partake from the tree of life and live forever in our perfect redeemed condition (Revelation 22:14). How wonderfully amazing and gracious!

Full Authority and Dominion Was Won Back By Jesus

"What is man that you are mindful of him, the son of man that you care for him? You made him a little lower than the heavenly beings and crowned him

with glory and honor. You made him ruler over the works of your hands; you put everything under his feet" (Psalm 8:4-6).

Jesus came to get it all back! Have you ever wondered why Jesus came as a human to redeem mankind? It is because the world was given to Adam, man's representative. When it passed to Satan in the garden, the only way to lawfully get it back under the system that God ordained, was for mankind to win it back. This is why God said in Isaiah, *"The LORD looked and was displeased that there was no justice. He saw that there was no one, he was appalled that there was no one to intervene; so his own arm worked salvation for him, and his own righteousness sustained him. He put on righteousness as his breastplate, and the helmet of salvation on his head; he put on the garments of vengeance and wrapped himself in zeal as in a cloak" (Isaiah 59:15b-17).* God was waiting for a righteous man to interview, but as He looked He knew sin had defeated us and we were hopeless and condemned. So His own right arm, Jesus, was sent to regain what was lost to the kingdom of darkness in the fall.

From the time of Adam, sin snowballed and each generation became more and more defeated by it. This is why Jesus had to become flesh and blood, so that He was subjected to the same rules that applied to mankind. He had to be born under Satan's kingdom in order to redeem it lawfully. This shows the amazing grace and love that God has for us to subject His only Son to humanity.

Jesus regained full authority and dominion from Satan at Calvary. He did this by living a perfect, sinless life. All of the rules that applied to mankind, applied to Jesus and yet sin never defeated Him. Satan tried to tempt Him and cause Him to stumble but Jesus looked toward the cross as the goal. The goal was to die in our place as the perfect sin sacrifice in order to restore mankind. Jesus became the second Adam (Romans 5:12-21). He became mankind's representative before God just as Adam had been initially. The same law that plunged the entire world into sin was the very law that allowed Jesus to undo it. This is called the Law of Substitution. *"Consequently, just as the result of one trespass was condemnation for all men, so also the result of one act of righteousness was justification that brings life for all men. For just as through the disobedience of the one man the many were made sinners, so also through the obedience of the one man the many will be made righteous" (Romans 5:18-19).*

True to God's nature and character, as soon as the world was redeemed by Jesus and authority and dominion returned, He once again gave it to us. *"Then Jesus came to them and said, "All authority in heaven and on earth has been given to me. Therefore go and make disciples of all nations, baptizing them in the name of the Father and of the Son and of the Holy Spirit, and teaching them to obey everything I have commanded you. And surely I am with you always, to the very end of the age" (Matthew 28:18-20).* As believers we have authority on earth. The kingdom of Satan has been destroyed (Colossians 2:14-15) and we have been raised and seated with Christ Jesus (Ephesians 2:6). Now we are co-heirs with Him (Romans 8:17). He has once again turned over authority on this earth to believers.

Everything is Subject to Jesus

"In putting everything under him, God left nothing that is not subject to him. Yet at present we do not see everything subject to him" (Hebrews 2:8b).

Through understanding this amazing truth of how the world works, hopefully you see that God cannot be blamed for sin, pain and suffering. The real culprit is Satan and the kingdom of darkness. When he gained control from Adam, he had the right to do whatever He wanted. Since he hates us he did not hold back with the evil that we see and this is why all of it exists today.

Now Jesus has regained control and God has placed everything under His feet. But Hebrews tells us that *"at present we do not see everything subject to him" (Hebrews 2:8b).* We still live in a fallen world because the physical world hasn't been restored and recreated yet. As believers, our spirits have been born again and restored to the state they were in before the fall, but the world is still suffering from the effects of sin until Jesus returns.

The good news is that Satan no longer has power over us unless we give it to him. Jesus broke that power and freed us from it (Colossians 2:15). Peter gives us the key to understanding how we have been freed, *"Be self-controlled and alert. Your enemy the devil prowls around like a roaring lion looking for someone to devour. Resist him, standing firm in the faith, because you know that your brothers throughout the world are undergoing the same kind of sufferings" (I Peter 5:8-9).* The King James Bible says that he is looking for someone he may devour, which means he has no power unless we give it to him. James gives us the key to resisting him, *"Submit yourselves, then, to*

God. Resist the devil, and he will flee from you" (James 4:7). Understanding this simple truth will put the devil in his place and he will be afraid of you!

In the end, when Jesus comes the second time, He will restore creation. Then we will no longer see sickness, suffering and death. When the end comes all of that will physically be destroyed and removed from our presence. Then we will be offered the tree of life which was present in the garden with Adam and Eve and now resides in heaven with God (Revelation 22:14). Imagine what it would have been like if they would have eaten of this tree in the first place instead of the other one. We would have skipped all of this and would be enjoying paradise right now. Thankfully Jesus offers us a second chance. Thankfully He became our second Adam to restore us back to God where He waits for us to join Him for eternity.

Jesus is the Only Way to Heaven

"But we see Jesus, who was made a little lower than the angels, now crowned with glory and honor because he suffered death, so that by the grace of God he might taste death for everyone" (Hebrews 2:9)

Several years back I was in a small group discussion and the topic was salvation. Most everyone in the group believed the same thing about Jesus. But there was one individual that did not believe in absolute truth, so the fact that Jesus was the only way to heaven was impossible for her to accept. Rather she believed that there were several ways to get to heaven and whatever you decided to follow would work for you. So if you liked the teachings of Buddha then by following His way, it was possible to achieve salvation. If the Hindu teachings are what you believed then somehow God honored that if you remained true to those things and wholeheartedly followed that way.

However the Bible says in Acts 4:12, *"Salvation is found in no one else, for there is no other name under heaven given to men by which we must be saved."* This is a hard truth for many, like my friend, but it doesn't nullify the fact; Jesus is the only way to heaven. To understand this, we will look at the punishment for sin and how Jesus experienced death for everyone so through Him we can be free from its accusation.

Jesus Tasted Death for Every Individual Person

With the fall of mankind, death entered into the picture. Not just physical death but eternal death; eternal separation from God. Sin ruined everything. God, being holy, could not tolerate sin and its effects, nor could He allow it to taint Heaven as it did this earthly creation. But He still loved us and wanted to fellowship with us just as He did with Adam and Eve. This is why He sent Jesus to deal with the issue of sin once and for all. I John makes this very clear, *"But you know that he appeared so that he might take away our sins. And in him is no sin" (I John 3:5).* John goes on to explain why He came to do this, *"The reason the Son of God appeared was to destroy the devil's work (I John 3:8b).* He wanted the power of sin over us destroyed so it would no longer be a barrier between us and the Father.

The prescribed punishment for sin is death (Romans 6:23), so Jesus tasted death for everyone so that we could escape it. When He died for the sins of the entire world (I John 2:2), He took them on His body and essentially became sin (II Corinthians 5:21). He dealt with the sin issue once and for all. This is a radical statement for some, but sin is not an issue with God. Every sin, past, present and future has been paid for by Jesus and forgiven by God. The punishment for sin was placed on Jesus. He tasted death in our place. *"All this is from God, who reconciled us to himself through Christ and gave us the ministry of reconciliation: that God was reconciling the world to himself in Christ, not counting men's sins against them. And he has committed to us the message of reconciliation" (II Corinthians 5:18-19).* This is an amazing truth; God does not count mankind's sins against them. Even those who do not believe in Jesus are forgiven. All that remains then, is the requirement that we accept God's gift of forgiveness through Jesus.

This is why Jesus is the only way to God, because He is the only one who provided the way to be reconciled to the Father by taking our punishment for sin. *"For Christ's love compels us, because we are convinced that one died for all, and therefore all died" (II Corinthians 5:14).* If death is the prescribed punishment for sin, then by dying the punishment has been satisfied. Through Christ the penalty has been paid.

Sin Does Not Send You to Hell, Rejecting Jesus Does

"For God did not send his Son into the world to condemn the world, but to save the world through him. Whoever believes in him is not condemned, but whoever does not believe stands condemned already because he has not believed in the name of God's one and only Son" (John 3:17-18).

Many assume that sin is what sends a person to hell. But sin has been paid for by Jesus, therefore the only thing that condemns a person is rejecting the payment for sin. Jesus was the payment. God provided the way in Jesus so to reject Him you are rejecting the only way for salvation. This is a hard truth for some who look for multiple ways to heaven, but Jesus is the only one who tasted death in our place so we could be completely forgiven and righteous before God. God didn't see the need to provide a different way when He started with the perfect way.

Jesus Saves

"For if, when we were God's enemies, we were reconciled to him through the death of his Son, how much more, having been reconciled, shall we be saved through his life!" (Romans 5:10).

The most amazing thing about Jesus is the abundant life He offers to us. It is not just about getting to heaven as the end goal, it is certainly a plus, but it is about experiencing Him in this life. Jesus promised us a full and abundant life right now (John 10:10). By believing, clinging to and relying on Him we are saved and filled to fullness of God. When we were His enemies and ruined by sin, God sent Jesus. So now we can rest in the fact that we are completely forgiven and righteous before Him, and this perspective changes everything.

Jesus' Role as Our Faithful High Priest

"In bringing many sons to glory, it was fitting that God, for whom and through whom everything exists, should make the author of their salvation perfect through suffering" (Hebrews 2:10)

Do you wonder why Jesus suffered? For just a moment, take the fact that the Holy God became sin for us out of the equation. Why did He endure the suffering associated with humanity? Why did Jesus give up everything and enter into the world with nothing? Entering as a hostage under the dominion of Satan to redeem mankind from his control. This is an important question to ask because finding the answer will help you understand this amazing truth: Jesus suffered through the human experience to be perfectly equipped for His office as our High Priest.

The Role of a High Priest

The High Priest was responsible for certain things that the other priests were not. He presided over the Sanhedrin and was in charge of the temple rituals to make sure they were carried out according to the law. But most importantly the High Priest would make the annual sacrifice on the Day of Atonement (Yom Kippur). This means he would act as an advocate for the people before God. He was allowed into the Holy of Holies to make intercession for the people, meeting with God. The priest only had access on this day otherwise he, like the rest, was confined to the outer chambers forbidden from entering into the presence of God.

On the Day of Atonement he would take blood into the Holy of Holies to pour out on the mercy seat as an offering to God. This is how he interceded for the people. The blood was used as a covering for sin, although it couldn't cleanse them from sin, thus, it would have to be offered again and again. It is important to know that the High Priest also had to offer this sacrifice for his own sins, as well as for the sins of the people. This whole system was a foreshadow to Jesus and His role as our High Priest serving in the Heavenly Tabernacle (Hebrews 9:7-14).

Suffering Perfectly Equipped Jesus for High Priest Office

"For it was an act worthy [of God] and fitting [to the divine nature] that He, for Whose sake and by Whom all things have their existence, in bringing many sons into glory, should make the Pioneer of their salvation perfect [should bring to maturity the human experience necessary to be perfectly equipped for His office as High Priest] through suffering" (Hebrews 2:10 AMP).

Jesus was sinless, so He could not sympathize with us on that basis as in the case of the Levitical priesthood. However, Jesus knew the fullness of the human experience through suffering so that He could accurately intercede for us. *"For this reason he had to be made like his brothers in every way, in order that he might become a merciful and faithful high priest in service to God, and that he might make atonement for the sins of the people. Because he himself suffered when he was tempted, he is able to help those who are being tempted" (Hebrews 2:17-18).* Because of His humanity and experience with suffering, He is able to relate to us in our time of need. The Amplified Bible tells us *"because He Himself [in His humanity] has suffered in being tempted (tested and tried), He is able [immediately] to run to the cry of (assist, relieve) those who are being tempted and tested and tried [and who therefore are being exposed to suffering]" (Hebrews 2:18 AMP).*

This is amazing! When Satan brings accusation against us before God, we have Jesus sitting at the right hand of the Father giving our defense. He can sympathize with us because He himself underwent the full human experience. He suffered so that He could perfectly intercede for us, drawing from that experience. This is an amazing look into the character and nature of God, who subjected Jesus to the worst humanity has to offer so that He would faithfully reside as our high priest extending mercy to us in every circumstance.

Jesus' Office as High Priest is Guaranteed By an Oath

"The former regulation is set aside because it was weak and useless (for the law made nothing perfect), and a better hope is introduced, by which we draw near

to God. And it was not without an oath! Others became priests without any oath, but he became a priest with an oath when God said to him: "The Lord has sworn and will not change his mind: 'You are a priest forever.' "Because of this oath, Jesus has become the guarantee of a better covenant" (Hebrews 7:18-22).

God has promised Jesus by an oath that He will not change His mind. Jesus is and will always be our High Priest. Jesus will always reside at the right hand of God making intercession for us because of the covenant that God made with Jesus. Therefore, we know that we are forgiven, cleansed from sin, accepted by God, holy, blameless, pure and set apart because of this oath. *"But because Jesus lives forever, he has a permanent priesthood. Therefore he is able to save completely those who come to God through him, because he always lives to intercede for them" (Hebrews 7:24-25).*

God in his brilliance sent Jesus to experience the fullness of humanity so that through this suffering He would be able to perfectly reside as our High Priest. And if that wasn't enough, God made a covenant with Jesus that He would always have this office to faithfully and mercifully intercede for us. This is truly a more perfect and better covenant than the forefathers had under the law. *"For the law appoints as high priests men who are weak; but the oath, which came after the law, appointed the Son, who has been made perfect forever" (Hebrews 7:28).*

Because of the Oath We Have Direct Access to God

"Therefore, brothers, since we have confidence to enter the Most Holy Place by the blood of Jesus, by a new and living way opened for us through the curtain, that is, his body, and since we have a great priest over the house of God, let us draw near to God with a sincere heart in full assurance of faith, having our hearts sprinkled to cleanse us from a guilty conscience and having our bodies washed with pure water" (Hebrews 10:19-22).

On the Day of Atonement the High Priest entered into the Holy of Holies. He was the only one allowed and he only had access once a year. Every other day a large heavy veil blocked passage into this chamber, this separated them from the presence of God. Now that Jesus has come, we are able to enter into the Holy of Holies through the veil of His body and into the very presence of God. We can join Him in the throne room, sit on his lap and enjoy His company. Jesus makes this possible (Hebrews 10:19-22).

redemption.

Because He is our faithful High Priest and because of the oath sworn to Him by God we can have confidence to enter in to that place (Hebrews 4:16). We can draw near to God with a sincere heart with no consciousness of sin because we have been washed clean by the blood that saves us. All of this is because Jesus was perfected through suffering to faithfully and mercifully reside as our High Priest forever.

Jesus Calls Us Brethren in the Presence of God

"Both the one who makes men holy and those who are made holy are of the same family. So Jesus is not ashamed to call them brothers. He says, "I will declare your name to my brothers; in the presence of the congregation I will sing your praises." And again, "I will put my trust in him." And again he says, "Here am I, and the children God has given me" (Hebrews 2:11-13)

Have you ever played matchmaker for a friend? You know, setting up the introductions for people who might hit it off? You describe one friend to another until the time they meet to see for themselves if they are compatible? Jesus is like that. As believers, He has introduced God the Father to us and in the same way; He stands before God calling us brothers and sisters, what an amazing thing!

Jesus is the one who has made us holy by cleansing us with His blood. And we who are sanctified belong to the same family of God. In fact, Jesus identifies us as His brethren in the presence of God, the angels, and in the heavenly realm. He is not ashamed to call us family. Hebrews 12 tells us that He looked forward to the cross with joy because He knew the outcome was our reconciliation and the resulting relationship to God (Hebrews 12:2). He did everything possible to make the first introductions.

In the same way, Jesus came to earth to show mankind the Father in a way we hadn't understood Him before. The first chapter of Hebrews tells us that Jesus is the exact representation of God (Hebrews 1:3). He is the perfect imprint of God. He shows us God's full nature and character. He came to straighten out our idea of who God is and introduce Him personally to us so that we can know Him in an intimate relational way.

redemption.

Jesus is the one who played matchmaker for us. Paul said in Ephesians, *"God raised us up with Christ and seated us with him in the heavenly realms in Christ Jesus, in order that in the coming ages he might show the incomparable riches of his grace, expressed in his kindness to us in Christ Jesus" (Ephesians 2:6-7)*. God had Jesus make the introductions so that He could pour His love on us throughout all eternity. This is why Jesus stepped into humanity, to bring us to the Father so He could express His love to us.

When I think about being in the same family as Jesus I am overcome with gratitude. It has nothing to do with who I am, but rather everything to do with who Jesus is. He is not ashamed to call us brothers in the presence of God and He willingly reveals the Father's love to us every day of our lives.

Jesus Shared in Humanity to Destroy the Power of Death

"Since the children have flesh and blood, he too shared in their humanity so that by his death he might destroy him who holds the power of death—that is, the devil— and free those who all their lives were held in slavery by their fear of death" (Hebrews 2:14-15)

Growing up in the late eighties and early nineties it was not uncommon to hear about a hijacked plane or a hostage situation. It seemed every time you turned on the news there was another breaking story of this kind. It was so prevalent even a good friend of mine was a passenger on a plane that got hijacked. He was leaving for basic training and ended up in Cuba under armed escort.

Hijackers take hostages to have negotiating power. Holding the power of life and death they barter lives for their objective. The same was true for humanity. Satan held mankind prisoner to use as a bartering chip. Jesus saw the helplessness of mankind which is why He stepped into humanity to rescue us. *"You see, at just the right time, when we were still powerless, Christ died for the ungodly" (Romans 5:6).* When Jesus took on human form, He fell under the jurisdiction of that kingdom, the same as mankind. He literally became Satan's hostage the moment He left heaven.

Jesus Disarmed Death from the Inside Out

"He was delivered over to death for our sins and was raised to life for our justification." (Romans 4:25).

Jesus shared in humanity to destroy death and the one who held the power of death. I John tells us that, *"The reason the Son of God appeared was to destroy the devil's work" (I John 3:8b)*. He did this by trading His life for ours. He rescued us by becoming hostage in our place and defeating the devil. Do you know how Jesus defeated Him? The Resurrection. He died as payment for our sins so we could be right with God, but He defeated the power that held us captive in slavery overpowering it by rising from the dead. Once the power is broken it no longer holds control. The proof of the resurrection shows that our sins are forgiven and the rescue mission worked. Death could not hold Jesus in the grave.

David prophesied this very thing, *"because you will not abandon me to the grave, nor will you let your Holy One see decay" (Psalm 16:10)*. He knew that God's Blessed Hope would one day defeat death and free those held captive by it. David looked forward to the time of Christ with hope because he knew death was not the final chapter. Jesus subjected himself to everything by which mankind was held prisoner so he could crush it and free us. Because of Jesus, death holds no power over us.

God's redemption plan was brilliant! I am sure that the powers of darkness were celebrating when they had Jesus hanging on the cross thinking they owned Him. But that was the beginning of the end. The cross was the means to defeat and overpower them, but they didn't understand this until it was too late. If they had realized, they would never have killed Him. *"None of the rulers of this age understood it, for if they had, they would not have crucified the Lord of glory" (I Corinthians 2:8)*. Once death had Him it was too late and it was over! The power living inside Jesus was too great to be held by anything, even death. When He arose, He ascended and led the captives free! (Ephesians 4:7-10).

We Have Been Set Free!

My friend, who ended up in Cuba with the hijacked plane, recounts that the hijackers were shot and killed shortly after landing in the foreign country. Then the passengers were freed and treated very nicely until the time they could be returned to the United States. With the threat gone, they were safe and in good hands, even though Cuba was an enemy of the U.S.

This is a good illustration of what happened for us. Christ defeated death and took every accusation against us nailing them to the cross where they stayed. *"When you were dead in your sins and in the uncircumcision of your sinful nature, God made you alive with Christ. He forgave us all our sins, having cancelled the written code, with its regulations, that was against us and that stood opposed to us; he took it away, nailing it to the cross. And having disarmed the powers and authorities, he made a public spectacle of them, triumphing over them by the cross" (Colossians 2:13-15).* As He ascended He passed through the heavens and every power and authority, making bold and public disgrace of them. He paraded them through the heavens as defeated, conquered and powerless.

This is an amazing truth; we have been set free! No longer do we live under the threat of death because we know that Jesus defeated and freed us from it. We know that we will rise again and live forever with Him simply by accepting the truth of Jesus. He traded His life for ours, becoming the hostage in our place so that we could be reunited with the Father. Jesus came in the flesh to destroy the works of the devil and disarmed all powers and authorities that opposed Him and held us captive (Colossians 2:15; I John 3:8b). Now He offers us the free gift of life, setting us free and giving us hope for a future!

God Helps Mankind; Not Fallen Angels

"For surely it is not angels he helps, but Abraham's descendants" (Hebrews 2:16)

This is an interesting verse. If you look at its context you will see that it is talking about both the fallen angels who rebelled against God and mankind after the fall of man. As I read and studied this passage I asked the Lord why He helped mankind and not the fallen angels. His answer to me was simple yet powerful, I created the angels to serve and worship me, but I created mankind for relationship.

Angels Were Created As Servants to Worship God

Angels are created beings the same as us. They were created to serve and worship God as well as minister and serve believers (Psalm 103:20; Hebrews 1:14). In God's goodness He created the angels with a free will just as He did mankind. The angels knew who God was, experienced His power, saw His glory, yet some rebelled. They made their choice in that moment knowing the full weight of their decision. In other words, there is no redemption for them because it was a willful decision to betray God.

Mankind Was Created for Relationship

After God created Adam and Eve, He walked with them in the cool of the evening. This means He fellowshipped with them, talked with them and knew them. They were created for relationship. Even after they disobeyed His command and were banished from the garden, He still walked and talked with them (Genesis 4). Sin didn't change this; they weren't out of fellowship with Him nor were they cut off from Him. After the fall, He still related to them just as He had in the garden.

The Bible records that *"Enoch walked with God; then he was no more, because God took him away" (Genesis 5:24)*. One day Enoch was caught up into heaven to live with God because they were so close they wouldn't be separated any longer. Enoch knew the intimate relationship that God designed humans to experience with Him.

In the same manner, God and Abraham were friends. God trusted Abraham and revealed the gospel in advance because He did not want to keep it from their friendship (Genesis 15; 17; 18:16-19). Abraham was the only Old Testament figure known as a friend of God (Isaiah 41:8; James 2:23). They had a relationship.

David was called a man after God's own heart (1 Sam 13:14; Acts 13:22). Not because his life was perfect or because he lived holy. In fact his life was a series of wars, unrest, adultery, murder, not to mention the ongoing trouble he experienced with his family. But he was called a man after God's own heart because He knew God. He knew God would rescue him. He knew God would forgive Him. He knew He could count on God. He knew that God should be the first person to run to in times of trouble. And He knew hope for the future because of their intimacy. Reading the words of David throughout the Psalms makes it clear that David enjoyed the relationship that God desires to have with us.

As believers we are all called friends of God (John 15:15). We have been brought into intimate unity with the Father, the Son and the Holy Spirit (John 17:22-23). We are called children of God (Romans 8:14-16). And co-heirs with Christ (Romans 8:17). This is an incredible truth. In the past, few ventured into a deep relationship with God, but through Jesus we have been united with Him in perfect unity (John 17:23). We have His Spirit living inside us reminding us of everything Jesus said (John 14:26; I John 2:20). God made it possible to have relationship with Him through Christ.

In all of these examples we see that God has befriended mankind and extended His love to us unconditionally. The fall of man didn't change His mind about us. He still loves us, desires relationship and provides the way of restoration. David saw this and wrote, *"What is man that you are mindful of him, the son of man that you care for him? You made him a little lower than the heavenly beings and crowned him with glory and honor" (Psalm 8:4-5).*

God Thinks Highly of Mankind

Jesus prayed an amazing thing for us in His High Priestly prayer in John 17. *"I have given them the glory that you gave me, that they may be one as we are one: I in them and you in me. May they be brought to complete unity to let the world know that you sent me and have loved them even as you have loved me" (John 17:22-23).* Jesus showed us the glory of God. The Greek word for glory is *Doxa*, which signifies an *"opinion, estimate, and hence, the honor resulting from a good opinion" (Vine's Expository Dictionary of New Testament Words).* God is the originator of every good thought. Jesus is saying that the thoughts, opinions and estimate of what God thinks about Jesus is what God also thinks about us. This is incredible!

Jesus came to reveal this truth to us. He prayed that we would understand this. He wasn't just praying for His disciples but everyone who would believe in Him through their message (John 17:20). God thinks highly of us. He is the originator of every good thought toward man. He loves us, created us for relationship and didn't spare His own Son so that we could be reconciled to Him. This is a powerful thing to consider when understanding the reason He came to earth was to destroy sin and the power of death that had held us captive (Hebrews 2:14-15).

Angels Long to Look into These Things

"Concerning this salvation, the prophets, who spoke of the grace that was to come to you, searched intently and with the greatest care, trying to find out the time and circumstances to which the Spirit of Christ in them was pointing when he predicted the sufferings of Christ and the glories that would follow. It was revealed to them that they were not serving themselves but you, when they spoke of the things that have now been told you by those who have preached the gospel to you by the Holy Spirit sent from heaven. Even angels long to look into these things" (I Peter 1:10-12).

We live in an amazing time period because we live after the time when Christ came to earth. As believers, we experience everything that the prophets foretold would happen after the Messiah came. We are born again with the Spirit of God inside of us, no longer having a sin nature (Romans 6:6-7), this changed everything. In fact David saw this and called us blessed. *"Blessed are they whose transgressions are forgiven, whose sins are covered. Blessed is the man whose sin the Lord will never count against him"*

(Romans 4:7-8; Psalm 32:1-2). God deals with us according to what Jesus did and not according to what we do. Peter said even the angels long to look into this wonderful salvation that has been given to mankind.

"Praise be to the God and Father of our Lord Jesus Christ, who has blessed us in the heavenly realms with every spiritual blessing in Christ. For he chose us in him before the creation of the world to be holy and blameless in his sight. In love he predestined us to be adopted as his sons through Jesus Christ, in accordance with his pleasure and will— to the praise of his glorious grace, which he has freely given us in the One he loves. In him we have redemption through his blood, the forgiveness of sins, in accordance with the riches of God's grace that he lavished on us with all wisdom and understanding. And he made known to us the mystery of his will according to his good pleasure, which he purposed in Christ, to be put into effect when the times will have reached their fulfillment—to bring all things in heaven and on earth together under one head, even Christ" (Ephesians 1:3-10).

Jesus Reached Out to Give Us a Helping Hand

"For this reason he had to be made like his brothers in every way, in order that he might become a merciful and faithful high priest in service to God, and that he might make atonement for the sins of the people" (Hebrews 2:17)

It is not trivial that Jesus entered into humanity as a man. Nor is it something He did lightly. Philippians 2:7 says that He emptied Himself of all divine privileges, born under the kingdom of darkness as a slave. He did this to give us a helping hand. He saw we were powerless to help ourselves because sin and its effect had completely destroyed us. For this reason He became a man, being made like us in every way to destroy the power that held us captive and in bondage to Satan's kingdom.

In doing this He accomplished two things, first He was able to empathize with us which is very important when you hold the title of High Priest and secondly He was able to make atonement for our sins.

In the Old Testament, the high priest made atonement for the people. He could empathize with them because he too was a man and sinned. In fact, he first had to make a sacrifice for himself and then for the people (Leviticus 9:7; Hebrews 5:3). This would go on year after year to serve as an annual reminder of sin. The blood of these animals would cover the person looking forward to the time of Christ.

When Christ came, His blood didn't cover us, it washed us clean. There is a huge difference. As our High Priest He was able to completely cleanse us from the effects of sin and free us from its grasp. In fact, He did something completely amazing, He became sin in our stead so that we could become righteous and stand before God completely justified (II Corinthians 5:21).

If this wasn't enough Jesus is able to identify with us because He too participated in the human experience. He was tested and tried while he was on earth yet was never defeated by sin. *"Therefore, since we have a great high priest who has gone through the heavens, Jesus the Son of God, let us hold firmly to the faith we profess. For we do not have a high priest who is unable to sympathize with our weaknesses, but we have one who has been tempted in every way, just as we are—yet was without sin. (Hebrews 4:14-15).* This is marvelous news for us because the writer goes on to say, *"Let us then approach the throne of grace with confidence, so that we may receive mercy and find grace to help us in our time of need" (Hebrews 4:16).*

Jesus' role as our high priest is to make intercession for us and give us access to God. Since He both cleanses and empathizes with us we know that we can approach God with confidence. What we will find is mercy and grace no matter what the circumstances are. Jesus makes this possible. And since He has risen from the dead, conquering death, we know that this promise is secure. *"But because Jesus lives forever, he has a permanent priesthood. Therefore he is able to save completely those who come to God through him, because he always lives to intercede for them. Such a high priest meets our need—one who is holy, blameless, pure, set apart from sinners, exalted above the heavens. Unlike the other high priests, he does not need to offer sacrifices day after day, first for his own sins, and then for the sins of the people. He sacrificed for their sins once for all when he offered himself" (Hebrews 7:24-27).*

This is why Jesus came as a man. It was essential that He be made like us in every way so that He could become a merciful and faithful High Priest in all things related to God.

Jesus is Able to Help Those Who Are Tempted

"Because he himself suffered when he was tempted, he is able to help those who are being tempted" (Hebrews 2:18)

There are many differences between Christianity and every other religion in the world. But the main difference and the thing that makes Christianity far superior to anything else is Jesus. Christianity is the only faith that has a Savior, everything else relies on the good works of the follower. There is no security in this. But because Jesus is the Savior of the World He has offered us grace, mercy and assurance to the things promised in the Bible. One of these wonderful truths is found in this passage of scripture in Hebrews 2. *"Because he himself suffered when he was tempted, he is able to help those who are being tempted" (Hebrews 2:18).*

No other religion offers a helping hand such as this. But Jesus stepped out of His home in heaven and into humanity to redeem mankind from the power of sin that held us captive. He underwent suffering and temptation in this world so that He was well equipped for His role as our High Priest. He offers us grace in every circumstance and is able to empathize (or, feel what we feel) when we suffer in this world. This is because He too suffered.

Jesus Didn't Suffer As a Sinner

Jesus wasn't tempted with evil, in other words He didn't suffer as a sinner because the lure of the world held something over Him. He suffered in humanity because He was sinless born into a world consumed and overpowered by transgressions. Jesus was tested and tried by each experience and interaction with people proving His faithfulness and steadfastness. This was where He proved He was able to be our faithful High Priest on our behalf.

Since Jesus suffered He is able to empathize with us when we undergo suffering and temptation in this world. This passage of scripture, as written in the Amplified Bible, magnifies the intent of meaning to what the author wrote so that we can gain full revelation into this wonderful truth. *"For because He Himself [in His humanity] has suffered in being tempted (tested and tried), He is able [immediately] to run to the cry of (assist, relieve) those who are being tempted and tested and tried [and who therefore are being exposed to suffering]" (Hebrews 2:18 AMP).* Jesus suffered on our behalf. He experiences everything that we are subjected to so that He is able to intercede for us. More than that, He will run to, relieve and assist us when we are suffering because this is His role as our High Priest.

With this in mind, it is important to look at Jesus in His humanity. Looking at His suffering, His testing and how He overcame them, will help us understand how He helps us when we suffer and are tested and tried. When we will look at the causes of suffering in this world, by looking at temptation, testing and suffering as a believer for the name of Christ, we will appreciate and understand Jesus intercession for us as High Priest. The result is knowing that we can run to Him in every circumstance and time of need.

The Testing of Jesus

Jesus was tested while on earth. The most memorable example is when He was tempted in the desert by Satan. Matthew records, *"then Jesus was led by the Spirit into the desert to be tempted by the devil. After fasting forty days and forty nights, he was hungry. The tempter came to him and said, "If you are the Son of God, tell these stones to become bread" (Matthew 4:1-3).* In this case Jesus was hungry, or a better way to put it is that He would have been starving. If there was ever a time when He would be weak in His humanity or tempted by the flesh this would be it. But look at His reply, *"Jesus answered, "It is written: 'Man does not live on bread alone, but on every word that comes from the mouth of God' "(Matthew 4:4).* Even in His hunger, He was not tempted to the point of sin and responded with scripture.

In the next instance the Bible records, *"Then the devil took him to the holy city and had him stand on the highest point of the temple. "If you are the Son of God," he said, "throw yourself down. For it is written: "'He will command his angels concerning you, and they will lift you up in their hands, so that you will not strike your foot against a stone.'" (Matthew 4:5-6).* Satan became aware that he could not tempt Jesus with fleshly desires so he raised the ante and used scripture to tempt Jesus into proving His lordship. *"Jesus answered him, "It is also written: 'Do not put the Lord your God to the test.'" (Matthew 4:7).* In other words, Jesus' understanding of the things of God trumped Satan's misuse of scripture. By having an eternal perspective He could not be tempted in this way either.

Lastly the scriptures record that *"Again, the devil took him to a very high mountain and showed him all the kingdoms of the world and their splendor." All this I will give you," he said, "if you will bow down and worship me"* (Matthew 4:8-9). The interesting thing about this is that Satan had the power to offer this to Jesus because the world was his; he obtained the lease to it in the garden from Adam. In the same way, by offering it to Jesus in exchange for His worship, Satan was attempting to seize control of Jesus' heavenly kingdom. Of all the things that might peak Jesus' interest, this would be it because this was the very reason He came to earth as a man, to regain control of what was lost in the garden. But Jesus could not be fooled. *"Jesus said to him, "Away from me, Satan! For it is written: 'Worship the Lord your God, and serve him only.' Then the devil left him, and angels came and attended him" (Matthew 4:10-11).* Jesus knew the Father and knew His plan so He could not be tempted in this way either. Jesus proved His faithfulness in being tempted. Satan got nowhere with Him and left at Jesus' command. Angels attended to Him afterwards as this trial was hard on Him, but He proved that sin, evil and the things of the flesh had no hold on Him. He could not be tempted with them.

However, this is not the only way that Jesus was tempted and tried while on earth, He was tested in many ways. At every turn the Pharisees were also there to test Him. In reading through the gospels you will see it everywhere, *"The Pharisees and Sadducees came to Jesus and tested him by asking him to show them a sign from heaven..." (Matthew 16:1); "Some Pharisees came to him to test him..." (Matthew 19:3); "But Jesus, knowing their evil intent, said, "You hypocrites, why are you trying to trap me...?" (Matthew 22:18).* The list goes on and on. In every case they were demanding answers from Him. They were looking for ways to entrap Him. They wanted to catch Him in their snare so they could accuse and kill Him.

He did this for us. He underwent these trials so He would be a faithful High Priest in all things related to God. Isaiah records the reason, *"after the suffering of his soul, he will see the light of life and be satisfied; by his knowledge my righteous servant will justify many, and he will bear their iniquities" (Isaiah 53:11).* He knew the result was bringing reconciliation and peace to us on God's behalf. He underwent testing, trials and temptation so that we would not have to. The result is He empathizes with us when we struggle and go through trials. Because of this He is able to run to us and help us in our time of need.

Jesus Helps Us When Tempted

"Because he himself suffered when he was tempted, he is able to help those who are being tempted" (Hebrews 2:18)

Jesus helps us in our time of need because He too suffered and experienced the full knowledge of being human. He knows and has a working comprehension of our weaknesses and struggles. Jesus shared in our humanity so He would be equipped to faithfully serve God, as our High Priest being both empathetic and merciful to us in every way. We do not have to bear the struggles of life alone. This is a promise that He will run to our rescue and help us when we are in need. What an amazing truth from God's word.

As believers we will undergo different types of temptation and suffering in this world. But understanding Jesus' role concerning this will equip us to come out on the other side unscathed. First we will look at temptation, or the things of this world that hold us. Next we will look at where temptation comes from so that we can understand our position of authority over it. Lastly we will look at being tested as a believer and how it is different than temptation. We will look at the cause of suffering and how it can prove our faith to be genuine, refined and, in the end, worth more than gold.

The Temptation of the Flesh

Just as Christ was not tempted by sin, as believers we too have been freed from the sin nature (Romans 6:6-7). He has provided the means for us to escape the desires of the flesh so that it does not hold us captive. This is a key principal for the Christian life, *"So I say, live by the Spirit, and you will not gratify the desires of the sinful nature. For the sinful nature desires what is contrary to the Spirit, and the Spirit what is contrary to the sinful nature. They are in conflict with each other, so that you do not do what you want" (Galatians*

5:16-17). We have been set free from the sin nature (Romans 6:6-7) and have been given a born again spirit that does not sin (I John 3:6, 9). But one third of our makeup is still flesh (I Thessalonians 5:23). Spirit, soul and body war against each other and the winner in this three-way tussle is the one where we place our focus and attention. So by focusing on the things of the Spirit, the things of the flesh will have no appeal or hold on us. By this principal, Jesus provided the means for effortless change.

Take the example of Jesus' temptation in the desert by Satan. When the devil told Him to turn stones into bread to prove that He was the Son of God, Jesus responded with what God said about it. He was hungry and hadn't eaten in forty days. However He would not be tempted into proving He was God by what He could do. Jesus chose to believe what God told Him rather than trying to prove it to satisfy His hunger. He was so consumed with the thoughts and words of God not even His physical need could redirect Him.

Temptation Does Not Come From God

A good thing to know is that God does not tempt us. This may come as a shock to many people but God does not trick, tempt or give us opportunities to sin. This is contrary to His nature. Jesus underwent this type of temptation and testing so we would not have to. After all, the Bible records that Jesus was led by the Spirit into the desert to be tested by the devil (Matthew 4:1; Mark 1:12-13; Luke 4:1-2). In this testing Jesus proved His faithfulness both to God, mankind and the truth. Since this was a victory, we will never be tempted by God. James makes this very clear, *"When tempted, no one should say, "God is tempting me." For God cannot be tempted by evil, nor does he tempt anyone" (James 1:13)*. Just as Jesus' temptation had no power and pull with Him, God cannot be tempted by evil and in the same manner would never tempt us with evil.

With this in mind it is important for us to understand where temptations come from. First, like with Jesus, it can come from the devil. But more likely it comes from our own desires that battle inside us. James went on to say immediately after declaring that God would never tempt us, *"but each one is tempted when, by his own evil desire, he is dragged away and enticed. Then, after desire has conceived, it gives birth to sin; and sin, when it is full-grown, gives birth to death" (James 1:14-15)*. He made it very clear that our own desires, when focused on and allowed to grow inside us, give birth to sin. Temptation starts in the heart before it is evident in our lives. This is why it is so important to focus on the Spirit and the things of God. Then these things will be evident in our lives instead of the desires of the flesh. Paul made this very point in Romans 8. *"Those who live according to the sinful nature have their minds set on what that nature desires; but those who live in accordance with the Spirit have their minds set on what the Spirit desires. The mind of sinful man is death, but the mind controlled by the Spirit is life and peace" (Romans 8:5-6).*

It is also important to understand that when temptation comes, God provides the way of escape. *"No temptation has seized you except what is common to man. And God is faithful; he will not let you be tempted beyond what you can bear. But when you are tempted, he will also provide a way out so that you can stand up under it" (I Corinthians 10:13).* This is an amazing truth, no matter how we are tempted, it all falls under the normal human experience. This is not to say that God gives His stamp of approval on every temptation that passes before us allowing them to happen. But when they do, God does not allow trials or situations to be beyond human resistance. Nothing will be more than you and I can bear. Plus, God is faithful to His Word and compassionate in nature so He can be trusted to not allow any temptation to exceed our ability to stand against it. If that were not enough, He will always provide a way of escape for us so that we can be removed from temptation, even in the midst of it.

God has given us sure-fire ways of escaping the things that can tempt us. First, if we are being tempted by Satan, James tells us in chapter 4, *"Submit yourselves, then, to God. Resist the devil, and he will flee from you" (James 4:7).* The truth is that Satan only has power over you if you give it to him. He is a defeated foe (Colossian 2:15). He is afraid of you because, as a believer, you are a co-heir with Christ and seated with Him in the heavenly realm holding a true position of authority (Romans 8:17; Ephesians 2:6). He has to flee. So in the midst of temptation, if we stop and recognize what is happening, then we will have victory. James gives us the key, submit yourselves to God and resist. What a wonderful combination and sure fire way of overcoming this type of temptation.

Secondly, if our temptation comes from our own desires then escaping these is done by the Spirit. *"So I say, live by the Spirit, and you will not gratify the desires of the sinful nature" (Galatians 5:16).* Living by the Spirit is being consumed with the things of God. Planting His Word in your heart, letting His truth and guidance overtake and consume you. We are to live like strangers in this world. When you walk after the Spirit this world and all its allure has no hold over you. It pales in comparison to the goodness and glory of God.

Lastly, a key to overcoming temptation is understanding God loves you, He died for you and He will never leave or forsake you (Hebrews 13:5-6). This is so important to know and understand with every fiber of your being. So many times in life we try to replace our desire to be loved and accepted with material things, alcohol, drugs or relationships. But this insatiable desire grows from your inherent longing for God. Everyone is born with it and unless you know the only One who can fill this void, you will try to fill it in many other ways. Many of which are destructive because this need is so great. But once you get a revelation of God's love for you then contentment and peace will overtake you. They fill you to overflowing. You will dwell in a state of acceptance, love, forgiveness and grace, and those things will pour out of you as well. The things of this world become insignificant in contrast to God's love. Abundant Life fills the void until it overflows and you will no longer look for things to fill that space. You will experience firsthand the goodness of God.

Temptation vs. Testing, What's the Difference?

God does not tempt us but God does test us, or a better way to put it is that He entrusts us. What's the difference? Temptation is being enticed or allured to sin. God will not tempt us with sin because He is good and no evil is found in Him (James 1:13). Testing, on the other hand, is God trusting us to make the right choice. Look at Deuteronomy 30 for example, God gave the Israelites a choice, *"This day I call heaven and earth as witnesses against you that I have set before you life and death, blessing and curses. Now choose life, so that you and your children may live" (Deuteronomy 30:19)*. He presented them with a choice, He wanted their buy-in, but He also gave them the answer, *"now choose life, so that you and your children may live"* then He gave them the reasons, *"that you may love the Lord your God, listen to his voice, and hold fast to him. For the Lord is your life, and he will give you many years in the land he swore to give to your fathers, Abraham, Isaac and Jacob" (Deuteronomy 30:20)*. This is an incredible promise from Him. He gave the Israelites full disclosure. He gave them a choice, gave them the answer and gave them the reasons for it. He wanted them to choose correctly and entrusted them to make the right choice.

In the same way, the Lord provides us with choices as believers wanting us to make the right decisions as well. This is not to say that if we don't choose wisely He will punish us. But He entrusts us with kingdom principles watching how we respond and act. Faithfulness in these tests are the road to promotion in His kingdom because He knows He can trust us to do what He has instructed. Money is a good example of this type of testing. Everything is from Him and He wants to trust us with it. So He watches how we use what we have to see if we are trustworthy. If we prove faithful in this area then He is more likely to give us more seed to sow (II Corinthians 9:10). The reason is not to become rich, instead it is to have the means to be generous in every occasion, the result is to bring glory and thanksgiving to God (II Corinthians 9:11).

Peter told us, *"His divine power has given us everything we need for life and godliness through our knowledge of him who called us by his own glory and goodness. Through these he has given us his very great and precious promises, so that through them you may participate in the divine nature and escape the corruption in the world caused by evil desires: (II Peter 1:3-4).* God has given us instruction on everything so that we can live set apart lives in the midst of this world. He has been very clear in how we should live and entrusts us to choose wisely. The key to all of this is knowing God and walking after the Spirit because we will know who we are in Christ and we will be strong in the power of His might. It is the perfect solution.

So, when temptation comes, we can know we can resist and be free of it (James 4:7). In the same way, when we are entrusted with the things of God we can find answers in His Word (II Peter 1:3-4; II Timothy 3:16-17). He has shown us His desires and gave us full instructions for life. Thankfully by knowing these wonderful truths, God has made this easy for us.

Suffering as a Believer for the Cause of Christ

It is easy to wrap temptation and suffering together into a nice little package because we experience both in this world, but they are very different. Temptation is the enticement to sin and suffering is a painful or distressing experience. Just as it is important to understand that God does not tempt us, God does not cause our suffering either. God is a good God; He loves us and sent Jesus to save us. So it is incompatible with His nature to imply that God allows or causes our suffering. But it still exists and as believers many times we suffer solely because we are Christians.

Believers are subjected to persecution and hatred because we bear the name of Christ. This should come as no surprise. Jesus told His disciples, *"If the world hates you, keep in mind that it hated me first. If you belonged to the world, it would love you as its own. As it is, you do not belong to the world, but I have chosen you out of the world. That is why the world hates you" (John 15:18-19)*. We are different, set apart and not of this world. So it is no surprise that Jesus told us that we would have trouble in this lifetime.

The good news in all of this is that good things can result in trouble and persecution. Peter told us to rejoice in these circumstances (I Peter 1:6-7) and James told us to consider them pure joy (James 1:2-4). This is because they knew that God was able to bring these things around for our benefit. When trouble and persecution comes our way, we can cling to the promise He made to Paul in such a circumstance, *"My grace is sufficient for you, for my power is made perfect in weakness..." (II Corinthians 12:9a)*. We can trust in the goodness and grace of God to get us through these incidents just as we can rely on Him to bring good out of them.

"In this you greatly rejoice, though now for a little while you may have had to suffer grief in all kinds of trials. These have come so that your faith—of greater worth than gold, which perishes even though refined by fire—may be proved genuine and may result in praise, glory and honor when Jesus Christ is revealed" (I Peter 1:6-7). The trials of this life work as a refining fire to burn away dross. Not only will we come out on the other side unscathed but we will come out with a genuine and proven faith. This is worth very much in the sight of God and results in His praise, glory and honor.

James tells us that God is able to perfect us through suffering. *"Consider it pure joy, my brothers, whenever you face trials of many kinds, because you know that the testing of your faith develops perseverance. Perseverance must finish its work so that you may be mature and complete, not lacking anything" (James 1:2-4)*. The King James Bible says that we will be *'perfect and entire'*. I cannot stress enough that God does not cause our suffering, but He is able to bring good from it. Our faith is developed, the character of perseverance is perfected and we are mature and not easily taken off course by the struggles and hardships of this life.

Through both temptation and testing in life we learn to rely on Jesus *"Because he himself suffered when he was tempted, he is able to help those who are being tempted" (Hebrews 2:18)*. He had the full human experience so He can sympathize with us in every circumstance. What a marvelous attribute in the High Priest who lives to make intercession for us. *"Therefore, since we have a great high priest who has gone through the heavens, Jesus the Son of God, let us hold firmly to the faith we profess. For we do not have a high priest who is unable to sympathize with our weaknesses, but we have one who has been tempted in every way, just as we are—yet was without sin. Let us then approach the throne of grace with confidence, so that we may receive mercy and find grace to help us in our time of need" (Hebrews 4:14-16).*

hebrews 3.

JESUS IS

GREATER THAN MOSES

Fixing Your Thoughts on Jesus

"Therefore, holy brothers, who share in the heavenly calling, fix your thoughts on Jesus, the apostle and high priest whom we confess" (Hebrews 3:1)

Christianity is the only religion in the world that has a Savior; this makes it special and unique. It is the only religion that is less about what you do for salvation and all about what Jesus did for you. When we confess that we are a Christian, we confess our faith and trust in Jesus as our personal savior and the only way to heaven. This is why it is important to look at Christ and constantly focus our attention on Him. When we do, He will keep our hearts and minds in perfect peace even in the midst of the trouble of this world.

In the gospel of Matthew, there is an account of Peter walking on the water (Matthew 14:22-36). The disciples were in the middle of the sea trying to cross over and they were buffeted by the wind on every side. They had been struggling and fighting the storm all night. It seemed like a hopeless and dangerous situation. Early in the morning they looked out and saw a figure walking toward them on top of the water and they were terrified. They screamed with fright assuming it was a ghost. But Jesus reassured them it was Him and told them to take courage. When Peter heard this he asked Jesus to tell him to come out to Him on the water. Jesus' answer was to come.

Peter stepped out of the boat and walked toward Jesus. I imagine he walked quite a ways. But the longer he was out on the water and the closer he got to Jesus, His mind began telling him that He shouldn't be able to walk on water. Then Matthew records *But when he saw the wind, he was afraid and, beginning to sink, cried out, "Lord, save me!" (Matthew 14:30).*

redemption.

What happened is he took his eyes off Jesus for a split second. He felt the strong wind and perceived the physical danger becoming frightened by it. Nothing had changed except his perception of the situation. Instead of looking toward Jesus and focusing on Him and His ability he was distracted by what was going on around him and it affected his ability to walk on the water.

Notice he began to sink, it was a gradual thing, and he didn't just fall into the water completely immersed. When he was focused and fixed on Jesus he walked across the water, but when his attention was on the storm he sank. He was very close to Jesus at this time too because the Bible records, *"Immediately Jesus reached out his hand and caught him."You of little faith,"* *he said, "why did you doubt?" (Matthew 14:31).* He was all but there. He showed marvelous faith in getting out of the boat. He walked a long way toward Jesus but near the end something changed. He became aware of the situation that walking on water was physically impossible. However, instead of understanding that it was Jesus who held him he looked to himself and failed. Thankfully Jesus was right there to rescue him. In the same way Jesus has promised to always be with us (John 14:18; Hebrews 13:5).

This is a parallel for life and something that the writer of Hebrews reminds us of in this passage. *"Therefore, holy brothers, who share in the heavenly calling, fix your thoughts on Jesus, the apostle and high priest whom we confess" (Hebrews 3:1).* If we are to get through life we need to constantly focus on Jesus as we can do nothing on our own. By thoughtfully and attentively considering Jesus in all things, we too can be a water walker.

Believers are Consecrated and Set Apart to God

In order to focus on Jesus and not get distracted by the world around us it is important to understand who we are in Christ. An amazing truth in all of this is that believers are consecrated and set apart for a higher purpose. The writer of Hebrews makes this very clear as he calls us holy brethren. Consecration means to declare or make something holy; it is associated with the idea of being sacred. What is awesome in all of this is that this declaration is made, not by us, but by God. He has consecrated us and set us apart for a higher purpose the moment we accept and trust in Jesus as our Savior.

Renewing our mind to this truth is of the utmost importance. We must know and understand who we are in Christ and who He is in us so that we can walk in the purpose to which we have been called and set apart. We are to look thoughtfully and attentively at Jesus considering His role as our High Priest in everything because He proved His faithfulness by sharing in our humanity and breaking the power of death that held us captive (Hebrews 2:14-18). In the same way, He will help us in our time of need. More than that He will empower and guide us through this life in all things. When we pay attention, then like Peter we stay on top of the water walking toward, beside and with Jesus all the way.

Peter learned this lesson well; this is why he wrote in his second letter, *"His divine power has given us everything we need for life and godliness through our knowledge of him who called us by his own glory and goodness. Through these he has given us his very great and precious promises, so that through them you may participate in the divine nature and escape the corruption in the world caused by evil desires" (II Peter 1:3-4).* We have been given the power to escape the lure of this world and it comes by knowing God and walking in His truth. This is why we have been set apart and consecrated, so that we may live the holy lives to which we have been chosen and called.

God has a plan for each one of us but it is up to us to walk it out in our lives. Knowing this gives us purpose and incredible value. God is entrusting us with a mission. We were set apart and sanctified for this very purpose. This is why it is so important to trust in and focus on Jesus, because the plan is not something we can do on our own. His desire for our lives is so incredible that we need His help every step of the way.

We can look at examples from scripture of people who knew their purpose in life and trusted in God to fulfill it. Jeremiah is a great example. *"The word of the LORD came to me, saying, "Before I formed you in the womb I knew you, before you were born I set you apart; I appointed you as a prophet to the nations." (Jeremiah 1:4-5).* Jeremiah was very young when God revealed His plan for him. But the plan came with promises. God promised him that He would not only give him the words to speak but He would perform them. Then He promised Jeremiah that He would make him a fortified city, an iron pillar and a bronze wall so that he would not be overcome by the people (Jeremiah 1:18-19). Jeremiah walked this out because God had set him apart for this very purpose and was with Him every step of the way.

The Apostle Paul is another great example. He started out hunting and killing Christians but thankfully his past didn't get in the way of his future. In Romans chapter 1 he wrote to the church, *"Paul, a servant of Christ Jesus, called to be an apostle and set apart for the gospel of God" (Romans 1:1).* He knew he was set apart for the purpose of preaching the gospel and in walking out this mission; he all but converted the known world at that time. He was chosen long before he was an enemy of the church, God knew what he wanted to do through Paul, so his past did not change God's mind or calling. He had chosen Paul and empowered him to be a prevailing witness to the world.

Lastly, by looking at Jesus we can see how powerful it is when one understands they are called, separated and consecrated to God's higher purpose in life. Jesus entered the synagogue on the Sabbath immediately after He was tempted by Satan. Here He made this mission known. *"The scroll of the prophet Isaiah was handed to him. Unrolling it, he found the place where it is written: "The Spirit of the Lord is on me, because he has anointed me to preach good news to the poor. He has sent me to proclaim freedom for the prisoners and recovery of sight for the blind, to release the oppressed, to proclaim the year of the Lord's favor." Then he rolled up the scroll, gave it back to the attendant and sat down. The eyes of everyone in the synagogue were fastened on him, and he began by saying to them, "Today this scripture is fulfilled in your hearing." (Luke 4:17-21).* Jesus had a mission like no one else. He knew what it was and focused all His attention toward it. He knew who He was, why He came and what He had to do. He knew the higher purpose to which he had been called and walked it out. His life made all the difference for humanity.

This is why we need to pay attention to Jesus and thoughtfully consider Him in everything we do. We should embrace Him as ours as we go through this life. Because He has chosen us, set us apart and has a wonderful plan for our lives. He will help us every step of the way. And like Peter, He desires for us to get out of the boat and walk out His supernatural plan. To do this we need to look toward Him and understand who we are by His grace and mercy.

Believers Share in the Heavenly Calling

Knowing that we are consecrated and set apart from birth does not guarantee success. Victory comes when we understand that we share in the heavenly calling because what we have been called into is a relationship. This is the single most important mission for your life, knowing God in an intimate way.

Jesus said in John 17, *"For you granted him authority over all people that he might give eternal life to all those you have given him. Now this is eternal life: that they may know you, the only true God, and Jesus Christ, whom you have sent" (John 17:2-3).* Our job is to know God and to know Jesus; this is the definition of eternal life. By experiencing an intimate relationship with God we are experiencing the abundant life Jesus promised to His followers (John 10:10). It is true, as believers, we will reign in eternity with Jesus, but knowing that our heavenly calling right now is to know God, we can enjoy and experience eternal life right here in this world, starting today.

Our mission is to know God because everything for the Christian life begins here. As we experience this relationship our hearts begin to change, aligning with His and the result is incredible and drastic. When our hearts change, our lives change as well, *"For as he thinketh in his heart, so is he" (Proverbs 23:7 KJV).* Meaning the true intentions and attitudes of a man come out in behavior and actions. To experience true change we must change what we think at the core level. The only way to do this is to allow God to rewrite His truth on our hearts, to let us see life as He sees it. To have His thoughts and values be ours. This is why cultivating a relationship with God is the single most important thing you can do, because this type of change is a byproduct of that relationship.

Busyness and Service is Not Our Heavenly Calling!

Since our heavenly calling is relationship it is important not to get sidetracked with other things even if these things are good. So many times, we believe that we need to do in order to be effective for the kingdom but God doesn't want our service He just wants us. Look at the example of Mary and Martha. When Jesus visited their home, Martha was busy preparing and serving the Lord and her guests while Mary sat at Jesus' feet and listened to Him. The Bible records that Martha was distracted; she probably didn't hear a word Jesus said. As she was occupied and busy she became upset at Mary because she wasn't helping. When she brought this to Jesus' attention, His response shows the importance He places on relationship versus service. *"Martha, Martha," the Lord answered, "you are worried and upset about many things, but only one thing is needed. Mary has chosen what is better, and it will not be taken away from her" (Luke 10:41-42).* Martha's things were good, they were needed and Jesus didn't condemn her for doing them. In fact, I'm sure He appreciated the hospitality He enjoyed while staying there. But Mary had chosen better, she chose to sit at Jesus' feet, enjoy His company and learn from Him.

Martha probably started out like Mary. The family was close to Jesus and He probably stayed with them whenever He was in the area. She probably started out listening and fellowshipping with the Savior when He was in town just as Mary did. As her love for Him grew she probably wanted to serve Him, make special meals for Him and make Him comfortable in her home. It is only natural for this to be the case. But somewhere in the midst of her preparations the focus was taken off Jesus and pleasing Him and it turned solely to the work at hand. The change, although slight was a matter of the heart. She became distracted, busy and overly occupied. At this point she didn't have time for the person of Jesus even though she was doing for Him. Mary on the other hand recognized the most important thing, which was sitting at Jesus' feet, realizing that everything else could wait.

Now, I am not bashing Martha, because I tend to be somewhere in the middle of Mary and Martha. Service is needed in the body of Christ; there is much work to be done. But when the focus switches from Jesus and serving out of gratitude to the busyness of what needs done then something must give. Like Peter, when he took his eyes off Jesus, he sank. We must return to the real focus of life, relationship with God. Looking to Him in everything, this is our heavenly calling.

The more we fellowship and know Jesus the more we will be equipped and ready to serve the body. Because His love will pour out of us and overflow to everyone we meet. We will share His wonderful truth and love with everyone that will listen. The Great Commission will also be fulfilled in our lives simply because we will want to share with others what we have. All of this comes from relationship. We must understand that the most important thing we can do is remove both busyness and distractions and simply focus on Jesus.

True Success Comes From Making Jesus Personal

It is amazing to know that we are called, set apart and share in the heavenly calling as believers. To maximize on this wonderful truth we must make Jesus personal in our lives. We should thoughtfully and attentively consider Him, seeking to understand who He is and what He has done for us. We should embrace Him as our very own in every sense of the word.

We were called into a relationship, but relationships cannot grow unless you get to know the other person. This is why we are to constantly consider Jesus, the Apostle of our faith. When we seek to understand His role as our High Priest we will gain insight into many workings of God. He is our personal advocate with the Father. He shared in our humanity conquering death so He could faithfully administer grace and mercy on our behalf. He was sent to rescue us. We can approach God with assurance when we understand this role. Because of Jesus, the writer of Hebrews reminds us, *"Let us then approach the throne of grace with confidence, so that we may receive mercy and find grace to help us in our time of need" (Hebrews 4:16).*

This is why it is so important to know Jesus and make Him personal in our lives. Just as Peter walked across the water when He looked to the Savior, we too will succeed in this life when we pay close attention to what He has done for us. All we need to do is seek Him. God has made us an awesome promise in his Word, regarding this; *"For I know the plans I have for you," declares the LORD, "plans to prosper you and not to harm you, plans to give you hope and a future. Then you will call upon me and come and pray to me, and I will listen to you. You will seek me and find me when you seek me with all your heart" (Jeremiah 29:11-13).* We can have confidence in this, knowing that God will be found by us. He will make Himself known to us. He will reveal Himself and become real in our lives.

Jesus Was Faithful to God Just Like Moses

"He was faithful to the one who appointed him, just as Moses was faithful in all God's house" (Hebrews 3:2)

The writer of Hebrews is calling our attention to the covenants. He is drawing a parallel between the faithfulness of Jesus compared to the faithfulness of Moses. Both men ushered in God's covenants, Moses with the Law, Jesus with abundant grace. The book of John tells us, *"For the law was given through Moses; grace and truth came through Jesus Christ" (John 1:17)*. Both were faithful to God with what He had entrusted to them.

Since the original audience of the book of Hebrews was primarily Jewish, this statement would have been quite radical. Moses held a place of honor with the people far above any other prophet in the scriptures because he gave them the Law. Moses proved faithful before God, administering this covenant. In fact God said this about him in Numbers, *"When a prophet of the LORD is among you, I reveal myself to him in visions, I speak to him in dreams. But this is not true of my servant Moses; he is faithful in all my house" (Numbers 12:6-7)*. Even though the Israelites were hard-hearted, refusing to believe God, wandering the desert for forty years, this didn't nullify Moses' faithfulness. He remains true to God and the covenant that was made.

Just like Moses, Jesus has remained faithful to the one who appointed Him Apostle and High Priest on our behalf. None of this bears weight on what we do, but everything depends on what He did. He has proven Himself a faithful steward with what God entrusted to Him. And now Jesus resides permanently over the house of God administering this covenant of grace. In fact, God has sworn an oath to Jesus that He will never change His mind, Jesus is a priest forever (Hebrews 7:21-22). Because of this oath, Jesus is the guarantee for a better covenant.

This is why the writer started chapter three reminding us to focus our thoughts on Jesus. Just like Moses, He has proven Himself faithful. Understanding the covenant of which He is the guarantor will bring us into a deeper revelation of grace. With this understanding, nothing will get in the way of the relationship that God has called us into.

Jesus Was Worthy of Greater Honor than Moses

"Jesus has been found worthy of greater honor than Moses,
just as the builder of a house has greater honor than the
house itself. For every house is built by someone, but
God is the builder of everything" (Hebrews 3:3-4)

When the Law was given, it was given to the people by Moses. He acted as a mediator between God and man. He was God's steward overseeing the administration of the written code. Moses was truly a faithful servant over God's house leading the Israelites by example. But Jesus is worthy of greater honor than Moses because He is not a servant entrusted with overseeing the covenant, Jesus is the covenant. Everything that the Law and the prophets foretold was about Jesus. He is the spoken Word of God and He was always the plan for redemption (Luke 24:44; John 1:1-3; Hebrews 1:1-3; I Peter 1:19-20; Revelation 13:8).

Covenants Are God's Way of Protecting Us

God has always made covenants with His people. If you look back through the scriptures you will see several accounts of these promises. The amazing thing is, these covenants were always initiated by God and based solely on His Word. In other words, mankind's behavior did not nullify the pledge God made to them. Take Abraham for example. God came to him and told him that his offspring would be as numerous as the stars in the sky and He would give him a great span of land as his inheritance. He asked nothing in return from Abraham. Then God ratified this covenant with a heifer, a goat, a ram, a dove and a young pigeon (Genesis 15). The only thing required on Abraham's part was believing God. The scripture records, *"Abram believed the LORD, and he credited it to him as righteousness." (Genesis 15:6).* Faith placed in the Lord and what He did was the only requirement.

The important thing to understand is that God is the one who initiates the covenant. He makes the promise, ratifies it and then stands behind it, never changing His mind. The New Covenant, which Jesus ushered in is in the same fashion as the covenant made with Abraham. It is not based on anything we can do, it is based on what God did. Ratification of this promise was made by Jesus' blood. Now Jesus is the guarantor of this covenant, since He lives, this promise offered to us can never be broken or revoked and God will not change His mind about it. Even though the world gets increasingly worse, with more evil and sin, God will never renege on this covenant of grace offered to us through Jesus.

Because of this, Jesus is truly worthy of far greater honor than Moses. Paul said in II Corinthians, *"Now if the ministry that brought death, which was engraved in letters on stone, came with glory, so that the Israelites could not look steadily at the face of Moses because of its glory, fading though it was, will not the ministry of the Spirit be even more glorious? If the ministry that condemns men is glorious, how much more glorious is the ministry that brings righteousness! For what was glorious has no glory now in comparison with the surpassing glory. And if what was fading away came with glory, how much greater is the glory of that which lasts!" (II Corinthians 3:7-11).* This is a comparison between the Law, written in stone and the administration of the Spirit written on our hearts through the covenant of grace. It is far superior and worthy of more honor than anything the Law did or could ever do.

John 1 tells us, *"From the fullness of his grace we have all received one blessing after another. For the law was given through Moses; grace and truth came through Jesus Christ. No one has ever seen God, but God the One and Only, who is at the Father's side, has made him known" (John 1:16-18).* The Law was meant to accuse us and show us our guilt before God (Romans 5:20; II Corinthians 3:6; Galatians 3:24-25) but the grace and truth that Jesus offers us shows us the love and forgiving nature of God. This message is incredible and since the bearer of this amazing news lives, seated at the right hand of the Father, we know that this promise is eternal. So in every sense of the word, Jesus is worthy of incredible honor and glory and He is the guarantor of our covenant of grace, initiated and offered by God, rarified and secured by Jesus forever. The only requirement is believing and accepting it. Then we too like Abraham are credited with righteousness (Genesis 15:6; Romans 4:23-24).

Moses Testified About the Christ

"Moses was faithful as a servant in all God's house, testifying to what would be said in the future. But Christ is faithful as a son over God's house. And we are his house, if we hold on to our courage and the hope of which we boast" (Hebrews 3:5-6)

Moses was truly a faithful servant. He oversaw the administration of the Law and led the people of God through the desert for all those years. However Moses' entire ministry was a testimony about Christ. Because everything the Law said, pointed to Jesus. The Law showed God's righteousness, His standards and His holiness. But what it couldn't do is make us right with God. Galatians tells us *"For if a law had been given that could impart life, then righteousness would certainly have come by the law"* (Galatians 3:21b).

In fact the Law did just the opposite; it accused us before God and showed our guilt because of sin. Paul went on to say, *"But the Scripture declares that the whole world is a prisoner of sin, so that what was promised, being given through faith in Jesus Christ, might be given to those who believe. Before this faith came, we were held prisoners by the law, locked up until faith should be revealed. So the law was put in charge to lead us to Christ that we might be justified by faith. Now that faith has come, we are no longer under the supervision of the law"* (Galatians 3:22-25).

Moses gave, in amazing detail, what the Christ would be when he gave the Israelites the Law. Every aspect of the written code showed God's righteousness and holiness. To fulfill it, you had to be perfect and sinless. It was an impossible standard for mankind which is why the true purpose was to point us to Christ. This is why Moses' entire ministry was revealed afterward when Jesus came. He spoke faithfully about what was coming and yet he never lived to see the promise fulfilled. Hebrews gives us amazing insight into this, *"These were all commended for their faith, yet none of them received what had been promised. God had planned something better for us so that only together with us would they be made perfect" (Hebrews 11:39-40)*. All of the men and women mentioned in Hebrews 11, because of their faith, saw and looked forward to the time of Christ, but we are truly blessed because we live after the time when Jesus entered into humanity.

Christ is Faithful as a Son Over God's House

Christ ushered in the New Covenant of grace, which comes to us by faith alone. Faith placed in what Jesus did to fulfill the Law of Moses. He obtained the righteousness that the Law could never give mankind. And now anyone who trusts in Jesus to save them is freely offered this righteousness in place of the guilt and shame which plagued mankind because of sin. Romans makes this very clear, *"But now a righteousness from God, apart from law, has been made known, to which the Law and the Prophets testify. This righteousness from God comes through faith in Jesus Christ to all who believe. There is no difference, for all have sinned and fall short of the glory of God, and are justified freely by his grace through the redemption that came by Christ Jesus" (Romans 3:21-24)*.

Through faith in Christ we gain the full revelation of what Moses spoke about. He showed us the righteousness of the Law, Jesus is the one who provided that righteousness for us, so the Law of God could be fulfilled in our hearts. Paul said in II Corinthians, *"God made him who had no sin to be sin for us, so that in him we might become the righteousness of God" (II Corinthians 5:21)*. Now that we have obtained this we become partakers in God's house where Jesus resides as the faithful Son over it.

Jesus has proven Himself trustworthy as overseer of the New Covenant God made with mankind. But He is not just a servant of this promise; He is the master and guarantor of the Covenant. It is ratified by His precious blood. Therefore the members of God's house, everyone who puts their entire trust in Jesus, can rejoice and hold fast to this promise of grace. We can experience confidence before God because of the hope we place in Christ. Since He was faithful to God when He entered humanity to redeem us, He will be faithful to us and every promise that has been made.

What Moses saw and spoke about is fulfilled in Christ. As long as the Son resides over God's Covenant we rest securely in this promise. We have hope `redemption.`

for every situation in life. We know Jesus is our advocate to sympathize and help in every situation. We also know the glory to which we are called and look forward in anticipation to the time when Christ returns.

Hardness of Heart Affects Our Understanding of God

"So, as the Holy Spirit says: "Today, if you hear his voice, do not harden your hearts as you did in the rebellion, during the time of testing in the desert, where your fathers tested and tried me and for forty years saw what I did" (Hebrews 3:7-9)

I'll never forget the moment it dawned on me that God didn't take the Israelites out into the desert to test them. In fact it was the other way around, they were the ones who tried God's patience, tested His forbearance all those years and never once did God fail the test. They saw the mighty things He did to bring them out of Egypt. He provided for them and personally led them through the desert. Yet that entire generation passed away never entering into the Promise Land. Why? Because of their hardness of heart.

They believed certain things about God. If you read back through this account in Exodus you will see by their words the thoughts and attitudes they held about God. A prime example is when Moses led the Israelites across the Red Sea, *"As Pharaoh approached, the Israelites looked up, and there were the Egyptians, marching after them. They were terrified and cried out to the LORD. They said to Moses, "Was it because there were no graves in Egypt that you brought us to the desert to die? What have you done to us by bringing us out of Egypt? Didn't we say to you in Egypt, 'Leave us alone; let us serve the Egyptians'? It would have been better for us to serve the Egyptians than to die in the desert!" (Exodus 14:10-12).* This shows the true heart of Israel. Instead of believing God had delivered them to bring them into the Land He promised to Abraham, they thought He had brought them into the desert to kill them.

Moses had a different understanding of who God was. Look at his reply, *"Moses answered the people, "Do not be afraid. Stand firm and you will see the deliverance the LORD will bring you today. The Egyptians you see today you will never see again. The LORD will fight for you; you need only to be still." (Exodus 14:13-14).* Each viewpoint in the midst of this intense situation was vastly different. The Israelites saw the army and their impending death wanting to surrender. Moses saw the army and knew they were completely outnumbered because God was on Israel's side. He told them to watch and see their deliverance first hand.

Time after time, God provided, protected and delivered the Israelites and yet they never recognized the mighty works He did. They had preconceived ideas about God and this blocked their ability to trust and rely on Him. They grumbled, complained and were completely ungrateful to the one who sustained them all those years. God's plan was to lead them out of Egypt and straight into the Promise Land. But because of their hardness of heart and unbelief they were unable to enter, giving it all up to wander in the desert the rest of their lives. God put up with the Israelites even after they accused him of trying to kill them time and time again. God was tested and tried for forty years by the Israelites and found faithful.

This is a lesson for us. *"So, as the Holy Spirit says: "Today, if you hear his voice, do not harden your hearts..." (Hebrews 3:7-8a).* This is why we are to pay close attention to the message of Jesus. He was sent to show us the full nature and character of God (Hebrews 1:1-2). Imagine if the Israelites had the mindset of Moses who understood God's intent. The book of Exodus would be completely different. The same is true with us. If we have a revelation of God and His character, then our lives will be drastically different as well. The Holy Spirit is sent to remind us of these things and to lead us into fullness of the truth and the knowledge of God (John 14:26). Our job is to keep our hearts soft, pliable and teachable with the Lord, who is willing to reveal himself to us. Jeremiah boasted of this wonderful promise, *"For I know the plans I have for you," declares the LORD, "plans to prosper you and not to harm you, plans to give you hope and a future. Then you will call upon me and come and pray to me, and I will listen to you. You will seek me and find me when you seek me with all your heart. I will be found by you," declares the LORD (Jeremiah 29:11-14a).*

Just as my preconceived notion about the trial in the desert made me think that God tested the Israelites, understanding His nature more clearly revealed the truth of this scripture to me. In the same way, our world views, religious backgrounds and heart attitudes can keep us from being able to accept the true loving nature of God. They will taint our view if we allow them to. This is why it is so important to allow the Holy Spirit to reveal these wonderful truths to us. If we keep our hearts soft, minds open and come before the Lord in expectation; He will be faithful in revealing Himself to us as well.

Heart Attitude Can Taint Your Perception of God

"That is why I was angry with that generation, and I said,
'Their hearts are always going astray, and they have not
known my ways.' So I declared on oath in my anger, 'They
shall never enter my rest'" (Hebrews 3:10-11)

Do you long for rest? Are you tired? Weary? Does life seem more than you can bear most days? As believers, we have a promise of entering into the Sabbath Rest of God but many times we miss this plan for our lives because we do not know it is available. We continue on with our lives and certain things hinder us from entering into the rest God has promised His children. We can look at the example from Israel's past to understand how to enter into this rest.

As the Israelites wandered through the desert they became increasingly hard of heart. They saw God's provision for many generations and yet in their defiance they refused to acknowledge Him choosing rather to grumble and complain about Him. The problem was not in their circumstances. It was not because they were wandering through the desert for all those years lacking in provision. The problem was in their hearts. The true attitude and intentions of their hearts were the cause of all their problems. Proverbs says, *"For as he [man] thinketh in his heart, so is he" (Proverbs 23:7a KJV).* Their hearts were sick. They could not recognize the wonderful works of God because this callousness blinded them to it. He provided them with food, water and protection. Miraculously their clothing and shoes never wore out the entire time they were in the wilderness (Deuteronomy 29:5). And yet the attitude of their hearts tainted their perception of God, continually.

The reason is because they never progressed into a true revelation of who God was. They never became acquainted with His ways. They did not strive to understand His character and they misinterpreted His actions concerning them. The Amplified Bible puts it this way, *"And so I was provoked (displeased and sorely grieved) with that generation, and said, They always err and are led astray in their hearts, and they have not perceived or recognized My ways and become progressively better and more experimentally and intimately acquainted with them. Accordingly, I swore in My wrath and indignation, They shall not enter into My rest." (Hebrews 3:10-11 AMP).* They never entered, not because God kept them out, they kept themselves out because of their unbelief (Hebrews 3:19). They believed the wrong things about God. They saw His work and instead of progressively coming into further understanding of His nature and becoming more intimately acquainted with Him, they held fast to their unbelieving viewpoints. These ideas drove them around the wilderness for forty years.

Lessons from the Israelites

From this lesson we can draw certain conclusions. First, we must let the truth of God rewrite any misconceptions we have about Him. As we search through scripture, we must pay close attention to the words of Jesus as He was sent to reveal God to us (John 1:17-18; Colossians 1:15; Hebrews 1:1-3).

Secondly, we must pay attention to what the Holy Spirit reveals to our spirits. Jesus said in John that one of the functions of the Holy Spirit is to remind us of everything Jesus told us. *"But the Counselor, the Holy Spirit, whom the Father will send in my name, will teach you all things and will remind you of everything I have said to you. (John 14:26).* He will point out the thoughts that hinder us and confirm the truth to us rewriting the thoughts and attitudes of our heart. He will enlighten our minds and bring understanding of God and His ways.

Third, we must understand that God wants to bring us into a deep and intimate relationship with Himself and reveal His fullness to us. Unlike the Israelites who were 100% flesh and blood and not born again with the Spirit of God, we must understand that we have the Holy Spirit living inside us to reveal God's will to us. Paul told us in Corinthians, *"However, as it is written: "No eye has seen, no ear has heard, no mind has conceived what God has prepared for those who love him"— but God has revealed it to us by his Spirit" (I Corinthians 2:9-10a).* At the time of salvation God puts His Spirit into us so that we can fellowship with Him on a different level, a spiritual level. Part of this is to rewrite misconceptions we have about God. Paul went on to say, *"The Spirit searches all things, even the deep things of God. For who among men knows the thoughts of a man except the man's spirit within him? In the same way no one knows the thoughts of God except the Spirit of God. We have not received the spirit of the world but the Spirit who is from God, that we may understand what God has freely given us"* (I Corinthians 2:10b-12). When we listen to the Holy Spirit and understand God's true nature we will not be like the Israelites whose hard heart shut them out of the promise land, we will walk in the abundant life Jesus offered to his followers (John 10:10).

Sanctification is a Process

One of the major problems the Israelites experienced was that their preconceived notions overruled their experience. God wanted them to trust Him. He proved Himself faithful year after year and yet the people were oblivious to it. They saw the works He did and instead of engaging in an intimate relationship with Him they ungratefully turned against God.

However, had they recognized even the smallest of things God did for them, their hearts would have become more sensitive to Him. They would have experienced Him as Moses did. Exodus reveals, *"The LORD would speak to Moses face to face, as a man speaks with his friend"* (Exodus 33:11a). God willingly offered friendship to Moses and in return Moses walked and talked, face to face with the Lord. This is why Hebrews tells us that Moses was a faithful servant over the house of God (Hebrews 3:5). When Moses first saw the burning bush, he did not know who God was. But at the end of his life he walked and talked with Him as a friend.

It is important for us to move on in our relationship with the Lord. We need to be sensitive and open to His direction for our lives. We need to attentively listen and understand His will for us and then walk in it. We should not be like the Israelites; hard and insensitive to His mighty works, but we should be like Moses who grew in familiarity and understanding every day of his life.

This of course, is a process, but it has to start somewhere. The only place to start is Jesus. Paul told of this process when speaking about his encounter with Jesus in Acts. Christ sent him to the gentiles *"To open their eyes and turn them from darkness to light, and from the power of Satan to God, so that they may receive forgiveness of sins and a place among those who are sanctified by faith in me"* (Acts 26:18). The first step is having our eyes opened. We cannot progressively move on with the Lord unless we have realized who He is as both God and Savior. Secondly, when we see this, we must repent, which means to turn and go the opposite way. It means leaving the sin nature behind and being born again by the Spirit of God. Next we are translated into God's kingdom. Colossians says *"For He has rescued us from the dominion of darkness and brought us into the kingdom of the Son he loves"* (Colossians 1:13). He brings us out from under the authority and control of Satan's Kingdom and places us into Jesus' kingdom.

The next step is receiving the forgiveness of sins. Sadly this is where many people get hung up in this process. They either do not know they are forgiven and washed clean by the blood of Jesus or they cannot forgive themselves for their past. Like the Israelites, having this viewpoint will taint your perception of God and His loving acceptance of you. It will keep you immobile in life failing to move forward in intimacy with the Lord. Instead of being accepted on the basis of Jesus, you will keep yourself at a distance, never walking in the relationship that God desires to have with you.

However, once you understand that you are totally accepted and forgiven by God you can progress into the next stage which is a place among the sanctified. Sanctification is the process of becoming holy. Paul said the Holy Spirit is what sanctifies us, *"God chose you to be saved through the sanctifying work of the Spirit and through belief in the truth"* (II Thessalonians 2:13b). God looks at us as holy and righteous the moment we place our faith in Jesus to save us. But aligning our hearts and minds to God comes in stages. It happens as the Holy Spirit reveals God's truth to us. Jesus told us *"But the Counselor, the Holy Spirit, whom the Father will send in my name, will teach you all things and will remind you of everything I have said to you"* (John 14:26). It is His job to speak God's truths into our lives and bring understanding to our minds. But we have a part in this, it comes by relationship. It comes by walking and talking with the Lord just as Moses did. It comes by the Word of God. Jesus prayed, *"Sanctify them by the truth; your word is truth"* (John 17:17).

The last step, takes a lifetime; it is a journey not a destination. But to start we must understand certain truths about God. We must remain sensitive to the leading of the Holy Spirit and we must participate in the relationship.

God's major charge against the Israelites was *"they have not perceived or recognized My ways and become progressively better and more experimentally and intimately acquainted with them. Accordingly, I swore in My wrath and indignation, They shall not enter into My rest." (Hebrews 3:10b-11 AMP).* He was broken hearted that they never wanted to know Him. From the Israelites example we understand that we are called into intimacy with God. They were not able to enter into His rest, which means there still remains a rest for the people of God.

Entering into His Rest

"There remains, then, a Sabbath-rest for the people of God; for anyone who enters God's rest also rests from his own work, just as God did from his. Let us, therefore, make every effort to enter that rest, so that no one will fall by following their example of disobedience" (Hebrews 4:9-11).

We are called into a Sabbath Rest as people of God. We enter into this rest when we accept Jesus by faith. He is the literal fulfillment of the Sabbath Day. Just as God rested after creation was finished because there was nothing left to create. Jesus rested after He redeemed mankind from the power of darkness (Hebrews 1:3). We enter into this rest when we look to Jesus to save us because it is done and complete. It is finished! Nothing else needs to be done in order to secure our salvation. Jesus is the guarantee of this promise. Since He is resting at the right hand of God because His work is complete, we too can rest securely in Him.

Israel did not enter this rest on the basis of unbelief, Hebrews makes this clear, *"so we see that they were not able to enter, because of their unbelief" (Hebrews 3:19).* God did not shut them out of the Promise Land, unbelief did. The next chapter gives insight, *"For we also have had the gospel preached to us, just as they did; but the message they heard was of no value to them, because those who heard did not combine it with faith. Now we who have believed enter that rest..." (Hebrews 4:2-3a).* So it is fair to say the only way to enter in is by faith. Faith placed in what Jesus did to secure your salvation. Jesus is our Sabbath Rest and remaining in Him is what brings rest to the people of God. Jesus told His disciples, *"Come to me, all you who are weary and burdened, and I will give you rest. Take my yoke upon you and learn from me, for I am gentle and humble in heart, and you will find rest for your souls. For my yoke is easy and my burden is light" (Matthew 11:28-30).*

Finding Encouragement in One Another

"See to it, brothers, that none of you has a sinful, unbelieving heart that turns away from the living God. But encourage one another daily, as long as it is called Today, so that none of you may be hardened by sin's deceitfulness" (Hebrews 3:12-13)

I received a phone call the from a young friend. It was a girl I've known for a while, I've watched her grow up as I worked for her dad for many years. She's just out of college, starting her career and looking forward to her future. She had just started attending a class at her church geared toward growing in the Word. Throughout this process the leaders were encouraging the members to find mentors while going through the program. Although we haven't had much contact in the past few years the Lord kept placing me on her heart. When I received the call I was immediately excited because I knew the benefit to such a relationship. I had several mentors throughout my young life and the outcome was both positive and life changing. I was honored and blessed that the Lord chose and entrusted me with this amazing gift.

Not only will she benefit from this relationship, but I will as well. The encouragement will be mutual and so will the growth. This is because Jesus promised us, *"For where two or three come together in my name, there am I with them" (Matthew 18:20).* This illustrates an important truth to operating in the kingdom of God. We must take the time to get together with believers to build each other up, as well as encourage and pray for one another. The writer of Hebrews says the same thing in the passage we are looking at, *"But encourage one another daily, as long as it is called Today, so that none of you may be hardened by sin's deceitfulness" (Hebrews 3:13).*

The Unbelieving Heart is Like a Cancer

We are warned to protect our hearts. This is because a sinful, unbelieving heart causes us to become insensitive to God. It is like cancer that slowly eats away at our ability to trust and rely on Him. This does not happen overnight but like a callous thickened by constant rubbing, our hearts can become hard and insensitive to the prompting of the Holy Spirit. This happens when we are swept away by the deceitfulness of sin. The Amplified Bible puts it this way, *"[Therefore beware] brethren, take care, lest there be in any one of you a wicked, unbelieving heart [which refuses to cleave to, trust in, and rely on Him], leading you to turn away and desert or stand aloof from the living God. But instead warn (admonish, urge, and encourage) one another every day, as long as it is called Today, that none of you may be hardened [into settled rebellion] by the deceitfulness of sin [by the fraudulence, the stratagem, the trickery which the delusive glamor of his sin may play on him]"* (Hebrews 3:12-13 AMP). Unbelief is the end result of a choice. The choice may seem insignificant at the time, but overexposure to the lure of this world will wreak havoc on your heart and your ability to trust God.

Daily Encouragement in Christ

If overexposure to sin causes hardness of heart, then being built up and encouraged daily will prove just the opposite. It will keep our hearts soft, pliable and receptive to the Lord. This is why the writer of Hebrews instructs us to find daily encouragement in one another, because it strengthens us for the day ahead. Encouragement of this type comes in experiencing the body of believers who we're meant to share life with. *"And let us consider how we may spur one another on toward love and good deeds. Let us not give up meeting together, as some are in the habit of doing, but let us encourage one another—and all the more as you see the Day approaching"* (Hebrews 10:24-25). Jesus promises to be in the middle of the relationship, when we share our lives with other believers. We will draw encouragement from each other because our relationships are built on faith.

Having Confidence in Christ

"We have come to share in Christ if we hold firmly till the end the confidence we had at first" (Hebrews 3:14)

In Christ we are built on a firm foundation. This foundation built the heavens, the earth and everything we see around us. Jesus is the sole expression of God's glory and holds the eternal position as Savior seated in the heavenly realm at the right hand of God the Father (John 1:18; Hebrews 1:1-4). As believers, we too have come to partake in Christ and all that He has for us if we hold firm until the end, the confidence we had at first.

Paul said in Colossians, *"So then, just as you received Christ Jesus as Lord, continue to live in him" (Colossians 2:6).* The only way to receive Christ is by faith. Faith placed in what He did to restore and redeem you. Faith is the action of our convictions. When we heard the gospel message, our hearts responded in faith toward this message of grace. The book of Romans demonstrates this key principal, *"That if you confess with your mouth, "Jesus is Lord," and believe in your heart that God raised him from the dead, you will be saved. For it is with your heart that you believe and are justified, and it is with your mouth that you confess and are saved" (Romans 10:9-10).* What you are confessing is your faith in Jesus, this is a demonstration of the belief of your heart. Salvation is a combination of God's grace and your faith placed in that gift of grace. Ephesians makes this very clear, *"For it is by grace you have been saved, through faith—and this not from yourselves, it is the gift of God— not by works, so that no one can boast" (Ephesians 2:8-9).*

Since we received Christ by faith, we are to continue in Him in the very same way. We start with faith and we will finish in faith. We are called to share in Christ holding confidently to the exact same faith that saved us.

As believers, our life is a faith journey. Our faith grows and changes but the foundation remains the same and everything is built upon it. Christ is that foundation. We have come to partake in Christ, to share in everything that He has for us; but to do this we must hold in faith to the very end. Why, because faith is the key that unlocks everything God has for us. This is why Hebrews says, *"Without faith it is impossible to please God because anyone who comes to him must believe that he exists and the he rewards those who earnestly seek him" (Hebrews 11:6).* To receive you must believe and believing takes faith.

What an amazing truth to know in this life all we need to do is focus on Jesus. If we look toward Him and continue in Him the exact same way we started, we will be successful. We will be rooted and established on a foundation that is firm, unshakable and able to present us before God pure and holy. The writer of Hebrews reminds us time and time again to focus our thoughts and attention on Jesus. Just as the entire book of Hebrews wraps up with this reminder, *"Therefore, since we are surrounded by such a great cloud of witnesses, let us throw off everything that hinders and the sin that so easily entangles, and let us run with perseverance the race marked out for us. Let us fix our eyes on Jesus, the author and perfecter of our faith, who for the joy set before him endured the cross, scorning its shame, and sat down at the right hand of the throne of God. Consider him who endured such opposition from sinful men, so that you will not grow weary and lose heart" (Hebrews 12:1-3).*

Unbelief Shut Them Out of the Promise Land

"As has just been said: "Today, if you hear his voice, do not harden your hearts as you did in the rebellion." Who were they who heard and rebelled? Were they not all those Moses led out of Egypt? And with whom was he angry for forty years? Was it not with those who sinned, whose bodies fell in the desert? And to whom did God swear that they would never enter his rest if not to those who disobeyed? So we see that they were not able to enter, because of their unbelief" (Hebrews 3:15-19)

Unbelief shut the Israelites out of the promise land. They saw the mighty works of God for many years in the desert and chose disobedience instead of trusting the one who provided for them. Because of their hardness of heart they were unwilling to rely on God and follow in the plan he had for them. The result was doing it their own way, which caused them to wander through the wilderness for forty years. During that time they provoked and blatantly disobeyed God. The result was not entering into the land He promised their forefathers. This was His plan and desire for them but their unwillingness to believe kept them out.

This example from Israel's past is good for us to pay close attention to. The same offer of entering into God's rest is available for us today (Hebrews 4:1). The writer of Hebrews says if we hear God's voice don't be like the Israelites, hard and insensitive. This comes from many years of choosing to ignore this voice inside until it is but a faint echo of what was. We choose to become complacent to the things of God, refusing to obey. The results are destructive because in essence we are walking away from God and the plan He has for us. We will never enter into His rest this way, unbelief will shut us out as well.

However, the point is not to let hardness of heart run rampant in your life. The Holy Spirit starts speaking and drawing mankind unto Himself from an early age (John 6:44). The Spirit starts speaking the truth of God's love and His desire for relationship to everyone. Some choose to respond to the message; some choose to ignore it, resulting in the fate of the Israelites, hard and insensitive to God. If unbelief can shut us out of God's promise of eternal life, then choosing to believe, rely and trust in God brings us unto this rest. What we trust in is Jesus; He is the rest that God promised. *"Therefore, since the promise of entering his rest still stands, let us be careful that none of you be found to have fallen short of it. For we also have had the gospel preached to us, just as they did; but the message they heard was of no value to them, because those who heard did not combine it with faith"* (Hebrews 4:1-2).

This is why the writer of Hebrews reminds us time and again in chapter three to pay attention to the message of Jesus and to keep our hearts sensitive to the Holy Spirit. He does not want us to miss the rest that God promised to the Israelites and to us as well. He does not want unbelief to shut us out as it shut them out. He wants us to enter into this rest by solely relying on Jesus and His amazing message of grace and love.

hebrews 4.

THE BELIEVER'S
REST

The Promise of
Entering His Rest

"Therefore, since the promise of entering his rest still stands, let us be careful that none of you be found to have fallen short of it. For we also have had the gospel preached to us, just as they did; but the message they heard was of no value to them, because those who heard did not combine it with faith" (Hebrews 4:1-2)

Did you know that faith is the only way to enter into the rest that God offers. This rest is still available today but it remains that some will enter and some will not. The deciding factor is faith. When we choose to believe and solely trust in Jesus then we enter into the rest that God promised His people.

Once again we look back on the Israelites as our example. The writer of Hebrews reveals an amazing truth about them, they also had the gospel preached to them, just as we have but it was of no effect because they did not combine the message with faith. The wonderful thing about the gospel is that it is the power of God. Paul spoke of this very thing in Romans, he said, *"I am not ashamed of the gospel, because it is the power of God for the salvation of everyone who believes: first for the Jew, then for the Gentile" (Romans 1:16).* When the gospel is presented the words go into our hearts and release power, the correct response is one of faith. Faith looking toward Jesus for His grace and mercy. Grace plus faith equals salvation (Ephesians 2:8-9). Salvation through Jesus equals entering into the Sabbath Rest of God, because Jesus is that rest. This is why the gospel is so powerful.

The Israelites heard the good news message but did not combine it with faith. This caused them to wander the wilderness distrusting and provoking the Lord continually. The message they heard was their deliverance from the bondage in Egypt. God brought them out and wanted to take them into immediate possession of the land He promised Abraham but their disdain for Him blocked any attempts to do this. The root was a heart issue. They did not lean on God in absolute trust and confidence of His power. They had no understanding of His character, nature and goodness toward them. They did not respond in faith and the result was being shut out of the promised land because of their unbelief and unwillingness to enter in (Hebrews 3:19).

This lesson from Israel's past is a foreshadow to our deliverance from the bondage of sin. Jesus has brought us out from under its rule and dominion by His victory on the cross (Colossians 2:13-15). Sin was defeated once for all (Romans 6:6-7). When we hear this good news message the correct response to have is one of faith. Looking to Jesus and putting our entire trust and confidence in His saving grace. This brings us into the rest that Hebrews 4 is talking about. It goes on to say later in the chapter, *"There remains, then, a Sabbath-rest for the people of God; for anyone who enters God's rest also rests from his own work, just as God did from his"* (Hebrews 4:9-10). What we rest from is trying to work out our own salvation because Jesus provided this for us. He is the true Sabbath Rest and remaining in Him brings us rest on all sides.

The promise of entering into this rest is still freely offered today. All that is required is faith because Jesus' part has been completed. We simply respond to the good news message of Jesus. We trust solely in Him and rest in absolute confidence that He will preserve us until the end. When we stop striving in this life is when we truly start to live!

It Takes Faith
to Enter into Rest

"Now we who have believed enter that rest, just as God has
said, "So I declared on oath in my anger, 'They shall never enter
my rest.'" And yet his work has been finished since the creation
of the world. For somewhere he has spoken about the seventh
day in these words: "And on the seventh day God rested from
all his work." And again in the passage above he says, "They shall
never enter my rest." It still remains that some will enter that rest,
and those who formerly had the gospel preached to them did
not go in, because of their disobedience" (Hebrews 4:3-6)

It takes faith to enter into God's rest. Faith placed in the finished work of Christ
and not in our works. God's rest is more than setting aside one day a week
to cease from labor, it is placing our entire trust and confidence in Christ to
save us. God's special relationship with Israel was not fulfilled because of their
disobedience, so it stands to reason that this rest through relationship is still
available for all who believe. If unbelief keeps you out, then faith brings you in.

When God created the world, the Bible says that He rested on the seventh
day. This was not because He was tired and couldn't create anything else; it
was because creation was finished. There was nothing left to create. He didn't
have to produce more fruit trees to feed Adam and Eve. He created everything
with seeds and the ability to reproduce. Everything was planned out before it
was created to sustain mankind. Afterward God rested because everything was
done.

In fact, Adam and Eve were created dwelling in the rest of God. There was no
labor involved. Sure they had jobs to do, naming the animals and overseeing
the garden, but God's rest has nothing to do with taking a break from work
and activities. It had everything to do with trusting God as their source. They

walked and talked with God enjoying His fellowship and trusted in Him for everything.

God created mankind to dwell in this rest right from the start, this was always His plan. God never desired for mankind to go through all we have experienced because of sin. He created us to live in a constant state of Sabbath Rest. He created us to love us, sin is what ruined this plan.

However, the fall of mankind did not catch God off guard; He had made provision long before it was a problem. I Peter tells us, *"For you know that it was not with perishable things such as silver or gold that you were redeemed from the empty way of life handed down to you from your forefathers, but with the precious blood of Christ, a lamb without blemish or defect. He was chosen before the creation of the world, but was revealed in these last times for your sake. Through him you believe in God, who raised him from the dead and glorified him, and so your faith and hope are in God" (I Peter 1:18-21).* Christ was chosen, foreordained and destined for the cross from the beginning of time before the world existed because God knew that sin would separate us and remove us from the resting place in which He created us to dwell. Sin is what separated us, but sin is no longer an issue through Christ's sacrifice, so there remains the promise of entering into God's rest through faith in Jesus.

Just as God rested because everything was finished, we can rest in the finished work of the cross. We too have been born again with the living and lasting Word which regenerates our spirit. Peter goes on to say, *"For you have been born again, not of perishable seed, but of imperishable, through the living and enduring word of God" (I Peter 1:23).* Jesus restores us to where mankind was before the fall. He has erased the guilt and shame that sin heaps on us. He has restored the relationship with the Father that we were created for. By trusting in Jesus as our source we too can enter into the rest that God desires for us. The rest in which He created Adam and Eve. Jesus is the Sabbath Rest for the people of God.

The Jews missed out on this promise because they chose not to trust in God after they heard the good news of their deliverance. He wanted to take them into immediate possession of the land He promised to Abraham. Instead unbelief kept them out (Hebrews 3:19). So it stands to reason that if unbelief keeps you out of this promise, faith brings you in. Faith placed in Christ and what He did to restore this relationship. Only you can keep yourself out of this rest.

The Promise of Rest
is Still Available Today

"Therefore God again set a certain day, calling it Today,
when a long time later he spoke through David, as was said
before: "Today, if you hear his voice, do not harden your
hearts." For if Joshua had given them rest, God would not
have spoken later about another day" (Hebrews 4:7-8)

An important truth to understand when reading the Bible, is that in the New Testament we see the literal and spiritual fulfillment of the events that happened in the Old Testament. This example from Israel's past in their pursuit into Canaan is something we must pay close attention to because this was a foreshadow of entering into the true promised land of God.

In fact the writer of Hebrews calls to our attention that this passage is not even speaking about entering into Canaan, it is speaking about entering into the rest that David saw and prophesied about in Psalm 95. This rest comes through faith in Christ Jesus. Because of this, David looked forward to the time of Christ and called us blessed because he saw the righteousness that Christ awards through faith (Psalm 32:1-2). Paul explains this in Romans 4, *"David says the same thing when he speaks of the blessedness of the man to whom God credits righteousness apart from works: "Blessed are they whose transgressions are forgiven, whose sins are covered. Blessed is the man whose sin the Lord will never count against him" (Romans 4:6-8).*

When David saw this, he instructed under the influence of the Holy Spirit not to let hardness of heart numb this amazing truth (Psalm 95:7b-8). He warned against being like Israel during their time in the wilderness; hard and insensitive to God. Rather, when we hear His voice and His offer of life we are to respond in faith accepting the good news of Christ which has the power to save (Romans 1:16).

The writer cites these scriptures from Psalm 95 over and over in Hebrews 3 and 4 emphasizing the importance of the condition of our heart. Israel is the example, but the offer of entering into this rest is still available today. David talked about another day because Joshua didn't give them the true rest that comes from God. It was a mere shadow of Jesus. As believers we have another opportunity of securing this rest through faith in Christ Jesus. Everyone who believes enters into this rest (Hebrews 4:3). Thankfully this offer is still available today! The only requirement is faith; faith placed in Jesus. He is the true and complete Sabbath Rest that God promises His children.

True Sabbath Rest Through Christ

"There remains, then, a Sabbath-rest for the people of God;
for anyone who enters God's rest also rests from his own
work, just as God did from his" (Hebrews 4:9-10)

I remember as a teenager the pastor of the church we attended spoke one Sunday about resting on Sunday. The point of his message was to set aside one day a week to rest and focus on God. He cited the example from the Old Testament about keeping the Sabbath. After the service several people came up to me asking me if I still planned to work on Sundays commenting that I shouldn't because the Bible said to keep the Sabbath holy. I worked a part time job at a local restaurant and worked when I was scheduled, which included Sunday evenings. Although the pastor meant well, he missed the point of Sabbath Rest, it is not one day a week set aside to rest from our labors; the Sabbath Rest is Jesus.

In the Old Testament, the Law gave instruction about the Sabbath. The Israelites set aside one day to cease from their labors when everyone around them strived seven days a week. Israel prospered above others because this rest was about trusting in God as their source and not trusting in human labor to provide for them.

Everything demonstrated in the Old Testament was a type and shadow of what we would have as New Testament believers (Hebrews 10:1). They were copies and illustrations of what would be provided in Christ. A shadow is a vague outline resembling what is to come. For instance, my shadow has the shape of me. If I were to come around the corner my shadow would arrive ahead of me. You could see it and understand that a person was coming. You could make out my shape and know certain things about my height, weight and even length of hair. But you wouldn't be able to fully interpret what I look like by my shadow; that is not until you see me face to face. The same is true with the Old Testament, the Law was a foreshadowing of what Christ would be and do. It gave guidelines and regulations but these served merely to point us to the Savior, the reality has always been found in Him. At the time when they looked they could see certain things about who the Savior would be but they did not have a clear picture, just the shadow of what was coming.

As New Testament believers, we can look back and fully understand these things and see Jesus woven throughout the entire scriptures. We have the real thing. We have the expressed image of God, everything the law and prophets spoke about (Matthew 17:3; Luke 24:44; Hebrews 1:1-3). Since we have the fulfillment of these things, there is no need to live under the shadow of what was coming. The same is true for the Sabbath day, *"Therefore do not let anyone judge you by what you eat or drink, or with regard to a religious festival, a New Moon celebration or a Sabbath day. These are a shadow of the things that were to come; the reality, however, is found in Christ" (Colossians 2:16-17).* We must look at the Old Testament through the filter of Jesus otherwise we will get bogged down in confusion and never progress into full revelation of who God is and what He has provided in Christ. Instead we will continue living under the very things we have been freed from.

The Sabbath was a symbol of Jesus and now it is a New Testament reality. We can trust in the finished work of Christ and rest continually in this. We don't have to set aside one day a week to cease striving; our entire lives as believers dwell in this place. When Jesus hung on the cross He said, *"it is finished" (John 19:30).* He had fulfilled everything in the law and provided the righteousness of the law to us as a free gift. We do not need to add one thing to it, Jesus provided the way and by trusting in this provision we rest from trying to make it on our own. This is the true Sabbath Rest that God desires for His people. This rest is so much more than most people's interpretation of the Old Testament scriptures about the Sabbath day. The Sabbath is fulfilled in Jesus and knowing this amazing truth will equip you for a lifestyle of trusting in God as your source and finding wholeness in Christ.

Making an Effort to Enter the Rest

"Let us, therefore, make every effort to enter that rest, so that no one will fall by following their example of disobedience" (Hebrews 4:11)

It takes effort to enter into God's rest, it takes faith. Resting in God's grace comes moment by moment, resisting the urge to trust in ourselves. This is a process in which the foundation hinges on God's character. Unless we lay a good foundation of understanding who God is and His will concerning us we will never be able to operate in the rest that God desires for us to experience in Him.

We are continually warned not to follow the example from Israel's past. The generation that came out of Egypt distrusted and provoked God. They were disobedient and unbelieving; therefore they never saw the promise of entering into Canaan fulfilled. The entire generation passed away in the desert. We are reminded to make every effort to enter into God's rest so we will not follow in their example.

God's main charge against the Israelites was they never understood or knew Him. They did not perceive nor recognize His way nor did they become intimately acquainted with Him. *"That is why I was angry with that generation, and I said, 'Their hearts are always going astray, and they have not known my ways'" (Hebrews 3:10).* They let their preconceived notions about God overrule His demonstration of goodness, love and mercy. Their hearts were dull and hard toward Him and the result was disobedience, not trusting in God choosing rather to complain about everything.

The good news for us is that we can take this example and learn from it. The Israelites were not able to enter into the promised rest because they were not familiar and intimately acquainted with God and His ways, but we can enter and remain by understanding and fellowshipping with God. We can experience rest simply by knowing Him and His promises toward us.

Part of the reason Israel failed in this is because they thought God brought them into the desert to kill them. It is hard to trust and obey someone when you believe they are out to harm you. Unless we understand God's love for us we will also fall prey to responding as the Israelites did, distrusting God. Instead, we must let the truth of scripture speak and minister to our hearts; bringing enlightenment of His true character and desires concerning us. We can learn to trust Him by knowing these things and progressing in our relationship with Him.

Jesus came to show us God's true and complete nature (Hebrews 1:1-2). Jesus is the picture of how great God's love is toward us. He was sent to bring us into a deep and meaningful relationship with the Father. His grace and mercy is poured out on us covering and washing us clean, restoring us to a state as if we had never sinned. This is the foundation of rest. Starting here will soften our hearts opening them up to receive a revelation of God. We are to strive to enter this rest that was promised. By becoming intimately acquainted with God and His promises throughout scripture, we will continually dwell in this place. Unlike the Israelites who grew increasingly hard of heart, we can be just the opposite, increasingly sensitive to the Holy Spirit and the Lord's direction for our lives.

The Word of God is Alive and Full of Power

"For the word of God is living and active. Sharper than any double-edged sword, it penetrates even to dividing soul and spirit, joints and marrow; it judges the thoughts and attitudes of the heart" (Hebrews 4:12)

Growing up I worked at a summer camp. Each year the camp had a theme Bible verse that was presented to the kids and taught on in the chapel services. The second year I worked, Hebrews 4:12 was the verse. Since then, this verse has stuck with me, making a profound impact on my life because it placed an importance on the Word of God. Thinking of it often, I understood early that the scriptures were there to help and guide me through life. In fact they became life to me because the Word that God speaks is alive and full of power, which makes it effective and life changing.

It is no coincidence that this verse is found in the middle of instruction on entering into God's rest through Jesus. Hebrews 4:11 gives warning to make every effort of entering into rest; not following in Israel's example of disobedience and unbelief. To do this we must learn who God is and understand His nature and will concerning us. This is accomplished through scripture. The Word of God has an active part in remaining in rest.

True Sabbath Rest is found in Jesus; we enter by trusting in Him and the finished work of the cross. But to remain and stay in this place takes effort, not because we must do something to remain saved, but because we have a tendency to take back control and strive in the midst of circumstances. Instead we must rely solely on the Lord; not trusting in ourselves when situations come against us. The more we let the truth of scripture speak into our lives, the more we will trust God when things beyond our control happen because we know His promises. He will remind us of the things He has said in His Word, bringing both encouragement and confidence.

The Difference Between the Soul and The Spirit

The Word is powerful because it is able to discern the difference between the soul and spirit. These two words are so similar that most understand them to be the same thing. Even our language uses them interchangeably, but the Biblical definition is vastly different. I Thessalonians 5:23 shows us that mankind is made up of three parts, a spirit, a soul and a body. Understanding this truth is a key to unlocking and understanding many scriptures.

Our spirit is our life force. It is the part of us that was born again when we put our faith in Jesus. The default sin nature was taken out and we were given a new spirit that is identical to Jesus (Romans 6:6-7; Ephesians 4:24; I John 4:17). The believer's spirit is the part that has been sanctified, sealed and redeemed (Ephesians 1:13-14; Romans 8:15-17). The spirit you have now is the same spirit you will have for all eternity, it is perfect (Romans 8; Hebrews 10:10, 14).

The soul can be described as your personality, your thoughts, your attitudes and what makes you unique. Perhaps this is why we use words like spirit and soul interchangeably because we cannot see either one, yet we understand that we possess something that makes up who we are as a person.

The body is the container for the spirit and the soul. It is the physical structure of a human. It is our flesh and blood. It is who we are when people look at us. This is the third part to mankind, without any one of these things, we cannot sustain life.

The spirit and the soul appear to be so similar that we group them together. But Hebrews 4:12 says the Word is capable of showing us the difference between the spirit and the soul. It is like a sharp sword that is able to penetrate and divide the two. The Amplified Bible puts it this way, *"For the Word that God speaks is alive and full of power [making it active, operative, energizing, and effective]; it is sharper than any two-edged sword, penetrating to the dividing line of the breath of life (soul) and [the immortal] spirit, and of joints and marrow [of the deepest parts of our nature], exposing and sifting and analyzing and judging the very thoughts and purposes of the heart" (Hebrews 4:12 AMP).*

This is an important concept because we look at certain scriptures and wonder who they are talking about. We read passages showing us that we are identical to Jesus in this world (I John 4:17), God considers us pure, righteous and holy (Ephesians 4:24; Hebrews 10:14) and we don't believe it because we look to the realm of our soul and assume that God has made a mistake. We quote passages saying we are raised and seated with Christ in the heavenly realm (Ephesians 2:6) but continue to struggle with hardship in our homes. This is because we haven't understood the differences between the spirit and the soul and this plays out in how we interpret and understand the Bible.

The born again spirit we received the moment we were saved is identical with Jesus (Ephesians 4:24; I John 4:17). This is how God sees us, He looks at our spirit. This is why He sees us a righteous, because the sin nature is gone (Romans 6:6-9; II Corinthians 5:17, 21). Consequently this is how the devil sees us also. He looks at us dressed in our full armor (Ephesians 6:10-18) and cannot tell the difference between us and Jesus (Isaiah 59:15-18). This is why he trembles when we are around. The spirit is truly who we are because of what Jesus did.

However, we look at ourselves through the eyes of our soul. We see where we struggle, we know the thoughts we have, we know how we mess up. So there is a huge disconnect when we read the Bible because we don't understand who we are in the spirit and how God looks at us. Then we get frustrated thinking we need to be holy and righteous when in fact we already are.

This is why this passage of scripture is so powerful because it shows us the Word of God is able to discern between the two. Knowing the difference between the spirit and the soul brings enlightenment to the scriptures because we are able to discern what part of our makeup is being talked about in passages. Paul wrote, *"May God himself, the God of peace, sanctify you through and through. May your whole spirit, soul and body be kept blameless at the coming of our Lord Jesus Christ" (I Thessalonians 5:23).* Our spirit is already blameless, but our soul, the thoughts, attitudes and intent of the heart, needs to be renewed and reminded of who we are in the spirit so we will experience them in the physical realm as well.

The Word Exposes Our Thoughts and Attitudes

How we think is dependent on many things, how we were raised, the values and world views we were taught, not to mention the circumstances of our lives. All of these things shape our attitudes and perceptions whether good or bad. No matter where we come from the Word is able to expose all these things so the truth of scripture can be rewritten on our hearts.

Paul said in Romans 12:2 that transformation comes by the renewal of the mind. The transformation he is talking about is metamorphosis, illustrated by a caterpillar becoming a butterfly. It is a complete change. The same illustration holds true for us. When we let the truth of scripture rewrite the thoughts and attitudes we possess then our soul realm is transformed displaying the amazing things that are contained in our born again spirits. Everything God said we are through Christ is exactly what will show up in our lives through this renewal.

Peter said, *"His divine power has given us everything we need for life and godliness through our knowledge of him who called us by his own glory and goodness. Through these he has given us his very great and precious promises, so that through them you may participate in the divine nature and escape the corruption in the world caused by evil desires" (II Peter 1:3-4).* He gave us everything we will ever need in our spirits, remember they are identical in Jesus' spirit and perfected (Ephesians 4:24; I John 4:17). Unlocking these things comes through the knowledge of Him and renewing our minds to the truths found in scripture.

This is why God's word is alive and full of power! It is able to discern and release truth into our lives. It exposes, judges and analyzes the purposes of the heart. Then it rewrites, renews and changes our perceptions of reality aligning it to God's view. This is an amazing truth! This is why Paul told Timothy, *"Do your best to present yourself to God as one approved, a workman who does not need to be ashamed and who correctly handles the word of truth" (II Timothy 2:15).* We study not to show God that we are approved but to show ourselves that we are approved by God. Handling, releasing and teaching the word of truth with accuracy and skill.

Learning this verse from Hebrews 4 early on in life has made all the difference as I have grown and understand more clearly God's word. I see the wonderful things it contains and trust that God will reveal these truths

redemption.

to me. They contain life and have transformation power. Not only will my life resemble Christ's life in my born again spirit but it will also be displayed in my thoughts and actions as well. Knowing this amazing truth helps me dwell in a constant state of Sabbath Rest.

Nothing is Hidden
From God's Sight

"Nothing in all creation is hidden from God's sight.
Everything is uncovered and laid bare before the eyes of him
to whom we must give account" (Hebrews 4:13)

At first glance this verse seems scary depending on your view of God. If you believe God is waiting for you to mess up then a verse like this can be terrifying. Or, if you believe God is waiting for you to settle your sin account after death, then reading these words are less than reassuring. However understanding the context of this verse and God's loving nature toward us in the person of Jesus, we should see how wonderful this message is.

Nothing is concealed from God's sight, everything is open and exposed, but through Christ, this is not a scary thing. We feel secure in knowing that people don't really know our true thoughts and intentions, but the Bible says that God knows and scripture judges the heart. The verse prior to this passage says, *"For the word of God is living and active. Sharper than any double-edged sword, it penetrates even to dividing soul and spirit, joints and marrow; it judges the thoughts and attitudes of the heart" (Hebrews 4:12).* Since God knows and understands who we are, He also knows and understands the truth we need to hear to continue the transformation of our soul realm into the likeness of Christ.

The good news in all of this is; understanding that God loves us. He takes an active interest in our lives and desires for us to grow and develop through that love. As I was thinking about this passage and understanding the knee-jerk reaction to reading words such as this, Psalms 103 kept playing in my mind.

> *"The LORD is compassionate and gracious,*
>   *slow to anger, abounding in love.*
> *He will not always accuse,*
>   *nor will he harbor his anger forever;*
> *he does not treat us as our sins deserve*
>   *or repay us according to our iniquities.*
> *For as high as the heavens are above the earth,*
>   *so great is his love for those who fear him;*
> *as far as the east is from the west,*
>   *so far has he removed our transgressions from us.*
> *As a father has compassion on his children,*
>   *so the LORD has compassion on those*
> *who fear him" (Psalm 103:8-13).*

One thing I've realized through life is that God is so patient, loving and understanding. He knows the real us and loves us anyway. He knows what we need to change and uses the Word to do it. It comes just at the right moment exactly when we need to hear it, whether through a sermon, a friend or reading it for ourselves.

Even though everything is open and exposed before God we have a promise in this scripture as well because we have Jesus as our High Priest. The very next passage says, *"Therefore, since we have a great high priest who has gone through the heavens, Jesus the Son of God, let us hold firmly to the faith we profess. For we do not have a high priest who is unable to sympathize with our weaknesses, but we have one who has been tempted in every way, just as we are— yet was without sin. Let us then approach the throne of grace with confidence, so that we may receive mercy and find grace to help us in our time of need" (Hebrews 4:14-16).* Jesus has been there and understands everything about us. He is our personal advocate with the Father interceding continually on our behalf. We have confidence in approaching God to obtain grace and mercy because of what Jesus did for us on the cross. This truly is an amazing truth, to know that God knows everything about us, nothing being hidden, everything laid bare, exposed and naked and yet knowing that we have Jesus making a personal plea and defense for us. He is our eternal High Priest living to maintain the position of grace that we have through His name.

Holding Firmly to the Faith We Profess

"Therefore, since we have a great high priest who has gone through the heavens, Jesus the Son of God, let us hold firmly to the faith we profess" (Hebrews 4:14)

The resurrection of Jesus Christ was the pinnacle of history. The fate of mankind hinged on this one event. And as Jesus was raised from the dead He ascended through the heavens past every authority and spiritual force in existence. Nothing they could do stopped the ascension of our Savior and they watched in horror as life defeated death once for all (Philippians 2:9-11; Colossians 2:15).

Now Jesus is at the right hand of the Father making intercession for us. He is our personal advocate and the best defense attorney in the universe. Because this is a past event we hold firmly and confidently to this profession of faith in Christ, knowing that He lives to guarantee our lives as well.

Couple this amazing truth with the previous verses and you will understand the depth of God's love toward us. God knows us, He sees the inmost thoughts we possess. In fact verse 13 says, *"Nothing in all creation is hidden from God's sight. Everything is uncovered and laid bare before the eyes of him to whom we must give account" (Hebrews 4:13).* And yet in the very next verse it says, *"Therefore, since we have a great high priest who has gone through the heavens, Jesus the Son of God, let us hold firmly to the faith we profess" (Hebrews 4:14).* Nothing concerning our thoughts and actions surprise God. He sees and knows everything about us, but instead of pronouncing judgment we are instructed to hold firmly to our confession of faith in Christ. Grace and mercy abound as we are reminded that Jesus has ascended into heaven and is currently making intercession for us and on our behalf.

Jesus rushed to make our defense and His blood washed us clean of every offense. Paul said in Romans 5, *"For if, when we were God's enemies, we were reconciled to him through the death of his Son, how much more, having been reconciled, shall we be saved through his life!" (Romans 5:10).* God sent His only son for us when we were His enemies, now that we are redeemed and called beloved, how much more are we loved, forgiven and restored because of it? This is why we are reminded to hold firmly to our profession of faith, understanding that Jesus lives to intercede for us, knowing the most intimate details about us so He can accurately and completely uphold our defense.

Just as the pinnacle of history was Jesus' resurrection from the dead, our entire hope in life is still dependent on this significant event. If we hold firmly until the end this confession of faith, remembering that Jesus is our High Priest then we will have confidence and boldness to approach God on the basis of this faith (Hebrews 4:16). This is truly an amazing truth understanding the role that Jesus plays as our Savior and High Priest and letting this truth rewrite how we approach and relate to God.

Jesus Was Tempted in Every Way, Yet Without Sin

"For we do not have a high priest who is unable to sympathize with our weaknesses, but we have one who has been tempted in every way, just as we are—yet was without sin" (Hebrews 4:15)

One of the things that helps us relate to Jesus as a personal savior is that He has been there and can relate to us on the basis of humanity. Philippians tells us that He emptied himself of everything and entered into mankind in human form (Philippians 2:6-7). He stripped Himself of all divine privileges and dignity and assumed the guise of a slave born under the dominion of Satan's kingdom. He did this so He could rescue us.

Jesus started with nothing. He was born in the most humble of circumstances. Born to teenage parents in a lowly manger, reserved for animals. Not exactly the place for the King of Kings and Lord of Lords (Revelation 19:16). And yet Luke's gospel tells us that Jesus grew in wisdom, and the grace of God was on Him (Luke 2:40). Even from an early age, Jesus pursued and prepared for His role as the Savior of the World.

During His time on earth Jesus underwent temptation and trials so He would be fully equipped to serve as our High Priest. He dealt with difficult people and faced situations that are common in humanity and yet the Bible says that He was without sin. This is incredibly important because to defeat death we needed a perfect sin substitute. By conquering the grasp sin had on mankind He was able to free us from what held us captive. Since He emptied himself of all divine privileges and experienced the fullness of humanity He is able to understand and empathize with us in our weaknesses. There is no one better equipped to serve before God as our High Priest than Jesus.

The previous verse in Hebrews says, *"Therefore, since we have a great high priest who has gone through the heavens, Jesus the Son of God, let us hold firmly to the faith we profess" (Hebrews 4:14).* Since this is a past event and Jesus has ascended to the right hand of the Father, we can cling to this confession of faith in Jesus when trials and temptations seem to close in around us. He is there to provide help exactly when we need it. All we have to do is ask and believe that He will deliver us. Paul told us, *"No temptation has seized you except what is common to man. And God is faithful; he will not let you be tempted beyond what you can bear. But when you are tempted, he will also provide a way out so that you can stand up under it" (I Corinthians 10:13).* He is able to do this because He has been there and understands the common temptations that we faces.

What a marvelous truth knowing that Jesus was chosen as our High Priest. One who has been tempted and tried in every way imaginable and yet remained sinless throughout His course in life. He is able to run to our side and assist us in every circumstance because He has been there. And now, He is in heaven in a position to help us in every way because He humbled himself, becoming obedient to death to rescue us from the dominion of darkness. Because of this we can have boldness and confidence to enter into the throne room of God to find grace and mercy when we need it.

Approaching the Throne of Grace with Confidence

"Let us then approach the throne of grace with confidence, so that we may receive mercy and find grace to help us in our time of need" (Hebrews 4:16)

There was a period of time in my life that I was not living as I should. Everything spiraled downward and the blur of those years caused much guilt and shame later on in life. Although it was a short hiatus in my young life I struggled to get past a few events that happened in my late teens and early twenties. Every time I moved on with the Lord after that, it seemed the devil threw this stuff in my face to remind me of that shame. Each time I felt unworthy of the Lord and wanted to run and hide from Him instead of running to Him.

My pastor at one time shared an illustration about Satan and His minions being the best videographer around. They love to catch footage of our sin and replay it over and over for us. Hounding us so as to remind us that we mess up even when we call ourselves Christians. They glory in causing heartache and guilt over past events that are done and over with. This illustration came to a profound climax when He explained that Jesus takes this video footage and erases it by His blood. Then when the footage is played back it is blank with no condemning evidence.

Only when you understand the complete forgiveness from sins can you have confidence to enter into the presence of God and boldly draw near to the throne of grace. The only thing that keeps you from fearlessly approaching God is your consciousness of sin. But sin is not an issue with God because Jesus has made perfect provision for you, making you holy and blameless sanctified by His blood.

So as believers we should not have a sin conscience. The writer instructs that we can enter in to God's presence to receive mercy and find grace when we need it, even in the midst of struggling with sin. Mercy is not getting what we deserve. Grace is getting what we don't. Mercy is not receiving the punishment for our sins. Grace is receiving forgiveness, being restored to a state where it is as if we had never sinned in the first place. One drop of Jesus' blood was more than enough to cleanse and wash us clean. If we hold on to the memory of our sin, then we will never enter in to find this help and understanding from God.

Trouble comes when we don't understand this truth. I constantly dealt with the guilt and shame of my actions because I had no comprehension of the depth of His grace. I had taken over the playback of this video footage and each time it was erased I recreated it in my mind. It held me captive for many years and kept me from progressing into a deeper understanding of the Lord.

Freedom came when I saw the depth of God's love for me through the eyes of Jesus. I finally saw what He sees, not what I played back in my mind. He does not see a sinner saved by grace, He sees a woman who is righteous, holy, forgiven, loved, blameless and set apart. He does not see the sins that have been paid for and removed from both of our presence. He sees the blood of His Son, which has purified and restored.

I have taken the words of I John to heart, *"This then is how we know that we belong to the truth, and how we set our hearts at rest in his presence whenever our hearts condemn us. For God is greater than our hearts, and he knows everything. Dear friends, if our hearts do not condemn us, we have confidence before God"* (I John 3:19-21). If ever I struggle with guilt, then I remind myself of the truth from God's Word and suddenly my heart experiences the peace of God. The things that previously held me captive cannot hold me anymore. The Lord has done an amazing work in my life, even the memory of several events are but a faint echo of what was. Not only has He erased the guilt and shame I experience but He has all but erased the memory of it as well. Now I can look at myself through His eyes and see as He sees. This gives confidence to boldly approach God's throne and be at rest in His presence.

hebrews 5.

JESUS IS THE PERFECT HIGH PRIEST

The High Priest Selected from Among Men

"Every high priest is selected from among men and is appointed to represent them in matters related to God, to offer gifts and sacrifices for sins. He is able to deal gently with those who are ignorant and are going astray, since he himself is subject to weakness. This is why he has to offer sacrifices for his own sins, as well as for the sins of the people" (Hebrews 5:1-3)

The sacrificial system was a type and shadow of what was to come (Hebrews 10:1). It was a rough outline, not the image itself. It represented a vague picture of the true sacrifice that would be made by the Messiah. It was used to remind those making the sacrifices of their sin (Hebrews 10:3). They experienced this symbolism year after year looking forward with anticipation to the Christ.

When making a sin offering the worshiper had to provide a perfect, spotless lamb. Laying their hands on it to symbolically transfer their sin and guilt, the animal was then sacrificed as a covering for sin (Leviticus 4). However the sacrificing of animals was never able to remove sin as evidenced by the conscience of the worshiper and the repetitive act of bringing sacrifices. Hebrews 10 describes this in detail, *"The law is only a shadow of the good things that are coming—not the realities themselves. For this reason it can never, by the same sacrifices repeated endlessly year after year, make perfect those who draw near to worship. If it could, would they not have stopped being offered? For the worshipers would have been cleansed once for all, and would no longer have felt guilty for their sins. But those sacrifices are an annual reminder of sins, because it is impossible for the blood of bulls and goats to take away sins"* (Hebrews 10:1-4).

The sacrificed animal couldn't take away sin because it was incapable of being the perfect substitute. In the same way, the priest selected from among men, could never be the perfect mediator for mankind. This is because they were subjected to the same faults and weaknesses as those making atonement. The priest would have to offer a sacrifice first for his owns sins and then the sins of the people. This is why the sacrificial system only served as a picture to remind the people that the perfect sacrifice and mediator was coming.

Hebrews 9 goes into detail, *"This is an illustration for the present time, indicating that the gifts and sacrifices being offered were not able to clear the conscience of the worshiper. They are only a matter of food and drink and various ceremonial washings—external regulations applying until the time of the new order"* (Hebrews 9:9-10).

The High Priest was appointed to act on the behalf of men in all things relating to God. They offered both gifts and sacrifices. They served as mediator between God and man. This picture gives us insight into the function of the high priest, helping to understand the role of Jesus as the mediator of the New Covenant. Paul said in I Timothy, *"For there is one God and one mediator between God and men, the man Christ Jesus, who gave himself as a ransom for all men—the testimony given in its proper time"* (I Timothy 2:5-6).

Jesus was both the perfect sin substitute and perfect mediator ratifying the New Covenant between God and mankind with His blood. He is the true picture and exact representation of what the sacrificial system portrayed. In contrast, we do not have a High Priest who is subject to the weaknesses of mankind, but one who is perfect in every way. This is why our covenant is much more superior in every way, because we have Jesus the perfect High Priest to intercede for us.

God Bestowed the Honor of High Priest on Jesus

"No one takes this honor upon himself; he must be called by God, just as Aaron was. So Christ also did not take upon himself the glory of becoming a high priest. But God said to him, "You are my Son; today I have become your Father" (Hebrews 5:4-5)

Jesus did not exalt himself to the position of High Priest, even though He was the only one qualified who could have easily assumed the role. Instead God appointed Him this honor. Since the introduction of the High Priest, it was God who chose who would serve at the altar. He chose Aaron and gave instruction that every high priest would be his descendant (Exodus 29:9). Aaron wasn't qualified when God chose him, having served as a slave in Egypt his entire life. Nevertheless, God chose and equipped him to intercede on Israel's behalf.

However, being human, the High Priest was never able to make intercession effectively. Both because they were subjected to the weakness of the flesh and because death prevented them from continuing in office (Hebrews 5:1-3; 7:23). Because of this, the Levitical priesthood could only serve as a vague representation until the time of Christ. The sacrifices and intercession was only a covering for sin, it never dealt with the issue of sin. Isaiah tells us, "*The LORD looked and was displeased that there was no justice. He saw that there was no one, he was appalled that there was no one to intervene; so his own arm worked salvation for him, and his own righteousness sustained him*" *(Isaiah 59:15b-16).* God saw that mankind was incapable of bringing reconciliation between God and mankind. This displeased him, so Isaiah records that God's own right arm, Jesus, worked salvation for mankind.

Jesus is the person that God chose. He chose the very best right from the start. There was not a backup plan because the perfect plan was set into motion from the very beginning. I Peter records, *"He [Jesus] was chosen before the creation of the world, but was revealed in these last times for your sake" (I Peter 1:20)*. Jesus' redemption of mankind was so perfect and complete, God appointed Him the honor of eternal High Priest and exalted His name far above everything in existence (Philippians 2:9-11; Hebrews 1:4). Aaron portrayed a picture of the true High Priest, helping us to understand this role, but Jesus is the embodiment of the image. The difference is that Jesus is currently making intercession for us, in heaven, in the presence of God. *"Now there have been many of those priests, since death prevented them from continuing in office; but because Jesus lives forever, he has a permanent priesthood. Therefore he is able to save completely those who come to God through him, because he always lives to intercede for them" (Hebrews 7:23-25)*.

David prophesied about this in the Psalm, *"You are my Son, today I have become your Father" (Psalm 2:7; Hebrews 1:5; 5:5)*. Jesus was always the plan. He was the perfect atonement and He is the perfect High Priest. Romans tells us that *"God's gifts and his call are irrevocable" (Romans 11:29)*. Meaning, He does not change His mind. In fact, the position given to Jesus as High priest was given with an oath from God that it was an eternal position (Hebrews 7:21-22, 28). We can be confident in this, placing our entire faith in the one who died for us, who was raised to life for us and who lives interceding at God's right hand for us.

Jesus is a Priest
in the Order of Melchizedek

*"And he says in another place, "You are a priest forever,
in the order of Melchizedek" (Hebrews 5:6)*

Not only did God appoint Christ and exalt Him with the honor of becoming our High Priest, He also appointed Him a rank in the order of Melchizedek. This is extremely significant as human standards would never have allowed Jesus this position. And yet, God is the one who appointed Him as eternal High Priest after this order. There was a reason God prophesied these very words through David, *"The LORD has sworn and will not change his mind: "You are a priest forever, in the order of Melchizedek" (Psalm 110:4).* To understand this, we must look at who Melchizedek was and how Jesus is like him.

This account is found in Genesis 14. Abraham had just defeated the four kings and rescued Lot from their hand. As he is returning, Melchizedek the priest comes and blesses Abraham. *"Then Melchizedek king of Salem brought out bread and wine. He was priest of God Most High, and he blessed Abram, saying, "Blessed be Abram by God Most High, Creator of heaven and earth. And blessed be God Most High, who delivered your enemies into your hand." Then Abram gave him a tenth of everything" (Genesis 14:18-20).* In this short account we see a priest of God bless Abraham and he responds by giving him one tenth of all of his possessions. What is interesting is that the Law, with its priestly regulations wasn't introduced for another 430 years during the time of Moses and yet from the beginning there existed a priest of God Most High.

Hebrews 7 gives much more detail about this. *"This Melchizedek was king of Salem and priest of God Most High. He met Abraham returning from the defeat of the kings and blessed him, and Abraham gave him a tenth of everything. First, his name means "king of righteousness"; then also, "king of Salem" means "king of peace." Without father or mother, without genealogy, without beginning of days or end of life, like the Son of God he remains a priest forever" (Hebrews 7:1-3).* A lot of mystery surrounds this priest as he has no record of beginning, end or genealogy. Without these records, one could say he has always and will always exist. Known as both the king of righteousness and the king of peace, these names are descriptive of who he was.

Jesus shares the same attributes attributed to Melchizedek in Hebrews 7. First, He was appointed by God. The previous verses states, *"No one takes this honor upon himself; he must be called by God, just as Aaron was. So Christ also did not take upon himself the glory of becoming a high priest. But God said to him, "You are my Son; today I have become your Father" (Hebrews 5:4-5).* Secondly, we see through Jesus' recorded genealogy His eternal existence. Matthew and Luke give accounts of His physical lineage, but John gives His genealogy as eternal God. *"In the beginning was the Word, and the Word was with God, and the Word was God. He was with God in the beginning" (John 1:1-2).* Lastly, the names given to Melchizedek were also given to Jesus. It was Isaiah who prophesied that Jesus would be called Prince of Peace (Isaiah 9:6). And the author of Hebrews, quoting from the Psalm stated that righteousness would be the scepter of His kingdom (Hebrews 1:8; Psalm 45:6-7).

This is important to us because our faith rests in Jesus and the finished work of the cross. Our faith rests in the fact that He is alive and seated in heaven interceding on our behalf. *"Because Jesus lives forever, he has a permanent priesthood. Therefore he is able to save completely those who come to God through him, because he always lives to intercede for them" (Hebrews 7:24-25).* This is why it is important to understand how Jesus is a priest after the order and with the rank of Melchizedek. *"And what we have said is even more clear if another priest like Melchizedek appears, one who has become a priest not on the basis of a regulation as to his ancestry but on the basis of the power of an indestructible life. For it is declared: "You are a priest forever, in the order of Melchizedek" (Hebrews 7:15-17).* Jesus is able to save completely those who come to Him in faith because He is alive and resides permanently as High Priest of the Most High God.

Jesus Had a Choice

"During the days of Jesus' life on earth, he offered up prayers and petitions with loud cries and tears to the one who could save him from death, and he was heard because of his reverent submission. Although he was a son, he learned obedience from what he suffered" (Hebrews 5:7-8)

On this side of the cross we are used to hearing about Jesus' sacrifice for our sins so we forget this important truth, Jesus had a choice. The choice to redeem mankind, or let mankind pay the price for Adam's choice in the garden. Adam chose death, suffering and sin over God. As result, he plunged the entire world into this pattern of life and we were subjected to the destructiveness of un-regenerated man. Mankind needed someone to intercede which is why Jesus volunteered for the role as Savior of the world (I Corinthians 15:22; II Corinthians 5:19; I Peter 1:20; I John 2:2).

God is big on giving choices and letting us choose for ourselves. He does not force His will on us. In the same way, He did not force His will for redeeming mankind on Jesus. He gave Him the choice. This is beyond comprehension because God and Jesus are one and the same. They exist in a triune being of perfect love and unity. Father, Son and Holy Spirit, three distinctly different entities yet one in the same. II Peter 3 tells us that God is not willing that any should perish and desires everyone to come to repentance (II Peter 3:9). This means that Jesus holds this desire as well. Hebrews 1 tells us that *"The Son is the radiance of God's glory and the exact representation of his being..." (Hebrews 1:3a).* Meaning He is the exact image and picture of God. Everything God is, Jesus is. Everything God desires, Jesus desires. God's will is Jesus' will.

The plan from the start was Jesus. As He submitted to God's will, He became the lamb slain from the foundation of the world (Revelation 13:8). Jesus undertook this role even before there was a world to redeem. Then at the culmination of history He was made manifest in the flesh to complete this work once for all. It was a choice. No one took Jesus' life; He willing laid it down for us. John tells us, *"The reason my Father loves me is that I lay down my life—only to take it up again. No one takes it from me, but I lay it down of my own accord. I have authority to lay it down and authority to take it up again. This command I received from my Father."* (John 10:17-18).

The grace of God is more profound when you consider that Jesus could have backed out of this arrangement at any time. During His time on earth, Jesus could have said one word and God would have honored it. In the garden when Jesus was betrayed, Peter cut off the ear of the High Priest's servant. Jesus responded in this way, *"Put your sword back in its place,"* Jesus said to him, *"for all who draw the sword will die by the sword. Do you think I cannot call on my Father, and he will at once put at my disposal more than twelve legions of angels? But how then would the Scriptures be fulfilled that say it must happen in this way?"* (Matthew 26:52-54). Jesus understood the choice and knew God would honor and respond to His decision at any point in time. Which is why He submitted to God and learned obedience through this type of suffering.

Jesus' suffering was more than the physical aspects of being crucified. His suffering far exceeded this because He had the entire weight of sin, sickness and death placed on Him and then He was completely and totally separated from the presence of the Father. It took an act of obedience for a holy God to undergo this type of suffering. This is the point the writer of Hebrews is highlighting in this passage. The Amplified Bible puts it best, *"In the days of His flesh [Jesus] offered up definite, special petitions [for that which He not only wanted but needed] and supplications with strong crying and tears to Him Who was [always] able to save Him [out] from death, and He was heard because of His reverence toward God [His godly fear, His piety, in that He shrank from the horrors of separation from the bright presence of the Father]. Although He was a Son, He learned [active, special] obedience through what He suffered"* (Hebrews 5:7-8 AMP). The price Jesus paid was extremely high. He was removed from the very essences of God the Father and literally became sin, the very thing He abhorred, so that we could be righteous in God's sight (II Corinthians 5:21).

When looking at the accounts of Jesus in the Garden of Gethsemane right before His betrayal we see how the anticipation of being separated from God affected Jesus. Yet during the entire time He readily submitted to

God's will in spite of what He was facing. Mark's account is extremely insightful, *"He took Peter, James and John along with him, and he began to be deeply distressed and troubled. "My soul is overwhelmed with sorrow to the point of death," he said to them. "Stay here and keep watch." Going a little farther, he fell to the ground and prayed that if possible the hour might pass from him. "Abba, Father," he said, "everything is possible for you. Take this cup from me. Yet not what I will, but what you will" (Mark 14:33-36).* Jesus knew that on request God would save Him from this horrible death and from taking the weight of Adams choice on Himself as mankind's representative. In the same way, He knew that God had chosen Jesus as the first and only way to redeem mankind. So Jesus actively submitted to God's will and plan so that it would be finished.

Jesus completed everything that He was instructed to do. He fulfilled every scripture written about the promised Messiah. John records, *"Later, knowing that all was now completed, and so that the Scripture would be fulfilled, Jesus said, "I am thirsty." A jar of wine vinegar was there, so they soaked a sponge in it, put the sponge on a stalk of the hyssop plant, and lifted it to Jesus' lips. When he had received the drink, Jesus said, "It is finished." With that, he bowed his head and gave up his spirit" (John 19:28-30).* What an amazing picture of the love God has for us. Mark gives us more detail on what happened, *"It was now about the sixth hour, and darkness came over the whole land until the ninth hour, for the sun stopped shining. And the curtain of the temple was torn in two. Jesus called out with a loud voice, "Father, into your hands I commit my spirit." When he had said this, he breathed his last" (Luke 23:44-46).*

This act of obedience perfectly equipped Jesus for His role as our eternal High Priest, He accomplished everything God desired and became the source of eternal salvation for everyone who puts their trust in Him (Hebrews 5:9; 7:25). Jesus has been exalted to His rightful place as Lord and will remain in this position eternally. *"And being found in appearance as a man, he humbled himself and became obedient to death— even death on a cross! Therefore God exalted him to the highest place and gave him the name that is above every name, that at the name of Jesus every knee should bow, in heaven and on earth and under the earth, and every tongue confess that Jesus Christ is Lord, to the glory of God the Father" (Philippians 2:8-11).* This confession of Jesus' lordship brings glory to God because it was His desire from the beginning that we would be reconciled through Jesus. And Jesus honored God's request.

Jesus had a choice and He chose us. God still offers this choice today. The work of salvation has been accomplished and now it is freely given to us as a gift through faith in Jesus. It is His desire that we accept this gift, but God does not make us choose him. *"Yet to all who received him, to those who believed in his name, he gave the right to become children of God— children born not of natural descent, nor of human decision or a husband's will, but born of God" (John 1:12-13).*

Jesus is the Source
of Eternal Salvation

"and, once made perfect, he became the source of eternal salvation for all who obey him and was designated by God to be high priest in the order of Melchizedek" (Hebrews 5:9-10)

On the cross Jesus said *"it is finished"* right before He gave up His spirit. With these words, He was signifying that everything He came to do was accomplished, everything written about Him had been fulfilled and the redemption of the entire world was completed. Since there was nothing left to do He ascended into heaven and sat down at the right hand of the Father taking His rightful place as Lord (Mark 16:19; Acts 2:32-33; Romans 8:34; Ephesians 1:20; Hebrews 1:3; 10:12).

This is an important truth to understand because Jesus is Lord whether you have personally confessed His Lordship or not. Not recognizing His position does not change it as fact. Peter stated this very thing at Pentecost, *"Therefore let all Israel be assured of this: God has made this Jesus, whom you crucified, both Lord and Christ." (Acts 2:36).*

With one marvelous act of obedience on the cross, Jesus was perfectly equipped through this experience to become our High Priest in service to God. With this completed exercise He became both the author and source of eternal salvation to everyone who puts their saving faith in Him.

Everything we know and experience as humans has a beginning and an end. We are bound by time, distance and energy. We set aside periods of rest and recharging by eating, sleeping and drinking. This maintains our body's health and energy. In light of this, it is hard to wrap our brains around the fact that, Jesus is the source of eternal salvation. Which means that it originated with Him, it flows out of Him and He is the supply for its power. Jesus told this very truth to the woman at the well in John 4, *"Jesus answered, "Everyone who drinks this water will be thirsty again, but whoever drinks the water I give him will never thirst. Indeed, the water I give him will become in him a spring of water welling up to eternal life" (John 4:13-14).* Once you participate in this life that Jesus offers, He is able to sustain you and keep you forever because Jesus is the wellspring to eternal life and its supply will never be shut off.

This truth rings clear when we understand that Jesus has been guaranteed this position because God designated Him to be a High Priest in the order of Melchizedek. Hebrews 7 gives much more detail about this. *"And what we have said is even more clear if another priest like Melchizedek appears, one who has become a priest not on the basis of a regulation as to his ancestry but on the basis of the power of an indestructible life. For it is declared: "You are a priest forever, in the order of Melchizedek" (Hebrews 7:15-17).* With Jesus' resurrection from the dead, He broke the power of death, meaning He can never die again (Romans 6:9; Acts 2:24; Ephesians 1:20-23). Because He cannot die again, it means that He will live forever. *"Now there have been many of those priests, since death prevented them from continuing in office; but because Jesus lives forever, he has a permanent priesthood. Therefore he is able to save completely those who come to God through him, because he always lives to intercede for them" (Hebrews 7:23-25).* This is why it is so wonderful that God designated Jesus to be a priest after this order. *"For the law appoints as high priests men who are weak; but the oath, which came after the law, appointed the Son, who has been made perfect forever" (Hebrews 7:28).*

As if this wasn't enough, God promised Jesus by an oath that He would never change His mind, as so Jesus became the author and source of the salvation we so dearly cherish and cling to. *"And it was not without an oath! Others became priests without any oath, but he became a priest with an oath when God said to him: "The Lord has sworn and will not change his mind: "You are a priest forever."" Because of this oath, Jesus has become the guarantee of a better covenant" (Hebrews 7:20-22).* Understanding Jesus' role as our High Priest, knowing that He is the source of eternal salvation guaranteed by oath from God is an amazing truth that will encourage and bless you throughout your entire life.

You Need Milk, Not Solid Food

"We have much to say about this, but it is hard to explain because you are slow to learn. In fact, though by this time you ought to be teachers, you need someone to teach you the elementary truths of God's word all over again. You need milk, not solid food!" (Hebrews 5:11-12)

This is a word for the modern church. We have congregations of people that remain in infancy, hovering around the door of salvation without a desire to walk into the fullness of God, to which they have been called. Placing no importance on God's Word in their own lives, they cannot accept the deep things of God because they haven't strived to understand even the foundation.

This is exactly what the writer of Hebrews is chiding the reader about. The wonderful truth being explained of Jesus' priesthood being on the same order as Melchizedek's is hard to comprehend, not because it is impossible but because we are unable to receive it. This is due to dullness in our spiritual understanding and being undisciplined in God's word. The Amplified Bible records it this way, *"Concerning this we have much to say which is hard to explain, since you have become dull in your [spiritual] hearing and sluggish [even slothful in achieving spiritual insight]. For even though by this time you ought to be teaching others, you actually need someone to teach you over again the very first principles of God's Word. You have come to need milk, not solid food"* (Hebrews 5:11-12 AMP).

I believe this epidemic of infancy is twofold. First, since many teachers do not have a full understanding of the scripture as a whole, they spoon feed elementary truths again and again without offering to lead their congregations deeper in their understanding of God. Secondly, because of this, people have no desire to find out for themselves what God's Word says. They take at face value what they've been taught without verifying or knowing it for themselves. They do not allow themselves to feast on anything other than the milk of the Word. Because of this, we have congregations full of people who look more like the world, than like Jesus.

As believers we must place the utmost importance on knowing God's Word. Not just reading it to check it off the list, but studying it to gain spiritual understanding and revelation knowledge. This is our handbook for life. This is God's love letter to us to show us the person of Jesus Christ. John tells us that Jesus is the Word (John 1:1, 14), which means that these written truths are living and once we digest them they will activate within us and change us.

Peter said *"His divine power has given us everything we need for life and godliness through our knowledge of him who called us by his own glory and goodness. Through these he has given us his very great and precious promises, so that through them you may participate in the divine nature and escape the corruption in the world caused by evil desires" (II Peter 1:3-4).* Paul told Timothy, *"But as for you, continue in what you have learned and have become convinced of, because you know those from whom you learned it, and how from infancy you have known the holy Scriptures, which are able to make you wise for salvation through faith in Christ Jesus. All Scripture is God-breathed and is useful for teaching, rebuking, correcting and training in righteousness, so that the man of God may be thoroughly equipped for every good work" (II Timothy 3:14-17).* James said something similar, *"But the man who looks intently into the perfect law that gives freedom, and continues to do this, not forgetting what he has heard, but doing it—he will be blessed in what he does" (James 1:25).* All of these great men placed an importance on knowing the Word. Scripture was given to help us through this life. To remind us of everything Jesus said and did. To show us what is to come, and to protect us from everything that Jesus died to set us free of. The Bible is full of amazing truths and wonderful promises, but unless you know them you will never experience them.

The Bible is not hard to understand because we have a capable teacher. This is one of the functions of the Holy Spirit. I John 2 says, *"As for you, the anointing you received from him remains in you, and you do not need anyone to teach you. But as his anointing teaches you about all things and as that anointing is real, not counterfeit—just as it has taught you, remain in*

redemption.

him" (I John 2:27). The Holy Spirit will guide you to understand the Bible as you start to explore. He will speak these truths into your life, bringing understanding. All you need to do is start planting the seeds of life and He will do the rest.

Paul's charge to Timothy is a good one for us today, He told him, *"Do your best to present yourself to God as one approved, a workman who does not need to be ashamed and who correctly handles the word of truth" (II Timothy 2:15).* We study not to prove ourselves to God, but to show ourselves that we are approved by God. We will never be ashamed before Him when we accurately handle and skillfully teach the truths of the Word.

Solid Food is for the Mature

"Anyone who lives on milk, being still an infant, is not acquainted with the teaching about righteousness. But solid food is for the mature, who by constant use have trained themselves to distinguish good from evil" (Hebrews 5:13-14)

When a baby is born they are fed their mother's milk for the first six months of their lives. Then as they grow they are slowly introduced to solid food. First in the form of baby foods, pureed fruits and vegetables that are easy to swallow and digest. Then small amounts of prepared food, cut into little bits. Eventually they are given solid food, once their teeth have come in and they have learned to chew and swallow it. It is a natural process that one does not have to teach with much effort.

As children grow, they also begin to feed themselves. Every mother knows that at a certain point, the baby will not allow others to spoon-feed it any longer. The child wants to use the utensil to bring the food into their own mouth. What begins as a messy process is also a necessary one. They learn coordination from working the spoon when they eat. They develop skills, early on, to feed themselves for the rest of their lives. This is the way it should be. After all, no one would want to spoon feed a forty year old baby, it would be quite embarrassing.

The same natural principle can be used for Christians. At first, they should be gathered and taught the first principles of God's Word. They should be encouraged and led into these amazing truths by those who are older in Christ. As this happens, their own skills should start to develop for reading and understanding the Word for themselves. They should ask questions seeking comprehension of what they are studying. All the while being trained through the power of the Holy Spirit to understand what has been written to them in the Scriptures. As they do this, the Lord speaks

His powerful truths into their hearts illuminating their lives with this knowledge and truth.

This is a process which requires solid doctrine as its foundation. The footing must be set on the basic principles of God's Word to understand the other truths that are recorded for us. No one would give a child a steak; so in the same way, a new believer must start out on the milk of the word and grow in the knowledge and truth of God.

Problems arise because we have a multitude of Christians who are not progressing in the natural process of growing up. The writer of Hebrews is chiding the people for their laziness in understanding the principle he is writing about. He told them that they ought to be teaching others by this time and yet they are still feeding on the milk of the word, needing someone to teach them the very first principles over and over again (Hebrews 5:12). He goes on to say that anyone in this condition is not acquainted with the teaching about righteousness. The Amplified Bible puts it this way, *"For everyone who continues to feed on milk is obviously inexperienced and unskilled in the doctrine of righteousness (of conformity to the divine will in purpose, thought, and action), for he is a mere infant [not able to talk yet]!"* (*Hebrews 5:13 AMP*). These are harsh words, but the truth in them rings clear, just as it is not acceptable for an adult to continue to nurse, a believer should not remain an infant in the knowledge of the Word.

The remedy to this problem is growing up! It takes time and it takes discipline to get in the Word regularly. But Jesus is the one who said, *"The words I have spoken to you are spirit and they are life"* (*John 6:63b*). The written word is our handbook for this life, Peter said that everything pertaining to life and godliness is found there (II Peter 1:3-4). The writer of Hebrews closes chapter 5 with these words, *"But solid food is for full-grown men, for those whose senses and mental faculties are trained by practice to discriminate and distinguish between what is morally good and noble and what is evil and contrary either to divine or human law"* (*Hebrews 5:14 AMP*). As we grow, the more skilled we are in the word, the more we will understand these truths when we hear or read them. We will not need anyone to first explain the foundation again, instead we will build upon it entering into the fullness of God with the complete understanding that belongs to the spiritually mature.

hebrews 6.

A WARNING

AGAINST FALLING AWAY

Leaving Elementary Truths to Go on to Maturity

"Therefore let us leave the elementary teachings about Christ and go on to maturity, not laying again the foundation of repentance from acts that lead to death, and of faith in God, instruction about baptisms, the laying on of hands, the resurrection of the dead, and eternal judgment. And God permitting, we will do so" (Hebrews 6:1-3)

One of my favorite things to do is visit big cities. I love walking around town, taking in the skyscraper scenery and experiencing the hustle and bustle of big city life. New York is perhaps the most impressive of cities that I have ever visited. Every square inch is occupied by tall buildings and skyscrapers. Anything less than twenty stories dwarfs in comparison to what makes up New York City skyline. Considering the fact that all of this is housed on a tiny island, it makes sense that what you see above the surface is relative to what lies beneath. To support dozens of floors, each skyscraper must have footings that go deep into the earth. The foundation must be built right or the building would never support the addition of height.

The same is true for believers. Our foundation must be well constructed. We must know and understand certain things first in order to receive the deeper things of God later. The foundation always comes first. The cornerstone of our entire belief system is built on Jesus. Then as we get to know Him and read His Word certain principles are laid, solidifying the base we are building. What is being formed will support the many deep and wonderful truths of God in the future. But to build the sixteenth floor the foundation first has to be placed.

This passage of scripture is a call to start moving in the direction of maturity. The writer of Hebrews is still on the same thought as the ending of chapter 5. He ended this chapter rebuking the people for their laziness in understanding important beginning truths. Because of this, he is saying it is time to move on to spiritual maturity. They need to take the foundation of what they'd been taught and strive for more understanding.

This list of elementary truths found in the beginning of chapter 6 should be the foundation of our lives. These doctrines are important to know so well we could teach them to others. Understanding these things concerning repentance, faith, baptisms, laying on of hands, the resurrection and eternal judgment are the base things of God, they are beginning truths. But having these as our foundation of faith assures that the principles built on them will be secure and supported. This is why the writer says it is time to move on toward completeness and perfection belonging to the spiritually mature. And now, he aims to do just that. The next principles discussed in Hebrews can be hard to understand, and we will be proceeding into advanced teaching leaning on our foundational understanding to support these deeper truths.

Just as each floor of a New York skyscraper is built on the preceding one until the entire building is completed, we are to continue growing in the Word until the very end. It is not a one time read. Each time through brings more understanding and more revelation than the time before. As we plant these seeds in our hearts we can expect a return on our investment. David said we will be like a tree planted by the streams of water yielding fruit in season and prospering in everything we do (Psalm 1:2-3).

Subjecting the Son
to Public Disgrace

"It is impossible for those who have once been enlightened, who have tasted the heavenly gift, who have shared in the Holy Spirit, who have tasted the goodness of the word of God and the powers of the coming age, if they fall away, to be brought back to repentance, because to their loss they are crucifying the Son of God all over again and subjecting him to public disgrace" (Hebrews 6:4-6)

Growing up, I held tightly to the doctrine *once saved, always saved*. So you can imagine the ground shaking experience that occurred one summer at camp when my counselor co-worker challenged this idea. He was attending Bible college at the time learning all sorts of things. As he shared this knowledge, confusion about what I had always believed set in. I realize now what he was trying to say, but at that time, I wasn't able to reconcile this truth in full understanding. Even reading a verse such as this, can challenge our core belief system unless we understand several things. However, to comprehend the fullness of God's grace, having insight into a passage of scripture such as this is extremely important.

Every great truth in the Bible, appears to have a contradiction. This is why we get many divisions among believers who do not agree. However, there are always two sides to every truth and understanding both sides brings balance to each truth in the Bible. Each idea is usually not an either or but both. A good illustration I once heard a speaker use is that of a tightrope. If I was going to cross a divide on a tightrope I would need anchor points securely fastened on each side. I would want the tension and pull to be the exact same so I could walk the entire length of the rope without it losing structure. If they were not both pulling in opposite directions with the same force, walking across the rope would not be possible. In fact, it would be very dangerous.

This is a great picture in understanding why it is important to have equal and opposite truths that appear to contradict. Because it gives the pull needed to find balance between both ideas and both truths. Comprehending all facets will bring a deeper understanding of scripture and an intimate working knowledge of God and His infinite grace.

At first glance, this verse seems to be floating in this chapter out of nowhere. The writer is encouraging the reader to progress in their knowledge of truth. Then out of the blue He warns against falling away, noting it is impossible to be brought back again to repentance once this happens. This can be a little disconcerting because life carries us through ebbs and flows without the need to worry about losing one's salvation.

The Basis of Eternal Redemption

If it is possible to fall away, as this passage in Hebrews suggests, or in effect become again as an unbeliever without the regenerating work of the Holy Spirit, this verse seems to contradict others throughout scripture which talk about eternal redemption. So, it is important to first look at eternal redemption, what it is, what has been promised and who it is for; so we understand what the writer is saying in these verses concerning falling away.

Eternal redemption can be defined in this way; putting saving faith in the complete and perfect work of Jesus Christ, confessing Him as Lord, accepting the payment and forgiveness for your sins, trusting in Him to do what you cannot do. Once this happens you are saved, period. This is an eternal decision. You cannot lose what has been given to you as a gift.

Jesus made this quite clear. *"My sheep listen to my voice; I know them, and they follow me. I give them eternal life, and they shall never perish; no one can snatch them out of my hand. My Father, who has given them to me, is greater than all; no one can snatch them out of my Father's hand. I and the Father are one" (John 10:27-30).*

Paul asked a similar question in Romans 8, *"Who shall separate us from the love of Christ?" (Romans 8:35a).* His response, *"For I am convinced that neither death nor life, neither angels nor demons, neither the present nor the future, nor any powers, neither height nor depth, nor anything else in all creation, will be able to separate us from the love of God that is in Christ Jesus our Lord" (Romans 8:38-39).*

Besides these verses which clearly teach that no outside force can separate us from God, we have several promises from Jesus that show His intention for eternal redemption. First He offers us eternal life (John 3:16, 36; 10:10; 17:3; I John 5:11-13). Secondly He told us He would never leave us or forsake us (Deuteronomy 31:6, 8; Joshua 1:5; John 14:18; Hebrews 13:5). Next, He gave us the Holy Spirit as a deposit to ensure these promises (Romans 8:15-17; II Corinthians 5:5; Ephesians 1:13-14; II Timothy 1:14; Titus 3:4-6). Then, He gave us power and authority in this world and over the forces in the world (Matthew 28:18-20; Mark 16:15-18; Luke 10:19; Romans 8:17; Ephesians 2:6; I John 5:4-5). Lastly, He wrote our names in the Lamb's Book of Life and keeps a record in heaven of all of those who have placed faith in Him (Luke 10:20; Revelation 20:12, 15). These few things only scratch the surface when it comes to the promises that God made to us because of the finished work of Jesus Christ. And if this isn't enough, He promised Jesus on oath that He would never change His mind regarding these things (Hebrews 6:17-18; 7:21-22). So we can have confident hope in the things promised to us regarding eternal life and our redemption.

Another amazing truth is that this offer of salvation is for anyone regardless of what you have done or haven't done. Paul said, *"Everyone who calls on the name of the Lord will be saved" (Romans 10:13).* There was no qualifier to this statement, it is for everyone. All that is required is to ask, believe and receive. It doesn't get any simpler than this.

By considering all of these things, we can see how it is impossible to lose your salvation once you have placed saving faith in Jesus and what He did to bring you into fellowship with God the Father. You cannot lose it, you cannot misplace it and most importantly it cannot be taken away from you.

What Does it Mean to Fall Away?

We've established that you cannot lose your salvation, nor can anyone take it away from you, but Hebrews teaches that it is impossible to be brought back again to repentance once you've fallen away. If it is possible to fall away after being born again, it is important to look at this and understand what the writer is saying. Remember for every Biblical truth there is an equal and opposite truth that appears to contradict. Like our example of the tightrope, these truths pull in an equal and opposite direction to bring balance. In all cases it is not an either or scenario, but both. So understanding both sides of the apparent contradiction will expand your revelation of God's amazing grace and heighten your appreciation of the choice offered to you in Jesus.

Salvation is a choice and every person is offered this choice as a gift of God's grace. The choice is whether or not you accept Jesus as Savior and Lord and place your faith in Him. God does not make you chose Him although He desires it. He did everything possible to offer this to us but when it comes to the bottom line, we have a choice whether or not to accept this gift. John says, *"Yet to all who received him, to those who believed in his name, he gave the right to become children of God— children born not of natural descent, nor of human decision or a husband's will, but born of God" (John 1:12-13).* The only thing required is receiving this free gift.

So, if the only way into the kingdom of God is by choice, then it also makes sense that the only way out of the kingdom is by choice. Remember you cannot lose your salvation, no one can take it from you, God will never leave you or forsake you, but at any point you decide you no longer want to belong in this kingdom, you can renounce it and God honors that decision. God chose us and in return He wants us to choose Him. This is the highest form of relationship one can have, one of mutual choice.

This is why the writer of Hebrews advises us to get past the elementary truths of God and to gain knowledge and spiritual insight. Because the more you know about God and His loving nature toward you the less likely you will become complacent in this life concerning the things of God. The less complacent, the less hard of heart and more responsive toward the Holy Spirit and His leading in your life. In other words, the more you have an intimate working knowledge of God, the less likely you will be to fall away because of the snares of this world.

Peter also had something to say about this. *"If they have escaped the corruption of the world by knowing our Lord and Savior Jesus Christ and are again entangled in it and overcome, they are worse off at the end than they were at the beginning. It would have been better for them not to have known the way of righteousness, than to have known it and then to turn their backs on the sacred command that was passed on to them" (II Peter 2:20-21).*

This concept is mentioned in scripture to show us God's full nature of grace not to give us an out. His desire from the beginning has always been to have a relationship with us, which is why He sent Jesus to restore all things. It is our choice and always remains such. However, there are conditions on falling away or in essence becoming reprobate and renouncing salvation. It is not something one can do easily. Certain guidelines must first be met, in other words, one must be a mature Christian and fully aware of the decision and its result.

The Conditions of Becoming Reprobate

Every new believer has at one time or another struggled over this question of losing their salvation. They've messed up and assumed that what they've done proves they aren't saved. Of course the devil is right there planting these ideas into their head. But as we have already seen, you cannot lose your salvation, which was a gift. Neither will God take it back from you.

This should be a non-issue among Christians. It is in the scriptures to show us the incredible facets of God's nature, meaning He gives us a choice because this is the highest form of relationship one can have. Everyone in this kingdom is here by choice, personal choice. It is not a matter of losing it rather returning or renouncing it.

This is why the Lord outlined the guidelines for being mature enough to renounce such a great salvation. He will not hold you accountable unless you are fully aware of the decision. For instance, if when a child, I ran away from home and decided I no longer wanted to be a part of my family, the police would find me and return me to my parents. Even if I told them I wanted to change my name and cut all ties, they wouldn't allow such a decision from a child, even a teenager because there is no understanding of the long term effects of that decision. However, now that I am an adult, legally I could go down to the courthouse, change my name, renounce my birthright, cut off all association with my family and the courts would grant this decision in my favor. And the law would back me up. My parents would have nothing to say about it because legally, I am an adult and I am responsible and fully aware of the full weight of my decisions.

The same is true of God, He does not allow this decision to be made by a person unless certain requirements have first been met. Because verse 6 exclaims that they are crucifying the Son of God all over again and publicly shaming Him before the world (Hebrews 6:6). Since there was only one sacrifice for sin for all time (Hebrews 7:27; 10:10, 12, 14, 18), to reject this gift after experiencing it leaves a person in bad shape. There is no other salvation, which is why Peter said it would have been better for the person to never have known the way of righteousness than to know and turn back once again to the pollution of the world (II Peter 2:20-21). As in the previous example, one must be fully aware of the weight of their decisions to be held accountable, so certain requirements must be met.

"It is impossible for those who have once been enlightened, who have tasted the heavenly gift, who have shared in the Holy Spirit, who have tasted the goodness of the word of God and the powers of the coming age, if they fall away, to be brought back to repentance, because to their loss they are crucifying the Son of God all over again and subjecting him to public disgrace" (Hebrews 6:4-6).

First, the person has to be enlightened. The Greek word is *phōtizō*, which means *'to give light, to shine, to enlighten, light up, illumine, to bring to light, render evident' (Strong's Exhaustive Concordance of the Bible)*. It also denotes causing something to exist and come to light becoming clear to all. To enlighten spiritually with saving knowledge. The regenerating work of the Holy Spirit gives us a working knowledge of God. It's a revelation, it changes our entire way of thinking because we are new creations.

Secondly, the person has to have tasted the heavenly gift and shared in the Holy Spirit. This is more than being born again by the regenerating work of the Holy Spirit. This is operating in the kingdom. The word used for gift describes spiritual or supernatural gifts. The word for heavenly denotes things that take place in heaven not on earth. The word for tasted is defined as to partake of, enjoy, make trial of, or experience. In other words, the person actively participates in the kingdom by operating in the gifts of the Spirit (I Corinthians 12-14).

Next, the person must have tasted the goodness of the word of God. The Greek word used here is *rhēma,* the spoken word. The significance of *rhēma* as distinct from *logos* (written word) is not referring to the whole Bible as such, but to the individual scripture which the Spirit brings to our remembrance for use in time of need (Vine's Expository Dictionary of New

Testament Words). It is the ability to take *"the sword of the Spirit, which is the word of God" (Ephesians 6:17b)* and skillfully use it. This is our defense and offense here on earth. To use it, we must know and have spiritual insight into the scriptures. This comes through maturity and enlightenment by the Holy Spirit over time.

Lastly, the person must have experienced the powers of the coming age. The writer is talking about *dynamis* power, it is where we get the word for dynamite. It is defined by Strong's Concordance as '*inherent power, power residing in a thing by virtue of its nature, or which a person or thing exerts and puts forth. The power for performing miracles' (Strong's Exhaustive Concordance of the Bible).* The age being referred to is one of indefinite duration, eternity. This makes sense since the person is fully operating in the kingdom, its gifts and power.

These four things are required before God holds one accountable to make this decision. Notice, if after experiencing all of these things, hardness of heart takes over to the point they decide to renounce God, the reason they cannot be restored once again is because it is impossible for them to be brought back to repentance. If they'd repent, God would restore. But in this state of a reprobate mind the person basically becomes a God-hater.

This is why the writer of Hebrews begins this chapter instructing us to progress in our knowledge of the Lord Jesus. Because fellowshipping with the Lord protects the heart from the cares and worries of this world. Peter said, *"Like newborn babies, crave pure spiritual milk, so that by it you may grow up in your salvation, now that you have tasted that the Lord is good" (I Peter 2:2-3).* We should experience the Lord and enjoy Him and progress in our revelation of Him. In this way, we guarantee what has been promised to us through faith in Christ, protecting our hearts from forgetting what has been purchased for us. *"We want each of you to show this same diligence to the very end, in order to make your hope sure. We do not want you to become lazy, but to imitate those who through faith and patience inherit what has been promised" (Hebrews 6:11-12).*

Thorns & Thistles are Worthless and in Danger of Being Cursed

"Land that drinks in the rain often falling on it and that produces a crop useful to those for whom it is farmed receives the blessing of God. But land that produces thorns and thistles is worthless and is in danger of being cursed. In the end it will be burned" (Hebrews 6:7-8)

I am from Iowa, and in Iowa farming is very important to the economy. Every summer the entire state is covered by thousands of acres of corn and soy beans. Each spring farmers plant their crops to harvest in the fall. Around July and August there is always talk about the amount of rain needed for the crops to flourish and grow. While it is always a safe topic of conversation, the truth is God is the one who sends rain upon the earth to water it.

David spoke eloquently in Psalm 65, *"You care for the land and water it; you enrich it abundantly. The streams of God are filled with water to provide the people with grain, for so you have ordained it. You drench its furrows and level its ridges; you soften it with showers and bless its crops. You crown the year with your bounty, and your carts overflow with abundance. The grasslands of the desert overflow; the hills are clothed with gladness. The meadows are covered with flocks and the valleys are mantled with grain; they shout for joy and sing"* (Psalm 65:9-13).

The harvest is a blessing from the Lord. Amazingly, God also blesses those who are not of His kingdom. Jesus said in Matthew, *"He causes his sun to rise on the evil and the good, and sends rain on the righteous and the unrighteous"* (Matthew 5:45b). God is not partial and chooses to bless everyone whether they recognize it or not. The difference is how we respond to this blessing in our lives. If the farmers' fields repeatedly grew weeds instead of corn, eventually they might sell that land or let it return to prairie choosing to farm only in productive areas. The same is true of God. If a person repeatedly rejects Him and His blessings, producing thorns and thistles instead of what God desires and His blessings allow, then in the end they are in danger of their decisions in this life.

When Jesus explained the parable of the weeds to His disciples (Matthew 13:24-30, 36-43) He told them that the wheat and the tares were allowed to grow together until the harvest. At this time the weeds would first be gathered and burned. But all through the growing season the tares were allowed to grow with the wheat. They took the same nourishment from the soil, they enjoyed the same sunshine and benefited from the same rain drops that fell on the crops. However, the ending for the weeds was drastically different than it was for the wheat.

The writer of Hebrews is making this analogy directly after instructions about moving onto maturity in Christ. Weeds sprout because of neglect and sometimes it takes work to cultivate a good crop. However, Jesus gave us the key to a good harvest in John 15, *"I am the vine; you are the branches. If a man remains in me and I in him, he will bear much fruit; apart from me you can do nothing" (John 15:5)*. So it makes sense that believers will produce a kingdom crop by functioning as they were created while enjoying the many blessings from God. The fruit is always determined by the seed that is planted and cultivated, which is why it is so important to remain in the vine and recognize the many blessings of God.

Confident of Better Things

"Even though we speak like this, dear friends, we are confident of better things in your case—things that accompany salvation. God is not unjust; he will not forget your work and the love you have shown him as you have helped his people and continue to help them" (Hebrews 6:9-10)

Salvation is accompanied by lots of fringe benefits. In fact salvation is the entrance point for all the good things that God has in store for us. The moment we are born again every promise that has been made by God belongs to us as heirs of this kingdom. Although the warning at the end of Hebrews 5 and beginning of chapter 6 is a strong warning, the entire passage is really focusing on moving into maturity so as not to become complacent with the eternal life that has been given us. As believers we are not in danger of falling away, the writer simply mentioned it because what he wants to say needs a good foundation to understand and his audience was not training themselves to gain spiritual insight as they should have been.

Both knowledge and understanding is one of the many benefits that accompany salvation. John explained how this works, *"But you have an anointing from the Holy One, and all of you know the truth"* (I John 2:20). The King James Bible tells us that we have *"an unction from the Holy One, and ye know all things" (KJV)*. The root word used here is *'chrisma'*, and is translated both as anointing and unction, in which Strong's Concordance defines as *'anything smeared on, unguent, ointment, usually prepared by the Hebrews from oil and aromatic herbs. Anointing was the inaugural ceremony for priests' (Strong's Exhaustive Concordance of the Bible)*. Amazingly, John is referring to the Holy Spirit as the ointment covering for the believer, which grants them the means to possess knowledge and understanding of God's truth and walk in His ways.

John goes on to explain later in the very same chapter, *"As for you, the anointing you received from him remains in you, and you do not need anyone to teach you. But as his anointing teaches you about all things and as that anointing is real, not counterfeit—just as it has taught you, remain in him" (I John 2:27)*. We have the perfect teacher to lead us into all truths and unlock the scripture to us. When we don't understand, the Holy Spirit partners with us in bringing revelation knowledge concerning the things we have read or heard. This knowledge and understanding comes from within to illuminate our minds to the truth. This is one of the Holy Spirits many functions.

Being confident of better things, the writer also pauses to remind that God is not unjust. He notices the labor of love shown the world for His name sake. We are Christ's ambassadors on this earth (II Corinthians 5:20). He has given us full authority on this earth to act on His behalf, and God certainly notices and does not forget these acts of kindness. Which is why the writer finishes with this thought reminding us to persevere until the very end; *"We want each of you to show this same diligence to the very end, in order to make your hope sure. We do not want you to become lazy, but to imitate those who through faith and patience inherit what has been promised" (Hebrews 6:11-12)*. Through knowledge, spiritual insight and perseverance we will lay hold of the hope to which we have been called. This is why we take encouragement through these scriptures, chiding us to move forward in our knowledge and understanding of God, because we know the best is yet to come.

Showing Diligence Until the Very End

"We want each of you to show this same diligence to the very end, in order to make your hope sure. We do not want you to become lazy, but to imitate those who through faith and patience inherit what has been promised" (Hebrews 6:11-12)

Perseverance is a necessary characteristic for believers. Judging by the world around us it would be easy to become discouraged by the events continually surrounding us if we did not know the hope we have in Jesus and cling to it until the very end.

We are encouraged to show the same diligence as those who went before us in realizing and inheriting the promise. Paul noted in Corinthians, *"Do you not know that in a race all the runners run, but only one gets the prize? Run in such a way as to get the prize" (I Corinthians 9:24)*. Forget what surrounds you, run to win. Look to the future with tunnel vision, otherwise this world can distract from us accomplishing our mission. We need to be diligent and steadfast until the end to make this hope a reality.

We can look to the scriptures for examples of those that went before us and draw encouragement from them. Many of them only saw the promise of Jesus in the future, never realizing it while they were still alive. *"All these people were still living by faith when they died. They did not receive the things promised; they only saw them and welcomed them from a distance. And they admitted that they were aliens and strangers on earth" (Hebrews 11:13)*. But they continued steadfastly because they knew faith would eventually get them there. *"These were all commended for their faith, yet none of them received what had been promised. God had planned something better for us so that only together with us would they be made perfect" (Hebrews 11:39-40)*.

redemption.

Our hope in Jesus has been realized which is why we follow in the patriarchs example of perseverance through faith. We have already inherited what was promised and as we continue to grow in the grace of God we will naturally move into maturity just as the writer of Hebrews has been instructing at the closing of chapter 5 and beginning chapter 6. *"For everything that was written in the past was written to teach us, so that through endurance and the encouragement of the Scriptures we might have hope" (Romans 15:4).*

Abraham Received What Was Promised

"When God made his promise to Abraham, since there was no one greater for him to swear by, he swore by himself, saying, "I will surely bless you and give you many descendants." And so after waiting patiently, Abraham received what was promised" (Hebrews 6:13-15)

I remember going to Sunday school as a child and learning about Abraham. We learned about the birth of Isaac and how it came about because God promised him a son. I remember a teacher bringing a jar of sand to the class and asking us to count it. Of course we couldn't but the object lesson rang true, Abraham was blessed by God and his descendants were going to be numerous.

Since that time, I think often about Abraham and how he waited a long time to see this promise fulfilled. He was one hundred years old, Sarah was ninety yet he considered the One who promised him, faithful. That is why he held to the hope of having a son and also saw fulfillment of it.

The amazing thing about all of this is that Isaac was really just the down payment of the promise. Even the great number of people descending from Abraham was merely one of the blessings that came along with the promise. The real implication of this promise was that through the line of Abraham and Isaac the Messiah would come (Galatians 3:7-9, 16; Genesis 12:2-3; 13:14-17; 17:3-8). Galatians makes this very clear, *"The promises were spoken to Abraham and to his seed. The Scripture does not say "and to seeds," meaning many people, but "and to your seed," meaning one person, who is Christ"* (Galatians 3:16). This was a great promise and with it God announced the gospel in advance to Abraham when He made this pledge (Galatians 3:8).

God promised this to Abraham with an oath. In court, when giving testimony, the witness is sworn in with the Bible, the promise is that they will tell the truth and the object used is the guarantor of the promise. Scripture says God swore by Himself since there was nothing greater to guarantee His promise to Abraham (Hebrews 6:13). This pledge was backed by His namesake, His word and His power. This means that it would be fulfilled at all cost. Abraham may have gotten the down payment with Isaac, but we have seen fulfillment in Jesus.

The great thing about Abraham is that he believed God and it was credited to him as righteousness (Genesis 15:6; Romans 4:3; Galatians 3:6; James 2:23). Scripture mentions this four times which means it is incredibly important for us. He took God's guaranteed promise, backed by an oath, and knew that it would come to pass. He believed God and was justified by faith the same way we are today. *"This is why "it was credited to him as righteousness." The words "it was credited to him" were written not for him alone, but also for us, to whom God will credit righteousness—for us who believe in him who raised Jesus our Lord from the dead" (Romans 4:22-24).* Abraham is called the father of faith for a reason. His faith has truly blessed the world as it was the conduit for the promise of God to come to pass.

It is Impossible for God to Lie

"Men swear by someone greater than themselves, and the oath confirms what is said and puts an end to all argument. Because God wanted to make the unchanging nature of his purpose very clear to the heirs of what was promised, he confirmed it with an oath. God did this so that, by two unchangeable things in which it is impossible for God to lie, we who have fled to take hold of the hope offered to us may be greatly encouraged" (Hebrews 6:16-18)

Even in today's society an oath is sacred. To take an oath is to swear that what has been promised is true, binding all parties by this vow. We even have notaries who mark their seal on the oath certifying the vow. In the legal system willingly giving false information when making an affidavit is the crime of perjury. In other words, making an oath is sacred and guarantees the oath taker's honesty and integrity in the matter under question.

When God made the promise to Abraham that he would have a son, make him into a great nation and the Messiah would come through his line, since there was no one greater for God to swear by, He swore by himself on oath (Hebrews 6:13). He vowed the promise to Abraham would come to pass. He did this to show the unchanging nature of the promise. Meaning every blessing would be fulfilled and the promise would never be revoked. Even today we live under the blessings of this vow made to Abraham.

Amazingly both of these things, the promise and the oath, will always exist together because they are tied to God's nature and integrity. Just like water, both hydrogen and oxygen must be present, otherwise it is just elements, not substance. The oath made to Abraham makes it impossible for God to lie, prove false or deceive us. This is because the oath rests on the character of God. In fact since the world was spoken into existence by Jesus and it is held together by His word of power (Genesis 1; John 1:1-3; Colossians 1:16-17; Hebrews 1:2-3). If God lied, the world would cease to exist because His Word holds all things together. If God were ever proved false, His Word would be broken and there would be no power to sustain the universe. Which is why He confirmed His promise to Abraham with an oath. The stakes were incredibly high and He wanted to show the unchanging nature of the promise. What He said would come to pass.

We can draw strong encouragement from this since we too live under the blessing promised to Abraham. Everything God has said, has come to pass. Even in the midst of the trials of this world we have a hope that is unparalleled by any other. This hope is an anchor for the soul and it is guaranteed by both the promise made and the oath taken (Hebrews 6:19-20). In the midst of life we can rest securely knowing that our future is secured, our hope sure and our God faithful.

Hope Brings Us into the Inner Sanctuary with God

"We have this hope as an anchor for the soul, firm and secure. It enters the inner sanctuary behind the curtain, where Jesus, who went before us, has entered on our behalf. He has become a high priest forever, in the order of Melchizedek" (Hebrews 6:19-20)

Anchors have been around since the beginning of nautical travel. An anchor holds a ship in place in the midst of the most tumultuous seas. This has always been a safeguard for vessels keeping them from being thrown to shore in the middle of a storm.

As believers we also have an anchor that is steadfast and secure, it is hope. This hope is placed upon Jesus Christ Himself. This is because this hope rests on God's promise to Abraham and the oath taken that this promise would come to pass (Hebrews 6:13-18). Since the two, the promise and the oath, are intermingled and dependent on each other, we know that our hope is steadfast and secure. This acts as an anchor for our soul keeping our hearts at rest so they cannot be tossed about or dislodged from a place of peace.

This hope ushers us into the very presence of God, behind the veil and into the Holy of Holies. In the past, the High Priest was able to enter into God's presence once a year with the sacrifice for atonement. There were many regulations that first had to be met. The High Priest did not enter in with confidence. In fact, the High Priest had to take a censer of coals and incense with him so the smoke would cover the mercy seat to shield him from seeing it, lest he die (Leviticus 16:12-13). This was sacred ground because God was present. Now, we have a hope that brings us into the very presence of God, a way opened up and paved by Jesus. Unlike the Israel's High Priest, we are to enter boldly, *"Let us then approach the throne of grace with confidence, so that we may receive mercy and find grace to help us in our time of need" (Hebrews 4:16).*

In fulfillment of both the promise to Abraham and the oath taken by God that it would come to pass, we have been invited to this place that was never accessible before. This is because Jesus went before us and operates as our High Priest before God having made atonement for us. *"Therefore, brothers, since we have confidence to enter the Most Holy Place by the blood of Jesus, by a new and living way opened for us through the curtain, that is, his body, and since we have a great priest over the house of God, let us draw near to God with a sincere heart in full assurance of faith, having our hearts sprinkled to cleanse us from a guilty conscience and having our bodies washed with pure water. Let us hold unswervingly to the hope we profess, for he who promised is faithful" (Hebrews 10:19-23).*

The reason we can enter boldly into the Holy of Holies is because Jesus is there waiting to welcome us. His blood has removed all traces of sin making us clean (Hebrews 7:27; 8:11-12; 9:26; 10:10, 12, 14, 18). As High Priest He makes intercession before God on our behalf (Hebrews 7:25; 9:24; 10:19-21). He eternally holds the rank of Melchizedek (Hebrews 5:6; 7:16, 24, 28) and has fulfilled the promise made to Abraham that through his Seed a great nation would be born (Galatians 3:16-17). As believers, we are the result of that promise. All of this combined gives us the hope needed to enter into God's presence. This is the anchor for our soul keeping us steadfast and secure no matter what life holds.

hebrews 7.

MELCHIZEDEK'S PRIESTHOOD

LIKE CHRIST'S

Melchizedek, Priest of the Most High God

"This Melchizedek was king of Salem and priest of God Most High. He met Abraham returning from the defeat of the kings and blessed him, and Abraham gave him a tenth of everything. First, his name means "king of righteousness"; then also, "king of Salem" means "king of peace" (Hebrews 7:1-2)

Four kings went to war against the kings of Sodom and Gomorrah and their allies. As the kingdoms fell to the four kings, the defeated people were carried off along with all of their possessions (Genesis 14). This included Abraham's nephew Lot because he was living in Sodom. When Abraham heard that his relative had been taken captive, he called together three hundred and eighteen trained men born into his household to pursue the kings. He divided his men into two groups and attacked them during the night recovering everything that had been taken. He brought back Lot, the women and the rest of the people that belonged with them.

Abraham restored and redeemed Lot and all the people when they were taken into captivity. He didn't keep anything for himself, but everything was returned to the kings and their people. As he was returning from this victory, Melchizedek, priest of the Most High God came out to meet him and blessed him.

Abraham recognized Melchizedek's position and in return gave him a tenth of the choicest portion of his possessions. This wasn't demanded of him, instead it was a natural response to the favor and blessing he received. This gift was outflow of his heart when Abraham recognized the greatness of Melchizedek. Even the writer of Hebrews marvels at this in verse 4, *"Just think how great he was: Even the patriarch Abraham gave him a tenth of the plunder! (Hebrews 7:4).* The priesthood of Melchizedek is a foreshadowing of the priesthood of Jesus. By comparing the two we can gain insight into the role that Jesus holds.

Melchizedek was called a priest of the Most High God. Throughout the New Testament, these words, *"Most High"* or *"highest"* are used in reference to Jesus. The term was used when the angel announced to Mary that she would conceive the Messiah. *"He will be great and will be called the Son of the Most High. The Lord God will give him the throne of his father David"* *(Luke 1:32)*. It was prophesied by Zechariah that John the Baptist would be His forerunner, *"And you, my child, will be called a prophet of the Most High; for you will go on before the Lord to prepare the way for him" (Luke 1:76).* The Demons recognized this position of *"Most High"* as Jesus went about teaching, preaching and healing, *"When he saw Jesus from a distance, he ran and fell on his knees in front of him. He shouted at the top of his voice, "What do you want with me, Jesus, Son of the Most High God? Swear to God that you won't torture me!" (Mark 5:6-7; Luke 8:28).* And the people recognized it when Jesus made His triumphal entry into Jerusalem, *"The crowds that went ahead of him and those that followed shouted, "Hosanna to the Son of David!" "Blessed is he who comes in the name of the Lord!" "Hosanna in the highest!" (Matthew 21:9; Mark 11:9-10; Luke 19:38).* It was recognizable to everyone that Jesus was sent by the Most High God.

Secondly, Melchizedek's name, when translated means *'King of Righteousness'.* Righteousness is the condition of being acceptable to God. To be righteous means that we attain a state approved and acceptable to God. Melchizedek was called the King of Righteousness, Jesus also owns this title. In the first chapter of Hebrews, the writer, quoting from Psalm 45 says, *"about the Son he says, "Your throne, O God, will last for ever and ever, and righteousness will be the scepter of your kingdom. You have loved righteousness and hated wickedness; therefore God, your God, has set you above your companions by anointing you with the oil of joy" (Hebrews 1:8-9).* To be the king of something means that your rule is characterized by it. Both Melchizedek's and Jesus' kingdoms are signified by righteousness, which means the subjects of those kingdoms also partake in the state of being approved and acceptable to God.

Lastly, Melchizedek was the King of Salem, which many believe was the ancient name for Jerusalem, when translated it means *"King of Peace".* Peace is a state of tranquility. Peace is the absence of turmoil in the midst of trouble. Peace to the believer is the tranquil state of the soul assured, secure and content before God. Melchizedek was called the King of Peace, just as Isaiah prophesied about the Messiah, *"For to us a child is born, to us a son is given, and the government will be on his shoulders. And he will be called Wonderful Counselor, Mighty God, Everlasting Father, Prince of Peace" (Isaiah 9:6).* To be the King of Peace means that your subjects enjoy the state of peace. The angels, when announcing Jesus' birth heralded, *"Glory to God in the highest, and on earth peace to men on whom his favor rests" (Luke 2:14).* This peace didn't exist in the natural realm among mankind; the peace that was announced was peace toward mankind on behalf of God because the Messiah had just been born.

Like Melchizedek, Jesus is a priest of the Most High God and we can ascertain characteristics of this role by looking at what the scriptures say about Melchizedek. Like Abraham, we should also recognize the position of Jesus when encountering the many blessings of God. Gratitude for the gifts bestowed on us is the natural response to such blessings. Gaining insight into all of this helps us to understand the role of Jesus, who serves continually as our High Priest before God.

Without Beginning
of Days or End of Life

"Without father or mother, without genealogy, without
beginning of days or end of life, like the Son of God
he remains a priest forever" (Hebrews 7:3)

I was talking with a friend who has always struggled over the significance of Melchizedek. He wasn't sure why he was mentioned in the Scriptures and didn't understand why it was important to us today. He wrote off this quest for understanding after his Sunday School teacher told him it wasn't that important, after all Melchizedek is only mentioned three times in Scripture. I on the other hand believe that understanding who Melchizedek was and why Scripture mentions him so many times is very important, especially since Jesus became a High Priest after and with the rank of his order (Psalm 110:4; Hebrews 5:6; 7:17).

This passage in Hebrews 7 is quite an amazing statement because it says Melchizedek had no beginning or ending. There are no records of his father, mother or ancestral line. In the same way there are no records of his death. This is odd because genealogy is very important to Jewish heritage. If you've ever read through Scripture chances are you eventually read through some long lists of genealogy. Even Jesus' genealogy was covered from every angle. Both Matthew and Luke cover Jesus' physical ancestry while John showed His connection to God as His one and only son. But Melchizedek has no records.

The writer of Hebrews makes this connection that without records, Melchizedek had no beginning or ending of life. In other words, he will always exist. Because of this, he remains a priest forever as the position of High Priest was a lifetime position (Numbers 35:25).

redemption.

This is extremely significant to us because Jesus has been appointed our High Priest after the order of Melchizedek, not the order of Aaron who was a High Priest on the basis of the Law. The Levitical priesthood was subject to and interrupted by death because mankind is subject to death. But Jesus' priesthood was after the pattern of one who did not die, which means that His priesthood is forever and as such He will always be able to intercede for us (Hebrews 7:25). Death has no power to remove this office from Jesus.

Because Jesus is of Melchizedek's order, we can ascertain certain expectations about Christ and His priesthood. First, as mentioned it is an eternal position (Numbers 35:25; Hebrews 7:25). Secondly, it is based not in ancestry, but according to the power of an indestructible life (Hebrews 7:15-16). Next, the change in priesthood also changes the law and its requirements (Hebrews 7:12; Galatians 3:13; Colossians 2:13-14). Lastly, just as Melchizedek met Abraham and blessed him, through Christ we have been blessed in the heavenly realms with every spiritual blessing (Ephesians 1:3).

Adding up all these things helps us to understand why Melchizedek is mentioned in Scripture and why it is important. He is the pattern that shows us the incredible office that Christ Jesus holds. Understanding Jesus' role as our High Priest brings us to a place where we can boldly approach God through faith. When we do, we know that we will find grace and mercy to help us in our times of need (Hebrews 4:16).

The Greatness of Melchizedek

"Just think how great he was: Even the patriarch Abraham gave him a tenth of the plunder! Now the law requires the descendants of Levi who become priests to collect a tenth from the people—that is, their brothers—even though their brothers are descended from Abraham. This man, however, did not trace his descent from Levi, yet he collected a tenth from Abraham and blessed him who had the promises. And without doubt the lesser person is blessed by the greater" (Hebrews 7:4-7)

No one would dispute the greatness of Abraham. Throughout the entire Scriptures he is mentioned, his covenant with God is referred to and his faith is talked about. He was the only Old Testament patriarch that was called a friend of God. We can learn a lot from Abraham. His faith paved the way for righteousness to be credited to all who believe.

As Abraham returned from redeeming Lot from captivity, Melchizedek went out to meet him. As great as Abraham was he still recognized the greater one and paid due respect. As Melchizedek blessed him, Abraham gave him one tenth of the choicest portions of the spoils. He responded appropriately to Melchizedek's position and greatness.

The interesting thing is that the covenant and promises of God belonged to Abraham (Genesis 15). He even established circumcision as the sign of this covenant with Abraham and his descendants signifying that it was an everlasting covenant (Genesis 17). God went as far as to change both Abraham and Sarah's name to reflect the promise (Genesis 17). This is why Abraham is called the Father of Many Nations because everything we have as believers stems from this covenant.

Abraham was a great man, which is why it is important for us to pay attention to what happened between him and Melchizedek. Abraham gave Melchizedek a tenth of everything. Now the law, which was introduced four hundred and thirty years later (Galatians 3:17) described the tithe (Leviticus 27:30-34; Numbers 18:23-28). The tithe was brought to God and then dispersed to the priests. The priests were of the line of Levi, who came from Abraham. Melchizedek was before this, without family ties without record of beginning or ending. So the gift Abraham gave was not out of obligation to the Law, it was a response to the greatness of Melchizedek.

Where blessings are concerned, the lesser person is always blessed by the greater person as is the case with Abraham and Melchizedek even though it was Abraham who possessed the promises. No one refutes the greatness of Abraham, so taking this into account we see how amazing Melchizedek was. This matters to us because Jesus is our High Priest after this order (Psalm 110:4; Hebrews 5:6; 7:17).

We too are the recipients of a great promise and covenant with God. Like circumcision, the seal given to us is the deposited Holy Spirit; guaranteeing the promise. Like Melchizedek, Jesus bestows on us every spiritual blessing in the heavenly realm (Ephesians 1:3). So our response should be that of Abraham, a gift from the heart not stemming from obligation. This encompasses far more than money. Our response to the greatness and awesomeness of Christ should be our lives. We can look at the priesthood of Melchizedek to gain insight into Jesus as he was the pattern of that which was to come. If Melchizedek was great then Jesus is awesome. And God has given us this precious gift to guarantee our intercession before Him. What less can we give in return to this blessing than a life fully devoted to our Savior and faithful High Priest?

Our Gifts End
Up with the Lord

"In the one case, the tenth is collected by men who die; but in the other case, by him who is declared to be living. One might even say that Levi, who collects the tenth, paid the tenth through Abraham, because when Melchizedek met Abraham, Levi was still in the body of his ancestor" (Hebrews 7:8-10)

One of the great things about being a believer is that we can serve God well in whatever station of life we are in. Throughout the Scriptures we see this example. Paul told the church in Colosse, *"Whatever you do, work at it with all your heart, as working for the Lord, not for men, since you know that you will receive an inheritance from the Lord as a reward. It is the Lord Christ you are serving" (Colossians 3:23-24)*. He told the Ephesians, *"Serve wholeheartedly, as if you were serving the Lord, not men, because you know that the Lord will reward everyone for whatever good he does, whether he is slave or free" (Ephesians 6:7-8)*. We do not have to be a missionary in Africa to bless the Lord and be used mightily. We can advance the kingdom from our cubical at work or our kitchen at home by putting this principal into action; whatever we do, we do it for the Lord.

This fundamental concept is explained in this passage in Hebrews. Abraham gave Melchizedek a tenth of his possessions when he saw the greatness of this High Priest. The author of Hebrews is drawing the connection that the gifts the Levitical priesthood received also ended up with Melchizedek because Levi, the father of this line, was still in the body of Abraham when this offering was made. This shows us that our gifts and offerings, when given in faith, really go to God.

As New Testament believers we can rest assured that when we give, our offerings become a sweet smelling aroma to the Lord (Philippians 4:18).

redemption.

Paul told the Philippian church that the gifts that were given were then credited back to their account. We also see this between Melchizedek and Abraham. As the offering was made, Abraham was blessed by Melchizedek.

This passage illustrates an amazing concept because it shows us that everything we do boils down to a matter of the heart. God said to Samuel when on mission to anoint the next king of Israel, *"The LORD does not look at the things man looks at. Man looks at the outward appearance, but the LORD looks at the heart" (I Samuel 16:7b).* When we give, we give as unto the Lord. When we serve, we serve as unto the Lord. When we work at our jobs, we do it for the Lord. We know that whatever we do in word and deed, we do it as if it is the Lord himself we are serving.

The Need for Another Priest

"If perfection could have been attained through the Levitical priesthood (for on the basis of it the law was given to the people), why was there still need for another priest to come—one in the order of Melchizedek, not in the order of Aaron?" (Hebrews 7:11)

When Adam and Eve were created, they were created into a perfect fellowship with God. They always enjoyed the Sabbath Rest, in which they were created, right from the beginning. They were blameless before God and enjoyed an intimate fellowship with him.

This is still the goal. This passage says if perfection, or perfect fellowship between God and mankind could have been attained by the Levitical priesthood, then there would not have been a need for another priest. However, it could never be achieved in this way so there was a call for another priest, not from the line of Aaron, who mediated on behalf of the law, but from the order of Melchizedek who retained his position on the basis of an indestructible life (Hebrews 7:15-17).

This is a profound statement. This shows us that a right relationship with God can never come through the law. In fact, the very next verse says, *"For when there is a change of the priesthood, there must also be a change of the law" (Hebrews 7:12).* This means the old law, the old system of doing things, no longer applies. Instead, we have a new High Priest and a new law. In fact, it is so radically different that we cannot even use the Levitical priesthood as a basis for understanding it, which is why there is nothing in Jesus' ancestry to connect Him to it.

"The former regulation is set aside because it was weak and useless (for the law made nothing perfect), and a better hope is introduced, by which we draw near

to God" (Hebrews 7:18-19). This hope is Jesus. The law merely served as an illustration, a type and shadow of Christ (Hebrews 10:1). But now that He has come, there is no longer the need for this illustration (Hebrews 8:13; 9:9-10).

"First he said, "Sacrifices and offerings, burnt offerings and sin offerings you did not desire, nor were you pleased with them" (although the law required them to be made). Then he said, "Here I am, I have come to do your will." He sets aside the first to establish the second. And by that will, we have been made holy through the sacrifice of the body of Jesus Christ once for all" (Hebrews 10:8-10).

Jesus' sacrifice atoned for the sins of the world which restored the perfect fellowship between God and mankind. (Hebrews 8:12; 9:26; 10:10, 12, 14, 18; I John 2:2). Jesus accomplished what the law could never do. Through faith we enter into the Sabbath Rest in which Adam and Eve were created and God promised to the Israelites (Hebrews 4:1-3). This is why there was need for another priest to come in the order and with the rank of Melchizedek; because He was able to restore this relationship. Jesus' death and resurrection brought about the forgiveness of sins making us holy by faith (I Corinthians 1:2; Ephesians 1:4; 4:24; Hebrews 2:11). If we are holy, then perfection, or the perfect fellowship between God and the worshipper has been restored. If it is restored, then we can approach God confidently through faith. *"Let us then approach the throne of grace with confidence, so that we may receive mercy and find grace to help us in our time of need" (Hebrews 4:16).*

The law could never do this because it reminded us of our sin making us unsure and guilty before God (Romans 3:20; Hebrews 10:1-4). However, Jesus restored our confidence by completely wiping away our guilt and shame. This is why Jesus is after the order of Melchizedek and not the order of Aaron.

Changing the Priesthood Means Changing the Law

"For when there is a change of the priesthood, there must also be a change of the law" (Hebrews 7:12)

About a year ago, I sat through a series at church about the Ten Commandments. Each week the pastor would give his message on the next commandment instructing the congregation how to follow it and live it out in their lives. I spent the entire time wondering why a teaching series like this existed. I came to the conclusion that the Church as a whole is missing vital information concerning everything that took place at Calvary. This passage declares that when there is change in priesthood by necessity there also must be a change in law. And if there has been a change in the law, why are we still acting as if there hasn't been?

Christians still want to live under the Old Testament Covenant which is why we have this hybrid of grace and works that permeates the Church. We teach salvation by grace but holiness by Law as in the example of the teaching series on the Ten Commandments. However Paul said in Colossians, *"So then, just as you received Christ Jesus as Lord, continue to live in him" (Colossians 2:6).* How did you receive Christ? The only acceptable answer is by faith. So it makes sense that we continue in Him in the very same way. In fact, Paul said in Galatians, *"All who rely on observing the law are under a curse, for it is written: "Cursed is everyone who does not continue to do everything written in the Book of the Law." (Galatians 3:10).* His point is that Jesus became the curse so we could be redeemed from the law's curse to live by faith (Galatians 3:13-14).

This is why we must pay attention to Jesus and everything that took place at His death and resurrection. *"Therefore, holy brothers, who share in the heavenly calling, fix your thoughts on Jesus, the apostle and high priest whom we confess" (Hebrews 3:1).* Why? Because the covenant of grace that He ushered in is far superior in every way than the old system of the law. *"But the ministry Jesus has received is superior to theirs as the covenant of which he is mediator is superior to the old one, and it is founded on better promises" (Hebrews 8:6).* If we, as New Testament believers, have better promises, then it only makes sense that we know what they are and operate out of them instead of the old system that is aging and ready to disappear (Hebrews 8:13).

This comes as a shock to many people but the old system did not work. Look at this passage from scripture. It actually says this very thing – the old system was broken *"For if there had been nothing wrong with that first covenant, no place would have been sought for another. But God found fault with the people and said: "The time is coming, declares the Lord, when I will make a new covenant with the house of Israel and with the house of Judah. It will not be like the covenant I made with their forefathers when I took them by the hand to lead them out of Egypt, because they did not remain faithful to my covenant, and I turned away from them, declares the Lord" (Hebrews 8:7-9).* The time for change came with Jesus.

The old system of Laws only dealt with the external (Hebrews 9:10) which is why it could never work. Take an apple tree, for example; when the fruit is ready to be picked you might find evidence that it had a worm. However if it is early enough in the season when you pick the apple, there is a chance that the worm is still inside. This is because the apple actual grows around the worm and the worm ruins the apple from the inside out. The law was geared toward the flesh, but since the core was bad, it showed us that we were already defeated and in need of a savior. This is why God had to deal with the heart of man, not merely external behavior which manifests because of what is inside. This is why there was a need for a new Covenant and new system.

"This is the covenant I will make with the house of Israel after that time, declares the Lord. I will put my laws in their minds and write them on their hearts. I will be their God, and they will be my people. No longer will a man teach his neighbor, or a man his brother, saying, 'Know the Lord,' because they will all know me, from the least of them to the greatest. For I will forgive their wickedness and will remember their sins no more." By calling this covenant "new," he has made the first one obsolete; and what is obsolete and aging will soon disappear" (Hebrews 8:10-13).

Jesus dealt with the core of mankind which is why we must be born again, so that our nature is no longer according to the flesh which is corrupt. Instead it is according to spirit fashioned after Jesus' in true righteousness and holiness (Ephesians 4:22-24). He put the law of God on the inside of us, writing them on our hearts and minds so that we can know all His ways, it becomes part of us; cleansing us from the inside out, not just a system of rules to live by. This is the change in law. It is not of the letter which condemns, it is of the spirit which gives life. *"He has made us competent as ministers of a new covenant—not of the letter but of the Spirit; for the letter kills, but the Spirit gives life" (II Corinthians 3:6).*

As believers, our covenant is glorious, which is why it seems inconceivable that anyone would choose to return to the old system of being under the law. *"Now if the ministry that brought death, which was engraved in letters on stone [The Ten Commandments], came with glory, so that the Israelites could not look steadily at the face of Moses because of its glory, fading though it was, will not the ministry of the Spirit be even more glorious? (II Corinthians 3:7-8).* The point here is that Jesus ushered in a new system with His priesthood, then gave us the Holy Spirit, which allows us to live in a completely different way. Not by a list of "dos and don'ts" but by His Spirit. *"The mind of sinful man is death, but the mind controlled by the Spirit is life and peace" (Romans 8:6).* Unlike the commandments which arouse the desire to sin (Romans 7:11), living by the Spirit of God actually produces the righteous requirements the law describes (Romans 8:4), which is why the new system under Jesus' priesthood actually works!

"Therefore, since we have such a hope, we are very bold. We are not like Moses, who would put a veil over his face to keep the Israelites from gazing at it while the radiance was fading away. But their minds were made dull, for to this day the same veil remains when the old covenant is read. It has not been removed, because only in Christ is it taken away. Even to this day when Moses is read, a veil covers their hearts. But whenever anyone turns to the Lord, the veil is taken away. Now the Lord is the Spirit, and where the Spirit of the Lord is, there is freedom. And we, who with unveiled faces all reflect the Lord's glory, are being transformed into his likeness with ever-increasing glory, which comes from the Lord, who is the Spirit" (II Corinthians 3:12-18).

So instead of spending ten weeks doing a study on the Ten Commandments, which actually puts a veil over our hearts and dulls our minds to the things of God, we should spend time focused on Christ and the change that came

redemption.

with His priesthood. We do not need to be told what the law is, through Christ, His law has been written on our hearts and exist in our minds and will be evident in our lives by walking and living by the Spirit of God (Jeremiah 31:31-34; Hebrews 8:10-13; 10:15-16). We should always look at the law through the filter of Christ which will always confirm what is spoken to us through the Holy Spirit. This is why by necessity there had to be a change in law when there was a change in priesthood. Through Christ a better hope is introduced by which we can draw near to God (Hebrews 7:18).

Jesus Descended
From Judah Not Levi

"He of whom these things are said belonged to a different tribe, and no one from that tribe has ever served at the altar. For it is clear that our Lord descended from Judah, and in regard to that tribe Moses said nothing about priests" (Hebrews 7:13-14)

Did you know that the office of priest as held by the Levites is actually patterned after what takes place in the heavenly sanctuary? (Hebrews 8:5). This is why Moses was warned to make everything according to what he had been shown to him on the mountain (Exodus 25:40). Christ's priesthood was not patterned after the Levitical institution, it was the other way around, they were patterned after Christ's eternal position as High Priest.

This is important to us because we must understand that this was the plan from the very beginning. The institution of Aaron's line merely showed us an example of how it worked. It was a physical representation of a spiritual reality. The institution of this priesthood helped us to understand and visualize what takes place in heaven. However, it was never able to clear the conscience of the worshipper and so all the following generations of priests who made sacrifices merely served to remind the people of their sin (Hebrews 10:1-4).

It is amazing that God kept the Levitical priesthood and Jesus' eternal priesthood in completely separate lines. He did this to show us that the law could never make us perfect so we would never rely on it for a means of justification (Romans 5:20; Galatians 3:10-11; Hebrews 10:1-4; James 2:10). Being justified can only come through faith in Christ (Romans 5:1; Galatians 3:13-14; 24-25). This is why Jesus had to come from a completely different and separate line. In fact, we cannot even understand Jesus' office in relation to the Levitical lineage because it is far superior in every way imaginable (Hebrews 7:15-16, 18-19; 8:6; 9:8, 14-15).

This is why Jesus came in the order and with the rank of Melchizedek. Not only was he High Priest of the Most High God, he was also a King (Genesis 14:18; Hebrews 7:1-2). The priesthood of Aaron never held this honor. However, Melchizedek and Jesus do. Which is why Jesus came from Judah and the royal line of King David, because it fulfilled scripture that the Messiah would come from David's line and rule forever (II Samuel 7:16; Psalm 89:3-4; Jeremiah 23:5; Micah 5:2; John 7:42). Being after the order of Melchizedek, afforded Jesus the right to the position of both High Priest and King.

The previous verse in Hebrews 7 records, *"For when there is a change of the priesthood, there must also be a change of the law" (Hebrews 7:12).* This is why Moses never mentioned anyone from the tribe of Judah serving at the altar, *"If he were on earth, he would not be a priest, for there are already men who offer the gifts prescribed by the law" (Hebrews 8:4).* So if there's been a change in the law with the institution of Jesus' priesthood, then there is no longer a need for the priesthood of Aaron.

The Levitical priesthood reminded us of our sin and reminded us that perfect fellowship between God and mankind didn't exist (Hebrews 9:9; 10:1-4). However, *"Christ did not enter a man-made sanctuary that was only a copy of the true one; he entered heaven itself, now to appear for us in God's presence" (Hebrews 9:24).* And He's entered once for all which indicates that He has now perfected the relationship between God and mankind bringing us back into fellowship with Him through faith (Hebrews 9:12, 14, 24-28; 10:9-10, 12-14, 18). This is why the priesthood had to switch lines so we could be made righteous and holy through Christ. He was the only one capable of bridging this gap and restoring us. *"For what the law was powerless to do in that it was weakened by the sinful nature, God did by sending his own Son in the likeness of sinful man to be a sin offering. And so he condemned sin in sinful man, in order that the righteous requirements of the law might be fully met in us, who do not live according to the sinful nature but according to the Spirit" (Romans 8:3-4).*

Jesus Became High Priest on the Basis of an Indestructible Life

"And what we have said is even more clear if another priest like Melchizedek appears, one who has become a priest not on the basis of a regulation as to his ancestry but on the basis of the power of an indestructible life. For it is declared: "You are a priest forever, in the order of Melchizedek" (Hebrews 7:15-17)

The Levitical priesthood was a lifetime position. Once a person became High Priest this position was retained until death (Numbers 35:25). However, each time the priest died a new priest would be appointed, so in another sense you might say this priesthood never had any permanence, death always interrupted it.

Jesus' priesthood greatly contrasts this because death could not hold Him captive and therefore the grave did not interrupt His appointment as High Priest. His resurrection from the dead, solidified this position permanently. *"For we know that since Christ was raised from the dead, he cannot die again; death no longer has mastery over him" (Romans 6:9).* Since the priesthood is a lifetime position, Jesus' resurrection guarantees that He eternally holds this position. *"Now there have been many of those priests, since death prevented them from continuing in office; but because Jesus lives forever, he has a permanent priesthood. Therefore he is able to save completely those who come to God through him, because he always lives to intercede for them" (Hebrews 7:23-25).*

This is good news for us because it means the sacrifice made for sin worked, the first and only time it was given. In other words the payment for sin completely wiped out and nullified the debt that sin created. Which is why death had no power to hold Jesus captive, the account had been settled and closed, permanently. And if the power of sin and death had no claim to Jesus after He died, it also means that it can hold no power over Him while He's alive. Therefore we know that Christ will live eternally. In the same way the power of sin is also broken over us who put saving faith in Jesus (Hebrews 7:24; 9:12, 14; 10:10, 14, 18).

"For this reason Christ is the mediator of a new covenant, that those who are called may receive the promised eternal inheritance—now that he has died as a ransom to set them free from the sins committed under the first covenant" (Hebrews 9:15).

All of this becomes clear when we understand that Jesus is after a completely different line than what was established through the Levitical priesthood. The book of Hebrews records four times that Jesus became our High Priest fashioned after the order and with the rank of Melchizedek (Hebrews 5:10; 7:11, 15, 21). This is extremely significant because Melchizedek had no record of beginning or end. The beginning of Hebrews 7 records *"like the Son of God he remains a priest forever" (Hebrews 7:3b).* It had nothing to do with ancestry but everything to do with the power required to sustain life indefinitely. Jesus holds this power which is why there has been a change in priesthood (Hebrews 7:11) and subsequently a change in the law (Hebrews 7:12).

The Law Was
Weak and Useless

"The former regulation is set aside because it was weak and useless (for the law made nothing perfect), and a better hope is introduced, by which we draw near to God" (Hebrews 7:18-19)

The solution to the chasm that sin created is not the Law. As this passage clearly declares using it in this way is weak, useless and ineffective. Paul called the Law the ministry of death (II Corinthians 3:7). So relying on it to bring us into fellowship with God, bridging the gap caused by sin, only brings us death and condemnation.

On the other hand, if it is used in accordance to its true purpose then we will be justified by it. *"So the law was put in charge to lead us to Christ that we might be justified by faith. Now that faith has come, we are no longer under the supervision of the law" (Galatians 3:24-25).* The Law was set aside when Jesus ushered in the New Covenant because it was useless in bringing a person into perfect fellowship with God (Hebrews 7:11). The Law defined our sin in relation to God's holiness. So in essence it accused us before God, bringing further separation instead of reconciliation. Which is why Paul told Timothy, the law was not made for the righteous man, but for sinners (I Timothy 1:8-10). It showed us the need for a savior. So trusting in Christ to save us is the better hope that this passage is describing by which we draw near to God for reconciliation.

Paul made this very observation about the purpose of the Law in Romans 7, *"What shall we say, then? Is the law sin? Certainly not! Indeed I would not have known what sin was except through the law. For I would not have known what coveting really was if the law had not said, "Do not covet." But sin, seizing the opportunity afforded by the commandment, produced in me every kind of covetous desire. For apart from law, sin is dead. Once I was alive apart from law; but when the commandment came, sin sprang to life and I died. I found that the very commandment that was intended to bring life actually brought death. For sin, seizing the opportunity afforded by the commandment, deceived me, and through the commandment put me to death. So then, the law is holy, and the commandment is holy, righteous and good. Did that which is good, then, become death to me? By no means! But in order that sin might be recognized as sin, it produced death in me through what was good, so that through the commandment sin might become utterly sinful" (Romans 7:7-13).*

The main point that the writer is making is that to draw near to God we must set aside the law, because the law strengthens sin in our lives increasing its hold on us instead of bringing us the reconciliation we need. Instead we should cling to the better hope by which we have full access to God.

This blessed hope is in the person of Jesus Christ who has paved the way for us to enter blamelessly into God's very presence (Hebrews 4:16; 10:19-22). His blood has completely wiped away the effects of sin in our lives once for all (Hebrews 9:12, 14, 26, 28; 10:10, 12, 14, 18, 22). This is why we have this access. Jesus imputed His righteousness to us when we believed; the righteousness required to fulfill the entire law. Adherence to the law couldn't make us righteous because of our sin nature (Galatians 3:21). However Jesus fulfilled it because He was sinless. Then He gave us His Spirit to replace that sin nature when we were born again, which is how He imputed His righteousness to us. This is why He is the better hope by which we can come before God.

When we understand this, it gives us boldness and confidence before God instead of uncertainly and fear. Under the law, the High Priest was allowed to enter into the Holy of Holies and into the presence of God once a year when he made atonement for the people. However, when Jesus was crucified on the cross the curtain that had separated the people from God's presence was torn entirely in two from top to bottom (Matthew 27:51; Mark 15:38; Luke 23:45). This was done by God himself showing us that Jesus paved the way for us to come with full assurance of faith and clean consciences (Hebrews 10:22). His body is now the curtain by which we can freely enter at will (Hebrews 10:20).

This is why the law is set aside when we are saved, because its purpose has been fulfilled in bringing us to Christ to be justified by faith. Now that Jesus is our High Priest, He assures this access eternally. *"For the law appoints as high priests men who are weak; but the oath, which came after the law, appointed the Son, who has been made perfect forever" (Hebrews 7:28).* Jesus is the better hope which gives us confidence before God.

Jesus is the Guarantee of a Better Covenant

"And it was not without an oath! Others became priests without any oath, but he became a priest with an oath when God said to him: "The Lord has sworn and will not change his mind: 'You are a priest forever.'" Because of this oath, Jesus has become the guarantee of a better covenant" (Hebrews 7:20-22)

Several times throughout the gospels the voice of God was heard over Jesus. The first instance is when He was baptized by John. *"A voice came from heaven and said, "This is my Son, whom I love: with him I am well pleased" (Matthew 3:17).* Another notable event was on the mount of transfiguration. While Jesus was speaking with Moses and Elijah a bright cloud enveloped them and a voice from the cloud said, *"This is my Son, whom I love; with him I am well pleased. Listen to him!" (Matthews 17:5b).* Lastly right before Jesus death, while He was praying in the garden He said, *"Father, glorify your name!" Then a voice came from heaven, "I have glorified it, and will glorify it again." (John 12:28).* Everyone there had different reaction to the voice of God, some said it had thundered and others said an angel had spoken to him. However look at Jesus' response *"This voice was for your benefit, not mine" (John 12:30).*

Every time God spoke audibly to Jesus it was for our benefit. Jesus understood God's nature completely because they are one and the same so the words were not said for Jesus' sake (John 1:1; Colossians 1:15, 19; Hebrews 1:1-3). However, He said these things about Jesus so we could have insight into this relationship between the two. Through it we see that God loved Jesus, God was pleased with Jesus and God's name was glorified through Jesus. These are important truths to know.

In the same way, the oath made between God and Jesus that He would eternally be our High Priest was made solely for our benefit so we could understand that the covenant made on our behalf was lasting and eternal. In fact, God wanted to make His intent very clear so He made us this promise and then confirmed it with an oath and hinged everything on His character, *"Because God wanted to make the unchanging nature of his purpose very clear to the heirs of what was promised, he confirmed it with an oath. God did this so that, by two unchangeable things in which it is impossible for God to lie, we who have fled to take hold of the hope offered to us may be greatly encouraged"* (Hebrews 6:17-18).

Because of this oath, through Christ we have full access to God. We have boldness to enter into the very presence of the Father to find grace and help in every circumstance of life (Hebrews 4:16). This is why the Law was weak and useless (Hebrews 7:18). It could not bring us into perfect fellowship with God the Father (Hebrews 7:11), however Jesus did. And because God promised Him on oath that He was a priest forever in the order of Melchizedek, He has become the guarantee of a better, stronger and more advantageous covenant (Hebrews 7:22). God wants us to know this; which is why He made this oath to Jesus. This is something we should constantly remind ourselves so that we can live in a state of peace, being assured that we are acceptable to God solely on the basis of what Jesus did for us. This is an amazing truth, which is why John said, *"This then is how we know that we belong to the truth, and how we set our hearts at rest in his presence whenever our hearts condemn us. For God is greater than our hearts, and he knows everything"* (1 John 3:19-20).

The oath made to Jesus was made solely for our benefit so that we would know and rest in the covenant that Jesus secures for us. Through Christ we have peace with God (Romans 5:1) and confidence to approach Him through faith (Hebrews 4:16). This is why the covenant of grace we have is far superior to the old covenant in every way imaginable and this new covenant is guaranteed eternally by the oath made on our behalf.

Jesus is Able to Save Completely Because He has Permanent Priesthood

"Now there have been many of those priests, since death prevented them from continuing in office; but because Jesus lives forever, he has a permanent priesthood. Therefore he is able to save completely those who come to God through him, because he always lives to intercede for them" (Hebrews 7:23-25)

One of the most amazing truths in the entire Bible is that Jesus is able to save completely, perfectly and to the uttermost because of His resurrection from the dead. In fact our entire belief system hinges on this truth. Without the resurrection we would die in our sin, shame and guilt. Paul said in Romans 4, *"He was delivered over to death for our sins and was raised to life for our justification" (Romans 4:25),* meaning that His resurrection is the positive proof that we have been restored to a state as if we had never sinned in the first place. The payment for sin was satisfied once for all when Jesus was delivered over to death to make atonement. Since it was satisfied and all debts forgiven, death no longer had claim on Jesus and had to release Him from the grave.

This has incredible implications for us, because through Jesus, the grave has no claim on us either. Jesus has been appointed by God as our High Priest on oath that He would remain as such eternally. Before this time, death had been a problem in the Levitical priesthood because it continually interrupted this office. The position of High Priest was a lifetime position (Numbers 35:25). So it was like starting over every time a new High Priest was appointed following the death of the previous High Priest. However, since death has no claim on Jesus (Romans 6:9), His priesthood cannot be interrupted, therefore He is able to complete the work assigned to Him as High Priest.

The High Priest's job was to make atonement for the people once a year. He was mankind's representative before God in all things. The problem was that he first had to sacrifice for his own sins, disqualifying him from approaching God to make atonement in the first place. Jesus on the other hand was sinless so His sacrifice for sin, when offering himself as payment, was more than enough to permanently wipe out the debt that sin created. In fact the writer of Hebrews has stated over and over that our sins are paid for, forgiven and forgotten (Hebrews 9:12, 14, 26, 28; 10:10, 12, 14, 18, 22). Which means that Jesus' atonement as High Priest worked the first and only time it was given. And if it worked, then by no means does it need to be made again (Hebrews 10:10-14). In fact, Jesus now sits at the right hand of God the Father because His work is finished and complete (John 1:18; Ephesians 1:20; Hebrews 1:3; 10:12).

Since this work is finished and death has no claim on Jesus, He resides as High Priest forever. And if He lives forever with this office, He is also able to save for all time and eternity those who come to Him by faith. In fact, God promised Jesus on oath that this would always be the case which is why He promised Him that He would provide a High Priest, not after the Levitical line perpetuated by death, but after Melchizedek who had no record of death (Hebrews 7:3).

This is incredible news and very important to know because it assures our hearts before God. In fact these things have been written to give us insight and confidence in approaching God by faith (John 20:31; Romans 15:3; I John 5:13). Knowing that we have been saved, forgiven and restored to a state where we are justified and righteous before God should give us boldness in approaching Him without the consciousness of sin and resulting guilt (Hebrews 4:16; 10:22). Then knowing that Jesus lives forever to assure this relationship, making petitions and intercession on our behalf, should usher us into a state of heart peace and empower us to live a life like no other. These truths have been written for our benefit; so that we may understand all that we have access to through Christ Jesus.

Jesus is the High Priest Who Meets Our Needs

"Such a high priest meets our need—one who is holy, blameless, pure, set apart from sinners, exalted above the heavens. Unlike the other high priests, he does not need to offer sacrifices day after day, first for his own sins, and then for the sins of the people. He sacrificed for their sins once for all when he offered himself" (Hebrews 7:26-27)

When choosing Jesus as our High Priest, God chose the very best. He did not withhold anything from us but sent Jesus who could perfectly fulfill the requirements of both the sacrifice needed for the forgiveness of sins and for the role of High Priest, who made offering and intercession for us. This is an amazing truth, mankind chose individuals based on ancestry who were subject to sin and death, and God chose Jesus, who was sinless and perfect (Hebrews 7:28).

One of the greatest goals of this letter to the Hebrews is to show the superiority of Christ's eternal High Priesthood as being different and far superior to the Levitical office. In fact, the writer does everything to connect Jesus with the priesthood of Melchizedek. The reason is because the Levitical line was flawed by the sin and death of the priests. It was perpetuated by death, never having permanence or perfection (Hebrews 7:16). This is why there was a need for another priest *"If perfection could have been attained through the Levitical priesthood (for on the basis of it the law was given to the people), why was there still need for another priest to come—one in the order of Melchizedek, not in the order of Aaron?" (Hebrews 7:11)*.

Jesus on the other hand is perfect, sinless, pure, holy, blameless and set apart from sinners (Hebrews 7:26). These qualifications alone show His superiority over the Levitical priests. Not only that but they are also the elements of a perfect sacrifice. Unlike the earthly priests, Jesus did not have to first sacrifice for His own sins before making intercession (Hebrews 7:27). This is because He was perfect and sinless, which already qualified Him to make intercession on our behalf. He was both the perfect sacrifice and the perfect intercessor.

This is why God chose Jesus to reconcile the world to Himself, because He was the only one qualified for the job. In fact, Jesus' redemptive work was so perfect that it only required one sacrifice to forever wipe away and forgive the sins of the entire world (Hebrews 7:27; 8:12; 9:14-15, 26, 28; 10:10, 12, 17-18; I John 2:2). The truth is that God loved us so very much that He sent Jesus to do what mankind could not in restoring the relationship between God and man (Isaiah 59:15b-18; John 3:16; Romans 5:1-2; I Timothy 2:5; I John 2:1). Through Jesus we are brought into a right standing with God, restored, forgiven and accepted solely on His account. This is why Jesus' priesthood is far superior to the Levitical priesthood in every way imaginable. This high priest is perfectly adapted to meet our needs which is why God chose the very best right from the start!

The Law vs. the Oath

"For the law appoints as high priests men who are weak;
but the oath, which came after the law, appointed the Son,
who has been made perfect forever" (Hebrews 7:28)

The entire book of Hebrews contrasts in one way or the other the vast differences between the Old Covenant and the New. Whether it is contrasting Jesus' priesthood with the Levitical priesthood or the outcome of those priestly duties, the result is the same, the New Covenant is far superior in every way imaginable (Hebrews 8:6).

The point of the entire book is to show us that the Covenant of the Law is inferior to the Covenant which Jesus ushered in and secures for us. In fact the writer goes to great lengths to describe that this Covenant is backed by an oath from God that it is eternal and permanent. Because of the oath, God will never revoke or change His mind concerning these promises (Hebrews 6:16-18; 7:18-22).

This particular verse is a prime example of this contrast. The law sets up men to intercede based on frailty and weakness, which is not very effective considering the job they are required to do. However, the New Covenant, based on the oath that Jesus is the one to make peace for us (Romans 5:1), is very effective because Jesus is already perfect and sinless. In other words, He fulfilled the requirements of approaching God in perfection, so He is able to perfectly intercede on our behalf (I Timothy 2:5). Not only is this so, but since He defeated death once for all His position is eternal since death no longer has claim over Him (Romans 4:25; 6:9). This give us both confidence and assurance of every promise made to us throughout the Scriptures because Jesus is the guarantee of everything written to us (Hebrews 7:22).

When you really break it down, the Law is what strengthens sin in our lives showing our guilt and shame (Romans 3:19-20; Galatians 3:10-11, 21). Then when you consider that those set up to make intercession are subject to the same weaknesses, we can see the need for a new system. *"The former regulation is set aside because it was weak and useless (for the law made nothing perfect), and a better hope is introduced, by which we draw near to God" (Hebrews 7:18-19).*

The better hope is Jesus. He is the only one that can make us righteous and acceptable to God (Romans 3:22; 4:5, 16; 5:1; II Corinthians 5:21; Titus 3:5-7). He took our sin and gave us His righteousness (II Corinthians 5:21) so that we can stand justified before God (Romans 8:30). Since we now can stand in His presence we also know that we have boldness in approaching Him by faith (Hebrews 4:16; 10:22). This is by far a more superior and advantageous covenant in every way imaginable.

This Covenant is backed by an oath, not the law, *"Because of this oath, Jesus has become the guarantee of a better covenant" (Hebrews 7:22).* And the oath is founded on better promises, *"But the ministry Jesus has received is as superior to theirs as the covenant of which he is mediator is superior to the old one, and it is founded on better promises" (Hebrews 8:6).* This is why the contrast between the law and the oath is so great and is very important to us to understand because we are heirs of the New Covenant, founded and secured in Jesus Christ. *"For the Law sets up men in their weakness [frail, sinful, dying human beings] as high priests, but the word of [God's] oath, which [was spoken later] after the institution of the Law, [chooses and appoints as priest One Whose appointment is complete and permanent], a Son Who has been made perfect forever" (Hebrews 7:28 AMP).*

hebrews 8.

THE SUPERIORITY OF THE
NEW COVENANT

Jesus Serves in the True Tabernacle Set Up by the Lord

"The point of what we are saying is this: We do have such a high priest, who sat down at the right hand of the throne of the Majesty in heaven, and who serves in the sanctuary, the true tabernacle set up by the Lord, not by man" (Hebrews 8:1-2)

One Christmas during my youth, my family received a large jigsaw puzzle which we started putting together that very afternoon. By the time New Years Eve rolled around we decided we wouldn't eat dinner until the puzzle (on which we had labored all week) had been finished. Each piece revealed the puzzle in more detail and soon we had a very large montage of thousands of gumballs. It seemed like a miracle when we finally finished it.

Just as a puzzle, made up of thousands of pieces, reveals the larger image, the Levitical priesthood and all elements of the Law were a glimpse of the true system in heaven in which Jesus owns the title and position of High Priest. The earthly system helps us visualize what is currently taking place in the heavenly realm. These pieces, when put together, reveal the entire picture. Now that we have a working knowledge from the previous chapters of how everything relates, it is time to bring it all together and look at the big picture.

First, Jesus is the High Priest God provided for us under the New Covenant. This is an amazing truth. The old system was flawed because of mankind's inability to keep the covenant, so God made a New Covenant and based it on His ability to fulfill it (Hebrews 8:6). Then He set up Jesus as the guarantor of these promises (Hebrews 7:22).

Secondly, Jesus serves in the true heavenly tabernacle. It's easy to lose sight of the fact that tabernacle worship as illustrated and outlined in the law was fashioned after the true temple worship currently taking place in heaven. How else do you think Moses obtained the pattern for what he was instructed to build? (Exodus 25:40; Hebrews 8:5). The heavenly tabernacle was created, not by mankind, but by God which is why the earthly tabernacle only served as a type and shadow of the true one (Hebrews 10:1). The heavenly tabernacle is where Jesus poured His blood on the Mercy Seat for us (Hebrews 9:11-12). It was a perfect offering, not given according to the law but according to the eternal priesthood that God ordained through Jesus.

Next, Jesus sat down because His work was finished and complete. Just as in the example from creation (Genesis 2:2), the rest that Jesus entered into was because everything was done. Not one thing was left unfinished.

Lastly, Jesus sat down at the right hand of God the Father because this is the place of honor. The book of Hebrews opens with this very idea, *"The Son is the radiance of God's glory and the exact representation of his being, sustaining all things by his powerful word. After he had provided purification for sins, he sat down at the right hand of the Majesty in heaven. So he became as much superior to the angels as the name he has inherited is superior to theirs" (Hebrews 1:3-4).* Jesus inherited the name above every name because God was so pleased with the redemptive work that Jesus completed. So Jesus has both the place of honor at the right hand of the Father and the name above every name (Psalm 110:1; Matthew 26:64; Acts 2:34; Romans 8:34; Philippians 2:9-10; Colossians 3:1; Hebrews 1:3-4; 12:2).

These things summarize the main point the writer is making concerning everything he has said about Jesus' High Priesthood in the last couple of chapters. First, it was Jesus who carried out the plan of redemption and acted as our High Priest chosen by God. Secondly, these things took place in the true heavenly tabernacle. Next, Jesus sat down because it was finished. And lastly, Jesus has the place of honor and the name above every name because the job He was given to do was done so completely. This shows how our covenant with the Lord is completely different and far superior to the Old Covenant and why Jesus' priesthood is one of the best gifts we've ever received.

The Gifts and Sacrifices Prescribed by the Law

"Every high priest is appointed to offer both gifts and sacrifices, and so it was necessary for this one also to have something to offer. If he were on earth, he would not be a priest, for there are already men who offer the gifts prescribed by the law" (Hebrews 8:3-4)

Jesus' priesthood is unlike any other. The writer of Hebrews goes to great lengths to disconnect Jesus' priesthood from the Levitical line. The picture he paints of the Levitical priesthood is a system that continually operates over and over without having permanence or resolution (Hebrews 7). In fact he mentions this very idea five times throughout the entire book, each time building on the last, making it more apparent that this system could not accomplish what Jesus could (Hebrews 5:1; 7:27; 8:3; 9:9; 10:11).

The book of Leviticus describes the required gifts and sacrifices the priests were to make on behalf of the people. There were burnt offerings, grain offerings, peace, sin and guilt offerings, each sacrifice had specific guidelines and rituals required when making them. However, the result was the same; when the offering was made it was accepted by the Lord and became a pleasing aroma to Him. The priests were the only ones able to offer these gifts and sacrifices. It was their primary duty.

In the same way, Jesus, our High Priest, was also required to offer both gifts and sacrifices. The difference is that Jesus' gifts and His sacrifice were far superior to the gifts offered according to the law. He did not bring animals to sacrifice as a covering for sin. He presented His body, which was prepared and given for this very purpose (Hebrews 10:5-7). His sacrifice completely and utterly wiped away sin and its effects, so there was not even a record of them to accuse us (II Corinthians 5:19; Hebrews 10:17-18; I John 2:2). The New Testament tells us that Jesus' sacrifice was a fragrant and pleasing aroma to God (Ephesians 5:2).

redemption.

In fact, Jesus' gifts and sacrifice did several things that the Levitical priesthood could never do and only hinted at. First, Jesus paid the debt left by sin, making our account balanced, absolving us from all guilt before God (Romans 4:25; Hebrews 10:10, 12, 14, 22). Secondly, He took our old sin nature and gave us a new life fashioned after His own (Romans 6:4; II Corinthians 5:17; Galatians 2:20; Ephesians 4:24; I Peter 3:18). Next, He died so we could live apart from the law while obtaining the righteousness described within the law (II Corinthians 5:21). This removed death's claim on us (I Corinthians 15:55; Ephesians 4:7-8; I Peter 3:18). Lastly through Jesus, not the law, we will experience the incomparable riches of His grace for all eternity (Ephesians 2:7). This is why Jesus' priesthood is unparalleled to any other.

In contrast to the Levitical line, Jesus only offered these gifts and sacrifices once. He did not do it over and over, once was all it took. In the same way that the writer of Hebrews describes the continual offerings of the earthly priesthood to show that the old system was inadequate, he points out many times how Jesus' sacrifice worked the one and only time it was given (Hebrews 5:9; 6:20; 7:24-25, 27; 8:12; 9:15, 26, 28; 10:10, 12, 14, 18, 22-23). This alone, shows how superior Jesus' priesthood is. We are eternally blessed by the fact that Jesus has been appointed as our High Priest before God, making intercession for us. Faith in the saving name of Jesus alone is all it takes to secure a hope and future with Him eternally.

A Copy and a Shadow of What is in Heaven

"They serve at a sanctuary that is a copy and shadow of what is in heaven. This is why Moses was warned when he was about to build the tabernacle: "See to it that you make everything according to the pattern shown you on the mountain" (Hebrews 8:5)

Growing up, my brother liked to build model planes. He would spend hours constructing a model patterned after a real plane. In fact, after the glue dried and the decals were applied the model looked very much like the real thing.

Old Testament temple worship was just like this. It was based on a pattern of the real thing that took place in the heavenly tabernacle. Moses was shown the entire thing when he met with God on the mountain (Exodus 25:40). Then God instructed Moses to recreate this tabernacle and its practices on earth with a warning to make it exactly as he was shone.

This speaks to how detailed God is. The tabernacle, set up according to what takes place in heaven, was to serve as an illustration helping the people understand. The earthly system was a copy and a shadow of the heavenly system. It wasn't a means in itself; it was a model or replica of the true system. It looked like it, it functioned like it, but it was merely a pattern and foreshadowing of the real thing. This is why Moses was told to make it exactly according to what he saw, because it was simply a model.

The main point the writer is making in Hebrews 8 is that Jesus, our High Priest, entered into the heavenly tabernacle to perform His priestly duties (Hebrews 8:2; 9:11). The model portrayed by the earthly priests, in the earthly tabernacle, is based on the pattern of the true tabernacle in heaven. The Levitical priesthood was given so we could visualize everything Jesus did there. Everything we learn from the Levitical priest is a foreshadowing to Jesus and His priesthood. God gave us these examples to teach us so we would have complete understanding of this true priesthood.

Just as the planes my brother built as a child helped him visualize how the real planes looked, they were never a substitute for the real thing. In the same way, we can gain a lot of understanding by looking at the earthly system as long as we understand that it is merely a copy and a shadow of the true system in heaven where Jesus resides seated at the right hand of God the Father because His work is perfect and complete.

Jesus' Covenant is Superior, Founded on Better Promises

"But the ministry Jesus has received is as superior to theirs as the covenant of which he is mediator is superior to the old one, and it is founded on better promises" (Hebrews 8:6)

Jesus is the mediator or guarantor of the Covenant of grace. This covenant is far superior in every way imaginable to the Covenant of Law. This is because it is founded on better promises and backed by an oath between God and Jesus that it will be lasting and eternal (Hebrews 7:21). In fact, King David himself looked forward to this covenant and congratulated the recipients, pronouncing a blessing on them, *"Blessed is he whose transgressions are forgiven, whose sins are covered. Blessed is the man whose sin the LORD does not count against him and in whose spirit is no deceit" (Psalms 32:1-2; Romans 4:6-8).*

The better promises on which this covenant is founded rest solely in the Lord Jesus. It is superior because of this, and unlike the first, it is not based on cause and effect. In other words, God is not limited in His interaction with us based on something we do or do not do. In fact, chapter 8 defines the differences of the New Covenant. First He put His laws in our hearts and minds so that we can be familiar and intimate with His ways and precepts (Hebrews 8:10). Secondly, He makes us His people, declaring that He will be our God (Hebrews 8:10). Third, He reveals Himself to us so that we do not need someone to tell us about God, we can experience Him for ourselves (Hebrews 8:11). Lastly He has forgiven our sins and goes a step further declaring that He will also forget them entirely (Hebrews 8:12). We have these amazing things as New Covenant believers, which is why our covenant is far superior than the previous one. This is what David saw and why he pronounced a blessing on us (Psalms 32:1-2; Romans 4:6-8).

To highlight our wonderful covenant it is important to understand that the Old Covenant of law was based on blessings and curses. Deuteronomy 28 lists both. The chapter starts out with these words spoken by the Lord, *"If you fully obey the LORD your God and carefully follow all his commands I give you today, the LORD your God will set you high above all the nations on earth. All these blessings will come upon you and accompany you if you obey the LORD your God" (Deuteronomy 28:1-2).* He then gives the list of blessing that were theirs by obeying Him. However it was conditional, *"The LORD will establish you as his holy people, as he promised you on oath, if you keep the commands of the LORD your God and walk in his ways" (Deuteronomy 28:9).*

In the same way, curses would befall the people when they were disobedient. *"However, if you do not obey the LORD your God and do not carefully follow all his commands and decrees I am giving you today, all these curses will come upon you and overtake you" (Deuteronomy 28:15).* The list of the curses is immense and disastrous. This is why the New Covenant is so wonderful, because He placed His laws and precepts inside us and gave us the Holy Spirit to teach us to follow and obey (I John 2:20, 27). This was not the case under the law of the Old Testament, they were subjected to the whims of the flesh. The Law strengthened sin against them arousing the desire for disobedience and the curses it brought (Romans 7:10; I Corinthians 15:56).

In the New Covenant, Jesus became a curse for us so we could have all of the blessings described in Deuteronomy 28 with none of the curses, *"Christ redeemed us from the curse of the law by becoming a curse for us, for it is written: "Cursed is everyone who is hung on a tree." He redeemed us in order that the blessing given to Abraham might come to the Gentiles through Christ Jesus, so that by faith we might receive the promise of the Spirit" (Galatians 3:13-14).* You can see how our Covenant is superior in every way. We receive all of the blessings and none of the curses. All because Jesus became the curse for us to redeem us from the law.

In the same way our mediator is also far superior. Jesus is the Mediator of this Covenant just as Moses was the mediator of the Covenant of the law. However Jesus has acquired a better ministry because He resides over it as a son, not a servant. *"Moses was faithful as a servant in all God's house, testifying to what would be said in the future. But Christ is faithful as a son over God's house. And we are his house, if we hold on to our courage and the hope of which we boast" (Hebrews 3:5-6).* Not only do we have a better and more advantageous Covenant based on nobler and higher promises, but we have a Mediator that is far superior in both title and position than that which was previously given. This is why the Old Testament patriarchs looked forward to the time we enjoy because God has done a work through Jesus Christ that is unparalleled to anything they experienced. This is why God enacted the New Covenant making the first one obsolete (Hebrews 8:13) so that we could be the people of God enjoying all of the blessings He bestows on us.

God Found Fault with the People Who Did Not Remain Faithful to His Covenant

"For if there had been nothing wrong with that first covenant, no place would have been sought for another. But God found fault with the people and said: "The time is coming, declares the Lord, when I will make a new covenant with the house of Israel and with the house of Judah. It will not be like the covenant I made with their forefathers when I took them by the hand to lead them out of Egypt, because they did not remain faithful to my covenant, and I turned away from them, declares the Lord" (Hebrews 8:7-9)

I've struggled in the past while reading these verses because what stands out to me is the last statement saying, *"they did not remain faithful to my covenant, and I turned away from them, declares the Lord" (vs. 9b).* The Amplified puts it this way, *"for they did not abide in My agreement with them, and so I withdrew My favor and disregarded them, says the Lord" (vs. 9b AMP).* These statements seem so foreign to the God I know. It is hard to imagine Him ever saying these things. Setting out to reconcile this idea in my heart has brought wonderful revelation of what this passage is truly saying.

The key lies in the idea that the first covenant was flawed because of mankind's inability to keep it, not because of God. This is why He found fault with the first covenant and brought about a new one. The first covenant was based on blessings and curses (Deuteronomy 28). It was not like the covenant that God made Abraham and it is certainly not like the covenant that God made with us through Jesus. It was behavioral based.

If they kept the commandments they received the blessings listed in the 28th chapter of Deuteronomy. If they disobeyed the commandments they received the curses listed. It was all spelled out, the Israelites were well aware of the terms when they agreed to it (Exodus 24:3).

Of course mankind, being one hundred percent flesh at that time, couldn't live up to it's rigorous guidelines. In fact the Israelites are the ones who turned away from their part of the agreement first. This released God from His part, although He always remained faithful to it. This passage in Hebrews is a quote from Jeremiah 31, with a slight difference near the end, *"The time is coming," declares the LORD, "when I will make a new covenant with the house of Israel and with the house of Judah. It will not be like the covenant I made with their forefathers when I took them by the hand to lead them out of Egypt, because they broke my covenant, though I was a husband to them" declares the LORD" (Jeremiah 31:31-32).*

The relationship that Israel and God had, was akin to the marital relationship. The covenant agreement was a marriage agreement. Israel continually prostituted themselves with other gods even though the Lord was a husband to them. This led the Lord to give them a certificate of divorce (Jeremiah 3:8). This did not annul God's relationship with them, it merely made an allotment for Him to usher in a new covenant to include those outside the nation of Israel. Even though He divorced them, He told them to return, so He could establish a New Covenant with them still declaring Himself as their husband. *"Return, faithless people," declares the LORD, "for I am your husband. I will choose you—one from a town and two from a clan—and bring you to Zion. Then I will give you shepherds after my own heart, who will lead you with knowledge and understanding" (Jeremiah 3:14-15).*

He did in fact give us this Shepherd, who is the radiance of God's glory and exact representation of His being (Hebrews 1:3). Jesus brought with Him an understanding and revelation of God that was previously unknown (John 1:14; II Corinthians 4:6; Colossians 1:15-20; Hebrews 1:1-3). In the first covenant, it was the Israelites themselves who caused all their suffering. God wanted to protect us from that because we could never live in the weakness of the flesh, which is why He sent Jesus to usher in a New Covenant and give us the Holy Spirit so we could be born again not fashioned after the flesh but after the Spirit of God Himself (II Corinthians 5:17; Ephesians 1:13-14; 4:24).

The entire point is this; the first covenant had not been without defect. The weakness of the covenant was the people themselves. It wasn't that God just disregarded them withdrawing His favor on a whim. God found fault with the people because their behavior showed how they choose everything else before God. The people broke the covenant agreement, not God. He is stressing in verse 9 that the New Covenant He ushered in will not be like the previous covenant. In other words, it will not be left to mankind to keep it, the covenant will entirely be dependent on God Himself to bring it to pass, to ratify it and to uphold it for all eternity. Mankind can freely enter into it, but our behavior does not affect the terms or the outcome. This is why God found fault with the first in order to usher the second. Then He based the entire thing on His character and His ability to keep it. This is an amazing truth!

The New Covenant

"This is the covenant I will make with the house of Israel after that time, declares the Lord. I will put my laws in their minds and write them on their hearts. I will be their God, and they will be my people. No longer will a man teach his neighbor, or a man his brother, saying, 'Know the Lord,' because they will all know me, from the least of them to the greatest. For I will forgive their wickedness and will remember their sins no more" (Hebrews 8:10-12)

A few weeks ago, a friend asked me about this passage of Scripture. As he was reading through Hebrews he came to these very verses, which puzzled him. As he read that no longer will man teach his neighbor he questioned why this was so and if we should not try to teach others from the scripture? I started to share that this wasn't what this passage was saying. These few verses are a marvelous synopsis of the New Covenant that God instated through Jesus. Part of this is that we now have a personal relationship with the Father no longer needing someone to mediate that relationship for us. In other words, we do not need someone to teach us about God, instead God reveals Himself directly to us.

The previous verses tell us that God found fault with the people and the first covenant so He brought about a New Covenant based on His ability to keep it, not the people's ability. Then He describes in a nutshell the main differences between the Old Covenant and the New. The differences are so drastic we cannot understand the new in light of the first. Not only is it completely different and far better, but it is also based on better promises and guaranteed by a better High Priest (Hebrews 8:6).

Here is what the New Covenant has that the Old one never possessed. First, God writes His laws in our minds and upon our hearts. The Old Covenant laws were written in stone. This is not the case with the New. God's law is now a part of us, not something external to accuse us, but it is written by the Spirit of God on the inside of us. Paul said the same thing, *"You show that you are a letter from Christ, the result of our ministry, written not with ink but with the Spirit of the living God, not on tablets of stone but on tablets of human hearts" (II Corinthians 3:3).* Since they are now written on the inside of us, they are a part of our new nature or you could say, they are now second nature to us. To go against God's law is contrary to who we are in Christ. The New Covenant made it so we don't have to strive to live according to God's laws; we simply live by the Spirit of God and His nature that dwells in us.

Secondly, He has declared that He will be our God and we will be His people. We will not need someone to teach us about God, He will reveal Himself directly to us. In the Old Covenant, the people had a mediator to represent them to God and to relay to them what God spoke. Moses is a perfect example of this. He spoke to God on behalf of the people and He spoke to the people on behalf of God. The only time God spoke directly to the Israelites, they begged Him not to. They were consumed with fear and begged God to only speak to Moses (Exodus 20:18-19). The New Covenant, because of Jesus' atoning blood, made it so that we could speak directly to God without fear and hesitation. He became a personal God to everyone who believes in Him. No longer do we need someone to teach us about God, instead God reveals Himself directly to us teaching us by the Holy Spirit dwelling inside (I Corinthians 2:10, 16; I John 2:20, 27). Isaiah prophesied about this very thing, *"All your sons will be taught by the LORD, and great will be your children's peace" (Isaiah 54:13).*

Lastly, the main difference between the two covenants is that God will not only forgive our sins but He will not remember them. *"I, even I, am he who blots out your transgressions, for my own sake, and remembers your sins no more" (Isaiah 43:25).* The Old Covenant gave instructions for a yearly sacrifice for sin. This looked forward to the time of Christ but only served as a reminder of sin (Hebrews 10:3). If you are constantly reminded of your sin then you will not experience peace or have confidence to approach God. This is why He ushered in a new covenant, because God could not have the personal relationship with us that He desired when we were so sin-conscious. However, in the New Covenant God made it so that the issue of sin was completely and permanently dealt with once and for all. Because of it we have been made holy and acceptable to God (Hebrews 10:10, 14). Since we are holy and acceptable we can approach Him in faith knowing that God will never hold our sin against us (Hebrews 4:16;

10:22). This is drastically different than what the Israelites experienced under the Covenant of Law.

No covenant was instated without blood. After the Commandments were read to the people and they agreed to the Covenant, many bulls were sacrificed on that day (Exodus 24:3-8). In the same way, blood was required to solidify the New Covenant God made with us. So Jesus shed His blood for us ratifying the promise. Jesus is the one who made this all possible and left this world comforting us with these words, *"This cup is the new covenant in my blood, which is poured out for you" (Luke 22:20b).*

We have a Covenant guaranteed through Jesus that is far better than anything the Israelites experience in the Old Testament. Jesus is our mediator and His blood cleanses us, forgives us and makes it possible for us to experience and enjoy God the Father in a completely new and different way. Perhaps David said it the best *"Blessed are they whose transgressions are forgiven, whose sins are covered. Blessed is the man whose sin the Lord will never count against him" (Romans 4:7-8; Psalm 32:1-2).*

The New Covenant Made the First One Obsolete

"By calling this covenant "new," he has made the first one obsolete; and what is obsolete and aging will soon disappear" (Hebrews 8:13)

Right now we have a whole generation of children growing up that are not familiar with some of the things we grew up with. Take a VCR for instance, most have seen one but in all likelihood have never used one. A record player would be another good example; enough advances have been made in this area that most children probably have never ever heard of one. In fact today's generation of kids do not know what the world is like without video games, computers, iPads and smartphones. The point is that advances in technology have made obsolete items of that which were once commonplace in our homes and lives.

The same is true with the Covenants. The intent of the New Covenant was to completely replace the first because it was aging and obsolete. After all, God found fault and set about to establish the new one based on better promises (Hebrews 8:6-7). We are not to live under a hybrid of the two Covenants mixing both law and grace. We solely live in the Covenant God instituted through Jesus Christ because the Old Covenant is out of use and annulled and ready to be dispensed with altogether.

God went to great lengths to bring about this New Covenant so that it would be completely different than the first. To start with, He set up Jesus as our new High Priest, who was not from the earthly priestly line (Hebrews 7:14). This in itself would nullify the first agreement. Secondly, He sent the Holy Spirit to dwell on the inside of believers so that the laws and precepts of God are a part of their new creation (Hebrews 8:10). Next, the Holy Spirit reveals God to people so that we can be fully acquainted in all His ways (Hebrews 8:11). And lastly, our sins are completely wiped out, forgiven and forgotten (Hebrews 8:12). These things are vastly different than what the Israelites experienced under the Covenant of Law. This is why we should fully embrace our Covenant by understanding and living it.

The New Covenant is so superior that it is meant to fully replace the first. Just like in the example of the record player and VCR, advancements in our Covenant make the first one obsolete and showing its age. It was retired a long time ago and is useless in comparison to the agreement we have through Jesus Christ.

This is an exciting and amazing truth! We are truly blessed to be a part of this wonderful covenant of grace based on better promises and guaranteed through Jesus Christ. God saved the best for last. The first is ready to disappear but our covenant will be a lasting and eternal memorial to our wonderful and faithful God.

hebrews 9.

THE OLD AND THE

NEW

Cherubim of Glory Overshadowing the Atonement Cover

"Now the first covenant had regulations for worship and also an earthly sanctuary. A tabernacle was set up. In its first room were the lampstand, the table and the consecrated bread; this was called the Holy Place. Behind the second curtain was a room called the Most Holy Place, which had the golden altar of incense and the gold-covered ark of the covenant. This ark contained the gold jar of manna, Aaron's staff that had budded, and the stone tablets of the covenant. Above the ark were the cherubim of the Glory, overshadowing the atonement cover. But we cannot discuss these things in detail now" (Hebrews 9:1-5)

Worship as directed under the first covenant was very detailed. Everything was laid out according to the pattern Moses was shone on the mountain. Everything included in the temple worship had special meanings and significance. Even the items themselves which were placed within the Most Holy Place represented God's supernatural ability to care for and lead the Israelites.

Behind the second curtain was the Ark of the Covenant, where God dwelt with the people. Inside the Ark was the gold jar of manna, a reminder of the bread that fed the Israelites for years while wandering through the desert in disobedience. Aaron's staff, which God used after a rebellion to show that Aaron and the Levites were His chosen priests (Numbers 17). And lastly, the Ark contained the stone tablets of the Ten Commandments to remind the Israelites of the Law.

Guarding the ark and the Most Holy Place were cherubim of glory. The Israelites could not enter because these creatures protected this area. In fact, only the High Priest could enter this room, and only once a year with blood which He poured on the mercy seat making atonement for the sins of the people. The priest made this offering directly before God. We know this from Moses' account inside the tent, *"When Moses entered the Tent of Meeting to speak with the LORD, he heard the voice speaking to him from between the two cherubim above the atonement cover on the ark of the Testimony. And he spoke with him" (Numbers 7:89).*

The writer of Hebrews is drawing attention to all of these details, but notice the last statement in verse 5 declaring that these things cannot be discussed any longer. Why? Because the creatures guarding the way into the Most Holy Place where God dwelt among His people are no longer there. This is an amazing truth! After Jesus entered into the more perfect tabernacle in heaven to make perfect atonement for us, there was no longer a need for warrior angels to protect the way to God. Jesus opened this up so that we could have direct access to God the Father (Hebrews 10:19-22). In fact, we are now to approach the throne of grace in confidence (Hebrews 4:16) in a way the Israelites never could.

This makes perfect sense considering the last verse of chapter 8, *"By calling this covenant "new," he has made the first one obsolete; and what is obsolete and aging will soon disappear" (Hebrews 8:13).* Jesus brought with Him a new way of approaching God. We can approach Him in faith washed clean by the body of Christ, unafraid of anything standing in our way because anything that could condemn or harm us has been removed by the blood of Jesus. Our covenant of grace is vastly superior and Jesus is the one who will forever protect and guarantee the way into the presence of the Father Himself.

The Most Holy Place Was Not Open While the First Tabernacle Was Standing

"When everything had been arranged like this, the priests entered regularly into the outer room to carry on their ministry. But only the high priest entered the inner room, and that only once a year, and never without blood, which he offered for himself and for the sins the people had committed in ignorance. The Holy Spirit was showing by this that the way into the Most Holy Place had not yet been disclosed as long as the first tabernacle was still standing" (Hebrews 9:6-8)

To understand everything that Jesus completed for us as our High Priest we have examples from the earthly Levitical priesthood to guide us in our understanding. Hebrews 9 uses examples from this system to show us how Jesus performed the very same acts on our behalf in the presence of God the Father in the heavenly tabernacle. We can glean so much wonderful truth from these passages of Scripture.

The writer is showing how entrance to the Holy of Holies was not accessible under the Old Covenant. The priests were able to enter into the outer portion of the tabernacle to carry out their daily duties. However, only the High Priest could enter into the Holy of Holies and he could only enter once a year. In fact, the High Priest wore bells around his ephod so that the sound of bells could be heard when entering before the presence of the Lord.

"The gold bells and the pomegranates are to alternate around the hem of the robe. Aaron must wear it when he ministers. The sound of the bells will be heard when he enters the Holy Place before the LORD and when he comes out, so that

he will not die" (Exodus 28:34-35). Bells were worn to give off sounds so everyone in the outer portions would know the High Priest's status when ministering. The Cherubim of Glory circled around the atonement cover protecting the entrance to the Most Holy Place (Exodus 25:22; Hebrews 9:5). So many guidelines were to be met before the priest could even enter, so the confidence level I'm sure, was extremely low when before the Lord.

The High Priest also had to enter with blood from animal sacrifices which he offered for both himself and Israel. It was offered for all sins, even the ones committed in ignorance and thoughtlessness. It was a covering for a time period but these sacrifices were to continually be made. There was no permanence to this covering.

This system was an illustration looking forward to the time of Christ. As long as this system was in place the new system was not enacted. In the same way, when Christ came, He fulfilled everything that the Levitical priesthood foreshadowed. In other words, when Jesus came and took the role as High Priest, there was no longer a need for the previous institution. Because the way into the Most Holy Place was thrown wide open by Jesus (Hebrews 10:19-20).

The amazing truth in all of this is that Jesus has made it possible to enter into the presence of God the Father. This was never the case while the first tabernacle was standing. However Jesus' blood has completely cleansed us so that we are able to enter into the throne room through the veil which is His body and boldly come before the Father (Hebrews 10:20-22). As believers, we are included in a wonderful heritage. Peter tells us, *"But you are a chosen people, a royal priesthood, a holy nation, a people belonging to God, that you may declare the praises of him who called you out of darkness into his wonderful light" (I Peter 2:9).* What was limited to a few because of a family line, has now been thrown wide open and offered to everyone who puts trust in Jesus.

The Sacrifices Offered Could Not Clear the Conscience

"This is an illustration for the present time, indicating that the gifts and sacrifices being offered were not able to clear the conscience of the worshiper. They are only a matter of food and drink and various ceremonial washings—external regulations applying until the time of the new order" (Hebrews 9:9-10)

On this side of the cross we celebrate certain things to remind ourselves of everything Jesus accomplished on the cross. Communion is a great example of this. As we symbolically partake in the body and blood of Christ Jesus we remind ourselves of the sacrifice God the Father and His son Jesus made on our behalf. We remind ourselves that His body was broken so that we may be whole. We remind ourselves that His blood was shed so that we can be forgiven. We do this to remember.

In the same way, the Israelites experienced and celebrated certain rituals that were aimed at looking forward to the time of Christ Jesus. They were by no means an end unto themselves; they served as an illustration of the new order, or the institution of Jesus' eternal High Priesthood.

Day after day, month after month, year after year, theses ceremonies were carried out. If this system could have worked, then the repetition would not have been needed, in other words, they would not have offered the same gifts and sacrifices over and over (Hebrews 9:9-10; 10:1-2). Understanding this, we see why the entire system served as an illustration. The sacrifices made never cleared the conscience of the worshiper. What was offered was never able to renew the inner man because it only dealt with external rules and regulations for the body. This is why a new order was needed, one that dealt with the heart of mankind.

The sacrificial system was meant to point the worshiper to the coming Messiah. Just as we look back to the cross, the Israelites entire system of worship looked forward to the Cross. In both cases, Jesus plays the lead role. Since He has come, there is no longer a need for this illustration because we have the real thing. Hebrews 10:1 sums up this very thought, *"The law is only a shadow of the good things that are coming—not the realities themselves. For this reason it can never, by the same sacrifices repeated endlessly year after year, make perfect those who draw near to worship"* (Hebrews 10:1). The shadow is inconsequential when the real thing is present. Unlike the illustration, Jesus is able to wash clean and clear the conscience of those who come to Him. This shows how vastly different and far superior the New Covenant is over the Old. I am thankful that we are on this side of the cross looking back in remembrance to Jesus' sacrifice, with no need for an illustration because what we have is the real thing.

Jesus Obtained Eternal Redemption

"When Christ came as high priest of the good things that are already here, he went through the greater and more perfect tabernacle that is not man-made, that is to say, not a part of this creation. He did not enter by means of the blood of goats and calves; but he entered the Most Holy Place once for all by his own blood, having obtained eternal redemption" (Hebrews 9:11-12)

One of the most amazing truths throughout the entire Bible and a marvelous theme in the book of Hebrews is that our sins are completely paid for, eternally forgiven, forgotten and removed from all records. In fact, the writer of Hebrews mentions this idea so many times in chapters 8, 9 and 10 that it is impossible to miss. Jesus has obtained eternal redemption for those who put saving faith in Him.

If we have been redeemed, it is important for us to understand what it is. In the Old Testament redemption was the process of buying something back. For instance if a person sold a piece of property to another, by law, the seller or a family member could redeem their land so that no family would be without their inheritance (Leviticus 25:23-25). If they didn't have the means to for redemption then everything was returned to them in the Year of Jubilee (Leviticus 25:28). This principle applied to land, people and possessions. The law made it possible for the next of kin, also known as *"kinsman redeemer"* to rescue a person or property (Leviticus 25:47-55). Redemption was a family matter.

Mankind was sold into slavery in the Garden of Eden. Adam, God's representative for mankind, had been given full authority and possession of the earth (Genesis 1:28-30). Everything belonged to him. He transferred this birthright to Satan when he ate from the tree that God instructed him not to (Genesis 2:16-17). According to the Law of the Kinsman Redeemer only a relative could redeem or purchase back that which was lost or sold. In other words, mankind was the only one who could provide this redemption. This is why Jesus came in the flesh, fully God and fully man (Isaiah 59:16; John 1:14). Jesus became our brother so Adam and all mankind could be redeemed (Hebrews 2:11)

Jesus has been called the second Adam because He was able to undo everything that the first Adam did. As God's second representative for mankind, He came and restored mankind's birthright through the redemption process. *"Consequently, just as the result of one trespass was condemnation for all men, so also the result of one act of righteousness was justification that brings life for all men" (Romans 5:18).* Jesus acted as our Kinsman Redeemer and purchased back everything that mankind lost in the garden.

Jesus is our Kinsman Redeemer, this is an amazing truth! He did not enter into the man-made tabernacle but into the Most Holy Place in the heavenly tabernacle in the very presence of God the Father to redeem us. His blood was the entrance fee to intercede on our behalf before God in Heaven (Hebrews 9:12). His blood was poured on the Mercy Seat to atone and cleanse us from our sin (Hebrews 9:14). He is the mediator guaranteeing our eternal inheritance because He died as a ransom to set free, rescue and deliver us from all transgressions under the first covenant (Hebrews 9:15). He has done away with sin once for all by His perfect sacrifice (Hebrews 9:26). And lastly He has restored the relationship between God and mankind eternally (Hebrews 10:19-22).

All of this was accomplished by the law of the Kinsman Redeemer. And because Jesus is the second Adam, He was able to eternally secure our redemption. His blood was the purchase price which paid for an everlasting release from sin, death and judgment. This makes Jesus the pinnacle of history, the most significant person in all of humanity. He is the eternal God and the Savior of the world. Jesus is the reason we have life and the reason we have eternally been redeemed!

The Blood of Christ Cleanses Our Conscience

"The blood of goats and bulls and the ashes of a heifer sprinkled on those who are ceremonially unclean sanctify them so that they are outwardly clean. How much more, then, will the blood of Christ, who through the eternal Spirit offered himself unblemished to God, cleanse our consciences from acts that lead to death, so that we may serve the living God!" (Hebrews 9:13-14)

Jesus came to give life. This is an amazing truth. We once were dead, but Christ came to give us life and the life He gives is abundant (John 10:10).

If the blood of bulls and goats sanctified the Israelites for the purification of the body just think how much more surely the blood of Christ cleanses us. The Israelites only experienced a momentary cleansing and this was only for the outside of the body. However, Jesus' blood works from the inside out. It purifies the heart of man, eliminating the eternal effects of sin and purging the conscience of the guilt and shame that results from sin.

This was possible because Jesus' blood was unblemished by sin. He was perfect and sinless. He fulfilled the letter of the Law which qualified Him for being the perfect sacrifice. He became our sin so that we could have His righteousness (II Corinthians 5:21). This is the best trade ever recorded in history!

The result for us is that we are able to serve the living God. We have been cleansed and our consciences have been purified from dead works. We stand before the Lord holy, righteous and completely justified. We are not like the Israelites who serve at an altar and continually adhere to lifeless observances and rituals. We come before the Most High God, changed and accepted. Cleansed and purified from within.

redemption.

"Therefore, brothers, since we have confidence to enter the Most Holy Place by the blood of Jesus, by a new and living way opened for us through the curtain, that is, his body, and since we have a great priest over the house of God, let us draw near to God with a sincere heart in full assurance of faith, having our hearts sprinkled to cleanse us from a guilty conscience and having our bodies washed with pure water. Let us hold unswervingly to the hope we profess, for he who promised is faithful" (Hebrews 10:19-23).

Christ is the Mediator
of a New Covenant

"For this reason Christ is the mediator of a new covenant, that
those who are called may receive the promised eternal inheritance—
now that he has died as a ransom to set them free from the
sins committed under the first covenant" (Hebrews 9:15)

The church I grew up in concluded a lot of their weekly services by singing the hymn, *Jesus Paid it All*. The refrain goes like this,

> *Jesus paid it all,*
> *All to Him I owe;*
> *Sin had left a crimson stain,*
> *He washed it white as snow.*

There is incredible truth in these words. Even as a young child I understood that Jesus made things right. I knew that He had settled the score, made the account balanced and washed us clean by His blood.

In fact, the previous verses in Hebrews 9 declare that the previous way of forgiveness, the shedding of the blood of bulls and goats, only cleansed on the outside. In contrast, Jesus' blood entirely cleansed the heart of mankind and was able to clear the conscience from the guilt of sin, once for all. The debt was completely and utterly wiped out by Jesus' sacrifice on the cross. The result was life, so that we could serve the living God (Hebrews 9:14).

Because of this, Jesus is the mediator of a New Covenant (Hebrews 8:6). A mediator is the representative between two parties. A mediator negotiates for both parties until a resolution is reached. Jesus' blood was the means to bring mankind and God together. Up until this time, mankind was held hostage under the accusation of death because of sin. At the right time,

redemption.

Jesus was born as a man, to die as a ransom for us. The cost was His blood, the result was redemption from all of the sins committed under the first covenant. If sins have been paid for, then there is no longer the threat of death.

Jesus' cleansing blood is the reason and the means by which He is eternally the mediator of the New Covenant. In fact, Hebrews 12:24 tells us that Jesus' blood speaks a better word for us than the blood of Abel. Abel was murdered by his brother Cain and his blood cried out to God from the ground (Genesis 4:10). If Abel's blood cried for restitution, then think how much more the blood of Christ speaks on our behalf before God. What it is saying is love, mercy, grace, favor, forgiveness and acceptance. What a marvelous thing!

Just as the words of the hymn declare, *'Sin had left a crimson stain, He washed it white as snow'*, Jesus' blood both washes us clean and guarantees the relationship we enjoy with the Father. Knowing that Christ is forever the mediator of the covenant of grace we enjoy, empowers us to live a life fully devoted to God, serving out of gratitude for all that He has done for us. Because Jesus Christ lives, we have received the fulfillment of the promise of an everlasting inheritance, He guarantees it!

Jesus' Death Made God's Will and Testament Valid

"In the case of a will, it is necessary to prove the death of the one who made it, because a will is in force only when somebody has died; it never takes effect while the one who made it is living. This is why even the first covenant was not put into effect without blood" (Hebrews 9:16-18)

Obtaining a family inheritance only comes after the death of the family member and after the will is read. The will provides the guideline for how the inheritance is to be dispersed. The will's originator is the one who dictates this by creating a last will and testament so that their wishes are known and honored. This is a legal binding contract and it is never put into effect before the death of the individual, although it exists in legal form before death. The same is true of both the Old and New Covenants. They were put into effect after death, and always with blood.

This is an amazing truth about the Covenant we enjoy through Jesus. His death put the will of God into effect and made it legally binding and in operation. It is important for us to know what this Last Will includes so that we will understand what we have inherited through Jesus. To do this we must look at what Jesus said His mission, or God's will for His life was. Luke describes this perfectly. *"The scroll of the prophet Isaiah was handed to him. Unrolling it, he found the place where it is written: "The Spirit of the Lord is on me, because he has anointed me to preach good news to the poor. He has sent me to proclaim freedom for the prisoners and recovery of sight for the blind, to release the oppressed, to proclaim the year of the Lord's favor." Then he rolled up the scroll, gave it back to the attendant and sat down. The eyes of everyone in the synagogue were fastened on him, and he began by saying to them, "Today this scripture is fulfilled in your hearing"* (Luke 4:17-21).

Jesus came to preach the gospel, free the prisoners, restore sight, release the oppressed and announce the Lord's favor to mankind. This was God's will concerning the life of Jesus. He came to bring us into fellowship with the Father through the gospel. The good news is that our sins are forgiven and paid for through Jesus, and that we have been redeemed and purchased back by His blood.

He has freed the prisoners. Jesus' blood paid for the debt that sin held against us. He died as a ransom for us so that we wouldn't (Mark 10:45; Hebrews 9:15). We have been rescued from bondage.

He restores the sight of the blind. This happens in a spiritual sense as well as in the physical, because we now can see and understand the Father by looking at Jesus (John 1:18; II Corinthians 4:6; Colossians 1:15,19; Hebrews 1:1-3). The fullness of God dwelt in Jesus and He has shown us an exact representation of God the Father.

He has released the oppressed. No longer are we subjected to the whims of the sinful nature, but we have been freed from it and given a new, born again spirit, fashioned after Jesus' in righteousness and holiness (Romans 6:6; Galatians 2:20; Ephesians 4:24).

He was sent to announce the favor of the Lord. This was the message of the angels at Jesus' birth, *"Glory to God in the highest, and on earth peace to men on whom his favor rests" (Luke 2:14).* God was in the world, reconciling the world to Himself, no longer holding man accountable for his sins (II Corinthians 5:17-21). Jesus' entire life was a proclamation of this amazing truth!

Just as Jesus declared in the synagogue that this Scripture had been fulfilled at their hearing, Jesus' death completed and put into effect the will of God. Eugene H. Petersen said it best in the Message version, *"Like a will that takes effect when someone dies, the new covenant was put into action at Jesus' death. His death marked the transition from the old plan to the new one, canceling the old obligations and accompanying sins, and summoning the heirs to receive the eternal inheritance that was promised them. He brought together God and his people in this new way" (Hebrews 9:16-17 The Message).* Jesus' death made God's will and testament valid and in operation. He guarantees it with the precious blood of our Savior Jesus Christ, so that we who hope in God have received the inheritance eternally promised to us.

Without the Shedding of Blood There is No Forgiveness

"When Moses had proclaimed every commandment of the law to all the people, he took the blood of calves, together with water, scarlet wool and branches of hyssop, and sprinkled the scroll and all the people. He said, "This is the blood of the covenant, which God has commanded you to keep." In the same way, he sprinkled with the blood both the tabernacle and everything used in its ceremonies. In fact, the law requires that nearly everything be cleansed with blood, and without the shedding of blood there is no forgiveness" (Hebrews 9:19-22)

Both the Old and New Covenants were put into effect by blood. The blood proved the death, thereby enforcing and enacting the will of the one who died (Hebrews 9:17). Leviticus 17:11 explains why the blood was used, *"For the life of a creature is in the blood, and I have given it to you to make atonement for yourselves on the altar; it is the blood that makes atonement for one's life" (Leviticus 17:11).* So it was necessary for both Covenants to be ushered in by blood, because first it proved the death because the blood is the life force. And secondly, it was given for atonement. So without it, there could be no forgiveness for sins.

Jesus' blood was shed to usher in the New Covenant. His blood proved that a death had occurred thereby enacting His last will and testament. His blood was the price necessary for this will to come to pass, in other words, it put this covenant into effect. The New Covenant is not only the will of Jesus, whose blood ushered it in, it is also the will of God. Throughout Jesus' time on earth He said over and over that His will was to do the will of the Father (John 6:38). He stressed that what He said was only what the Father told Him to say (John 8:28) and He did only what He saw the Father do (John 5:19). His words and teachings were not His own but from the One who sent Him (John 7:16). In fact John 6:38 summarizes this very nicely, *"For I have come down from heaven not to do my will but to do the will of him who sent me" (John 6:38).* The writer of Hebrews starts chapter 1 by declaring that Jesus is the exact representation of God the Father (Hebrews 1:3). Since they are one and the same, we can see that Jesus' blood was the life force that was able to usher in the will of God, which was the New Covenant.

Not only did Jesus' blood prove the death and put the Covenant into effect, part of the New Covenant that God spoke of through the prophets included the forgiveness of sins (Jeremiah 31:31-34; Hebrews 8:8-12; 10:16-18). Leviticus 17:11 says the life force is in the blood and this is used as a means for atonement. So Jesus' blood served multiple purposes, it enacted the Will of the Covenant and it was the cleansing agent for sin. If no blood was shed, there couldn't be any forgiveness for sins.

The Vines Dictionary of New Testament Words brings clarification to this point. There are two words used for blood in Hebrews 9. The first one is *haima*, which has many meanings, but in this case it denotes the blood of sacrificial victims (Hebrews 9:7). *"The "blood" of Christ, which betokens His death by the shedding of His "blood" in expiatory sacrifice; to drink His "blood" is to appropriate the saving effects of His expiatory death, John 6:53. As "the life of the flesh is in the blood," Lev 17:11, and was forfeited by sin, life eternal can be imparted only by the expiation made, in the giving up of the life by the sinless Savior" (Vine's Expository Dictionary of New Testament Words).* In other words, life had been forfeited because of sin, which is why Jesus' life was given so that He, as a sinless man, could impart eternal life through this sacrifice. Jesus himself said this, *"I tell you the truth, unless you eat the flesh of the Son of Man and drink his blood, you have no life in you. Whoever eats my flesh and drinks my blood has eternal life, and I will raise him up at the last day" (John 6:53-54).* Our life was forfeited because of sin, but Jesus' blood was shed to forgive and restore us to a state as if we had never sinned in the first place (II Corinthians 5:21; Hebrews 9:12, 26; 10:10, 12, 14, 18). What an amazing truth!

The second word for blood used in Hebrews 9:22 is *haimatekchysia*, which means the *"shedding of blood"*, to pour out. Jesus didn't just give His blood, He let it flow freely. In fact, it didn't stop until every last drop had been given. He was poured out unto death, which is what Isaiah prophesied about Him, *"Therefore I will give him a portion among the great, and he will divide the spoils with the strong, because he poured out his life unto death, and was numbered with the transgressors. For he bore the sin of many, and made intercession for the transgressors" (Isaiah 53:12).* His life force completely covered, cleansed and annulled sin. Our lives had been forfeited because of sin, however His blood completely reversed the effect of sin so that we could experience eternal life.

Jesus understood this which is why He spoke these words while reclining at the table with His disciples at the last supper. *"Then he took the cup, gave thanks and offered it to them, saying, "Drink from it, all of you. This is my blood of the covenant, which is poured out for many for the forgiveness of sins" (Matthew 26:27-28).* He knew the price to bring us to the Father and His own words testify to the fact that He would let the blood flow freely. He knew His blood would usher in the covenant and it would completely and utterly blot out and destroy the effects and stains of sins.

His perfect blood was shed to usher in both the New Covenant and the forgiveness of sins. Neither one could be accomplished without it which is why He freely gave Himself to the will of God. Jesus accomplished what we could not and because of His sacrifice we have been forgiven, freed and offered eternal life through the person of Jesus Christ.

Jesus Entered Heaven Appearing Before God on Our Behalf

"It was necessary, then, for the copies of the heavenly things to be purified with these sacrifices, but the heavenly things themselves with better sacrifices than these. For Christ did not enter a man-made sanctuary that was only a copy of the true one; he entered heaven itself, now to appear for us in God's presence" (Hebrews 9:23-24)

Every time the priest made atonement for the people, it was merely a dress rehearsal for the real thing. The High Priest was the *"stand in"* for the star. They merely showed a glimpse of what truly would take place at the pinnacle of history when Jesus entered into the heavenly tabernacle, in full view of God the Father Himself to offer a perfect sacrifice for us. This was the means to bridge the gap and usher in the New Covenant founded on, and made perfect in His blood.

This event was what the entire Levitical system looked forward to and revealed, by the types and shadows it portrayed (Colossians 2:16-17; Hebrews 10:1). The earthly items, which were copies of the real things, had to continually be purified by the blood of bulls and goats. In fact, these things happened over and over, which shows that it was merely a foreshadowing to the time when Christ Jesus would take over the role of High Priest. If these sacrifices could have worked, they would have long since stopped being offered (Hebrews 10:2). However, as it stood, they merely reminded the people that One was coming who would perfect this offering for sin once for all (Hebrews 10:3-4, 10, 12, 14, 18).

This is why Jesus didn't enter a man-made tabernacle, patterned after the heavenly one. He entered into heaven itself. His blood was the entrance fee (Hebrews 9:12). His blood was the cleansing agent (Hebrews 9:14), His blood sealed and ratified the New Covenant made by God on our behalf (Matthew 26:28; Hebrews 9:22). His blood took care of the sin issue once for all (Hebrews 10:10, 12, 14, 18). His blood bought us eternal redemption (Hebrews 9:12; 10:12, 14). His blood was the exchange that took our sin and bestowed on us His righteousness (II Corinthians 5:21). His blood made everything all right and since it was offered in the presence of God the Father it was a one-time deal (Romans 5:1-2). His blood undid everything that sin and death ever took, ruined or stained (Romans 5:15, 17, 21). And His blood gives us the confidence to approach God by faith so we can find grace and mercy just when we need it (Hebrews 4:16; 10:19-22).

This is why the entire sacrificial system was a dress rehearsal for opening night when Jesus entered into God's presence to purchase and redeem us, because Jesus was the only one who could do all of these things. His sacrifice on the cross for us made it all possible. Now we have a High Priest who owns the position above all things seated at the right hand of the Father securing our reconciled position of grace (Philippians 2:9-11; Colossians 1:18-20; Hebrews 1:3-4).

Christ Abolished Sin
by the Sacrifice of Himself

"Nor did he enter heaven to offer himself again and again, the way the high priest enters the Most Holy Place every year with blood that is not his own. Then Christ would have had to suffer many times since the creation of the world. But now he has appeared once for all at the end of the ages to do away with sin by the sacrifice of himself" (Hebrews 9:25-26)

This glorious truth rings out from the dawn of mankind until the time when our King will return to bring us home... our sins are completely, utterly and eternally blotted out from all record and we are forgiven through the Lord Jesus Christ! This is why the cross was a complete victory, it was the means to forever deal, once and for all, the issue of sin.

The writer of Hebrews stresses this truth so many times in chapters 8, 9 and 10 that it is impossible to miss. In fact, looking at the Scriptures as a whole, this is one of the most amazing truths that the Law and the Prophets foretold, Jesus talked about and the Apostles wrote about. It is a theme throughout the entire Scriptures. Jesus' sacrifice was so perfect and so complete that it only took one time to completely undo everything that sin corrupted. Peter tells us that we have to know this otherwise we will be ineffective and unproductive in life (II Peter 1:8-9).

In contrast to the Levitical system, two things stand out in this passage of scripture in Hebrews 9. First, Christ did not enter a man-made sanctuary (Hebrews 9:24). Secondly, He did not have to offer himself over and over again (Hebrews 9:25). Christ's priesthood and sacrifice were vastly superior to that of the first covenant. In contrasting the two systems in this way, it shows the New Covenant's superiority in which Jesus is the guarantor. In fact, all of this happened only once and when it happened, it occurred in heaven. If it happened only once, it means that it worked the first and only time the sacrifice was made.

If it worked, it means that Christ obliterated sin once for all, for all time, past, present and future. Otherwise, sin would still have the means to accuse us before God, but Hebrews says, *"let us draw near to God with a sincere heart in full assurance of faith, having our hearts sprinkled to cleanse us from a guilty conscience and having our bodies washed with pure water"* *(Hebrews 10:22)*. We've been cleaned and purified by the blood of the lamb and welcomed by the Father into His presence.

David saw this and prophesied, *"as far as the east is from the west, so far has he removed our transgressions from us"* *(Psalm 103:12)*. Isaiah saw this and prophesied, *"I, even I, am he who blots out your transgressions, for my own sake, and remembers your sins no more"* *(Isaiah 43:25)*. And Jeremiah prophesied this also, *"For I will forgive their wickedness and will remember their sins no more"* *(Jeremiah 31:34b)*. Oh, what a marvelous truth this is.

As recipients of the blessing of the New Covenant we have an obligation to our Savior to not let sin keep us captive. We've been freed by the precious blood of the Lamb, our lives have been redeemed and we are forgiven. Paul said, *"When you were dead in your sins and in the uncircumcision of your sinful nature, God made you alive with Christ. He forgave us all our sins, having canceled the written code, with its regulations, that was against us and that stood opposed to us; he took it away, nailing it to the cross"* *(Colossians 2:13-14)*. There is nothing to accuse any longer, it was nailed to the cross marked *'Paid in Full'*.

Therefore, we should live as those who have been freed and forgiven. Not taking liberty in the freedom, but living like who we are in Christ Jesus. A holy people, set apart, redeemed, favored, forgiven and free. This is why Jesus' sacrifice for sin was the consummation of the ages, because He abolished and obliterated sin for all mankind, for all time (I John 2:2).

Christ Will Appear
To Bring Salvation

"Just as man is destined to die once, and after that to face judgment, so Christ was sacrificed once to take away the sins of many people; and he will appear a second time, not to bear sin, but to bring salvation to those who are waiting for him" (Hebrews 9:27-28)

There are certain things in life we are assured of, just as we were born, we will also die. It was Ben Franklin who joked *"in the world nothing can be said to be certain except death and taxes"*. I would suggest, however, that there are a few other things we can also be certain of. Just as mankind is appointed to die and to be brought before God in judgment, so also Jesus was destined to come and bear the burden of sins of the world once for all (I Peter 3:18; I John 2:2). This is amazing news for us. Because this work was finished and completed, He is also appointed to return, not to bear sin again but to bring salvation to those who are eagerly waiting and expecting Him.

This is Christ's legacy. He dealt with the issue of sin once for all so all that is left to do is to come and gather His people to Himself. As believers we have been redeemed, we have been purchased and we have been given a new born again spirit but we are still waiting for the redemption of our physical bodies. When Jesus Christ returns He will be coming to bring final salvation. This is one of the things in life we can be assured of, Christ is coming back and when He comes, He will bring salvation to those who are waiting for Him!

This is an exciting thing; there is no fear in anticipating that day. Paul told the church at Thessalonica, *"For God did not appoint us to suffer wrath but to receive salvation through our Lord Jesus Christ. He died for us so that, whether we are awake or asleep, we may live together with him. Therefore encourage one another and build each other up, just as in fact you are doing" (I Thessalonians 5:9-11).* The only question that will matter is; What did you do with Jesus? For those who believe in Him, we will not suffer wrath but we will receive our salvation.

The Apostle John also comforts us with these words, *"In this way, love is made complete among us so that we will have confidence on the day of judgment, because in this world we are like him. There is no fear in love. But perfect love drives out fear, because fear has to do with punishment. The one who fears is not made perfect in love. We love because he first loved us" (I John 4:17-19).* In other words, when we stand before God in judgment we will be wearing the righteousness of Jesus. John said *"as he is so are we in the world" (I John 4:17 KJV),* meaning that there is no accusation of sin against us, because Jesus dealt with the issue of sin and we have accepted His payment for it. Through Jesus we have the righteousness we need, to stand before God free from accusation or condemnation. We also have His perfect love to reassure us in this truth.

Jesus told us that anyone who accepts His message of grace and forgiveness will have this salvation without condemnation. *"I tell you the truth, whoever hears my word and believes him who sent me has eternal life and will not be condemned; he has crossed over from death to life" (John 5:24).* The word for condemned is the same word for judgment. Christ came first to bear sins so that He could come back again to bring salvation for all those who eagerly, constantly and patiently wait and expect Him!

hebrews 10.

CHRIST'S SACRIFICE

ONCE FOR ALL

The Law Was a Shadow of Christ

"The law is only a shadow of the good things that are coming—not the realities themselves. For this reason it can never, by the same sacrifices repeated endlessly year after year, make perfect those who draw near to worship. If it could, would they not have stopped being offered? For the worshipers would have been cleansed once for all, and would no longer have felt guilty for their sins" (Hebrews 10:1-2)

This is a good question. For the time period this was written this would have made them stop and think. If the sacrifices, repeated endlessly, could have cleared the conscience and cleansed once for all, wouldn't they stop being offered? While we don't offer animal sacrifices today, this truth remains, as believers we spend a lot of time and energy wrapped up in traditions and doctrines instead of focusing on the person of Jesus Christ and in the finished work of the cross. While in reality, many of those things are realized in Christ and we are merely paying attention to a type and shadow of what has already come.

Here's the contrast. If I were to come around a building with the sun to my back, you would be able to see my shadow coming. You would be able to ascertain certain things about me. You could see if I was tall or short, fat or thin, if I had long hair or short hair, there would be many things that you could get a glimpse of by the shadow that was arriving around the building before me. However, once I appeared, you wouldn't need my shadow to determine how I look, you would have the real thing standing in front of you. The same is true for Christ. The law gave an outline of what Christ would be, but it merely served as a shadow to the real thing. Once Christ came, there is no need for the shadow. It is ridiculous to pay more attention to the shadow than the person.

This passage states this very clearly, *"The law is only a shadow of the good things that are coming—not the realities themselves"*. To bring the point home, the writer draws attention to the fact that if they could have worked, they would have only needed to make the offering once, instead of time and time again. Pointing out that the one sacrifice would have cleared the conscience and absolved them from the guilt associated with sin. But this was not the case. This proves that the law wasn't the means to an end, the reality of it could only be found in Christ.

Which is exactly the point made in Hebrews 10. The writer contrasts the endless sacrifices dictated by the law with the one sacrifice made by Jesus and stresses many times that it was all that was needed to forgive sins and cleanse those who draw near, by faith, without having any guilt or shame associated with sin.

"First he said, "Sacrifices and offerings, burnt offerings and sin offerings you did not desire, nor were you pleased with them" (although the law required them to be made). Then he said, "Here I am, I have come to do your will." He sets aside the first to establish the second. And by that will, we have been made holy through the sacrifice of the body of Jesus Christ once for all. Day after day every priest stands and performs his religious duties; again and again he offers the same sacrifices, which can never take away sins. But when this priest had offered for all time one sacrifice for sins, he sat down at the right hand of God. Since that time he waits for his enemies to be made his footstool, because by one sacrifice he has made perfect forever those who are being made holy. The Holy Spirit also testifies to us about this. First he says: "This is the covenant I will make with them after that time, says the Lord. I will put my laws in their hearts, and I will write them on their minds." Then he adds: "Their sins and lawless acts I will remember no more." And where these have been forgiven, there is no longer any sacrifice for sin" (Hebrews 10:8-18).

It is an incredible thing to grasp. The law was a rude outline expressing what was coming. Christ is the reality of it. And since He has come, there is no need to continue in the things that were a type and shadow. Paul confirms this in Colossians, *"Therefore do not let anyone judge you by what you eat or drink, or with regard to a religious festival, a New Moon celebration or a Sabbath day. These are a shadow of the things that were to come; the reality, however, is found in Christ" (Colossians 2:16-17).*

This is an amazing truth with which to renew our minds. Through Christ Jesus, we have been forgiven and cleansed of all guilt associated with sin (Hebrews 10:18-22). We have been freed from the sin nature that previously held us captive (Romans 6:6). And we have been given the Holy Spirit to assure our hearts before God (I John 3:19-20). Resting in the person of Jesus Christ is far better, in every way imaginable, than being wrapped up in the type and shadow of what has already come.

It's Impossible For the Blood of Bulls and Goats to Take Away Sins

"But those sacrifices are an annual reminder of sins, because it is impossible for the blood of bulls and goats to take away sins" (Hebrews 10:3-4)

One thing about the law was that it was great about building anticipation to the time of Christ. I imagine that every time a bull or goat was brought as a sacrifice, the people would stop and think about the promised Messiah, longing for Him to come; knowing that when He came there would no longer be the need for these endless sacrifices.

The previous verses state the entire sacrificial system was a foreshadowing to the good things that were coming (Hebrews 10:1-2). They couldn't clear the conscience of the worshiper but rather served as a reminder of sin. This is why these sacrifices were brought time and time again. The blood of these animals only served as a covering for the body and could never cleanse the entire person. In other words, the blood of bulls and goats were powerless to take away sin.

The Messiah on the other hand would be able to cleanse the entirety of mankind by the sacrifice of Himself. This is why the endless sacrifices served to bring a fresh remembrance of sin. It would prepare the people for Christ. In contrast to the blood of bulls and goats, His blood would take away sin.

When Jesus appeared, He did away with sin by the sacrifice of Himself (Hebrews 9:26). His blood was more than enough to cleanse the worshiper and bring each one into perfect fellowship with God the Father (Hebrews

10:19-22). This was what the sacrificial system under the law portrayed and looked forward to in Christ. Now that it is here, there is no longer a need for any other type of atonement. Jesus' blood worked to cleanse us of sin, the first and only time it was given.

Just as the Israelites looked forward to Christ in anticipation, we can look to Christ, trusting in the perfect redemption He provided. We can rest assured that we are forgiven and accepted through Him alone and that His blood was more than enough to justify us in God's eyes (Romans 5:1-2). Just as the blood of bulls and goats was an annual reminder of sin, the blood of Jesus reminds us that we are forgiven and free through faith in Him.

Jesus' Body Was Prepared To Be Our Sacrifice

"Therefore, when Christ came into the world, he said: "Sacrifice and offering you did not desire, but a body you prepared for me; with burnt offerings and sin offerings you were not pleased. Then I said, 'Here I am—it is written about me in the scroll— I have come to do your will, O God'" (Hebrews 10:5-7)

The plan from the foundation of the world was for God to provide redemption for His people. The Bible tells us that Jesus was the lamb slain before the foundation of the world (I Peter 1:20; Revelation 13:8). The redemption of mankind was never *"Plan B"*, it was intentional and thought out long before the world even existed.

As described in the previous verses, the sacrificial system was merely a type and shadow looking forward to the time when Christ would present His body as a perfect and holy offering. He came in the flesh with a human body that was prepared for this very purpose.

Looking back at the account of Abraham and Isaac in Genesis 22 gives us incredible insight into this. God told Abraham to take Isaac and sacrifice him on the mountain. So they set off, arrived and prepared for the sacrifice. When Isaac asked Abraham about the offering, Abraham's reply was that God would provide the lamb. Then he bound Isaac and placed him on the altar.

Hebrews 11 gives insight into Abraham's faith in God's provision, *"By faith Abraham, when God tested him, offered Isaac as a sacrifice. He who had received the promises was about to sacrifice his one and only son, even though God had said to him, "It is through Isaac that your offspring will be reckoned." Abraham reasoned that God could raise the dead, and figuratively speaking, he did receive Isaac back from death" (Hebrews 11:17-19).* God had promised Abraham that Isaac was the promise, so many times, that he was fully convinced that God would raise Isaac from the dead to fulfill the promise that his offspring would be as numerous as the stars in the sky and his Seed would bless every nation (Genesis 12:2-3; 13:6; 22:18; 26:4; 28:14; Acts 3:25-26; Galatians 3:16). God saw Abraham's faith while testing him, knowing he would do what God instructed even at the cost of his one and only son, the promise. So God intervened and provided a lamb.

This is an amazing story, but it gets so much better, because it really wasn't about Abraham and Isaac, it was about Jesus. The example of Abraham and Isaac is another example of type and shadow; just as Abraham was faithful to God and willing to sacrifice his one and only son, God Himself was faithful to His promise and actually did sacrifice His one and only Son, Jesus. *"The Angel of the Lord called to Abraham from heaven a second time and said, I have sworn by Myself, says the Lord, that since you have done this and have not withheld [from Me] or begrudged [giving Me] your son, your only son, In blessing I will bless you and in multiplying I will multiply your descendants like the stars of the heavens and like the sand on the seashore. And your Seed (Heir) will possess the gate of His enemies, And in your Seed [Christ] shall all the nations of the earth be blessed and [by Him] bless themselves, because you have heard and obeyed My voice" (Genesis 22:15-18 AMP).* God tested Abraham to see if he would withhold his son and because he didn't all nations are blessed because the Messiah was given through Abraham's seed.

In the place where Abraham received back Isaac and was provided a lamb in his place, he named the spot Jehovah-jireh, the *'Lord will Provide'*. And so the Lord has provided, He prepared a body for His one and only Son as a sacrifice for all mankind, for all time. Jesus was the lamb chosen before the foundation of the world (I Peter 1:20)and it was God's will that He provide redemption through the sacrifice of His body.

God provided the sacrifice; He equipped our Savior with the body necessary to make atonement. Like Abraham He did not withhold His one and only Son but freely gave Him so that we could be made whole and brought into fellowship with God.

Made Holy Through the Sacrifice of Christ Once For All

"First he said, "Sacrifices and offerings, burnt offerings and sin offerings you did not desire, nor were you pleased with them" (although the law required them to be made). Then he said, "Here I am, I have come to do your will." He sets aside the first to establish the second. And by that will, we have been made holy through the sacrifice of the body of Jesus Christ once for all" (Hebrews 10:8-10)

God was never pleased with, nor desired continual sacrifices and offerings. The law required them to be made, however the law's purpose was to be the catalyst which would point people to Christ (Galatians 3:24). In other words, the sacrifices were more for mankind's benefit, than God's. They were a type and shadow of the perfect sacrificial lamb and merely served as a reminder to look forward in faith to the Messiah (Hebrews 10:1).

Jesus, who was the Messiah, came to put God's will of the New Covenant into effect. By His perfect sacrifice, He fulfilled and completed all the requirements of the first Covenant, including the sacrifices of blood for the forgiveness of sins. *"By calling this covenant "new," he has made the first one obsolete; and what is obsolete and aging will soon disappear" (Hebrews 8:13).*

God's will *(as in; Last Will and Testament)* was activated with the death of Jesus. Hebrews 9 testifies to this fact, *"In the case of a will, it is necessary to prove the death of the one who made it, because a will is in force only when somebody has died; it never takes effect while the one who made it is living. This is why even the first covenant was not put into effect without blood" (Hebrews 9:16-18).* Since a death has taken place, the will is currently in effect and the will is that we have been made holy by Jesus' sacrifice once for all (Hebrews 10:8-10).

This is an amazing truth! Through faith in Jesus' sacrifice, which paid the price for the forgiveness of sins, God considers us holy as result. It is not something we must work at or try to be. Holiness was purchased and given to us by the precious blood of the Lamb. It is a done-deal because unlike the animal sacrifices, which happened over and over, Jesus' sacrifice only happened once for all time. Therefore we are made holy by the body of Jesus.

The Greek word used for holy in Hebrews 10:10 is *hagiazō*, which is also translated sanctified in many translations. The verb tense signifies *"expressing the definiteness and completeness of the Divine act"* (*Vine's Expository Dictionary of New Testament Words*).

The Strong's Concordance gives these definitions:

1. to render or acknowledge, or to be venerable or hallow
2. to separate from profane things and dedicate to God
   a. consecrate things to God
   b. dedicate people to God
3. to purify
   a. to cleanse externally
   b. to purify by expiation: free from the guilt of sin
   c. to purify internally by renewing of the soul

(Strong's Exhaustive Concordance of the Bible)

In the context of Hebrews 10:10, we see its effect on the believer in the death of Christ; we have been made holy and we are sanctified by His blood. By definition this happens both externally and internally. Externally, because Christ's blood purifies us from the effects of sin. And internally; because we are free from the guilt of sin. This purification has a renewing effect on our soul realm as well. So we learn an important truth, Christ put the New Covenant into effect by His blood and this blood has made us holy and accepted by God forever.

Renewing your mind to this amazing truth will keep you from striving to achieve what you already have through Christ. You don't need to work at holiness; you have been made holy by His blood. You are sanctified through His body and God completely accepts you on the basis of Jesus' sacrifice. Through faith in Christ you are the righteousness of God and have been fashioned after Jesus Christ in true righteousness and holiness (Ephesians 4:24).

Jesus Sat Down at the Right Hand of God

"Day after day every priest stands and performs his religious duties; again and again he offers the same sacrifices, which can never take away sins. But when this priest had offered for all time one sacrifice for sins, he sat down at the right hand of God. Since that time he waits for his enemies to be made his footstool, because by one sacrifice he has made perfect forever those who are being made holy" (Hebrews 10:11-14)

Pointing out the contrast between the continuous and repetitive acts of the priests compared with the one act of Jesus' sacrifice is the main theme of Hebrews chapter 10. What the priests did over and over, Jesus did only once. And since that time He has been seated at the right hand of God the Father because the work He was sent to do is finished and complete.

We see the same thing with creation. On the seventh day God rested from all His work (Genesis 2:2). Not because He was tired, but because He was done (Hebrews 4:10). He saw all He had made, declared it good, gave it the ability to reproduce and so He entered into rest. In fact Adam and Eve were created in that rest. There was no sin, it was a paradise and they fellowshipped with God in perfect unity, then came the fall of mankind.

After Jesus completed His restoration work on the cross, like God He sat down because everything was done. Redemption had been accomplished. Sins had been forgiven. The Sabbath Rest that God originally instated in the garden had been restored (Hebrews 4:1-11). In other words, Jesus rested because there was nothing left to do. Now He waits for His enemies to be made His footstool.

The book of Hebrews opens with this very idea, *"The Son is the radiance of God's glory and the exact representation of his being, sustaining all things by his powerful word. After he had provided purification for sins, he sat down at the right hand of the Majesty in heaven" (Hebrews 1:3).* Evidence that this is currently the case is that the universe is held into place by His powerful Word. Jesus is the glue that is holding everything together and this testifies to the fact that Jesus is seated in heaven at the Fathers right hand.

This is good news for us because it means that His one sacrifice, in contrast to the law's many sacrifices, worked. We, by this single offering are completely cleansed, perfected, consecrated and made holy once for all. Just like Jesus, we can enter into the rest that God desires for His people. This Sabbath Rest is in the person of Jesus Christ and comes through trusting in Him (Colossians 2:16-17; Hebrews 4:3; 9-10).

By His one sacrifice we have been made holy and the law has been fulfilled in our lives. *"For what the law was powerless to do in that it was weakened by the sinful nature, God did by sending his own Son in the likeness of sinful man to be a sin offering. And so he condemned sin in sinful man, in order that the righteous requirements of the law might be fully met in us, who do not live according to the sinful nature but according to the Spirit" (Romans 8:3-4).* All of this is guaranteed by witness that Jesus is currently in heaven occupying the seated position of right hand to God the Father. Everything has been done and His work is completed. In the same way, our job is to believe in the One that God has sent (John 6:29). When this happens our work is also finished and complete and we enter into the very rest that God promised His people right from the start.

The Holy Spirit Testifies to the New Covenant

"The Holy Spirit also testifies to us about this. First he says: "This is the covenant I will make with them after that time, says the Lord. I will put my laws in their hearts, and I will write them on their minds." Then he adds: "Their sins and lawless acts I will remember no more." And where these have been forgiven, there is no longer any sacrifice for sin" (Hebrews 10:15-18)

The Holy Spirit does so many things in our lives but one of His most important roles is to testify and confirm the New Covenant to us. It is His job to reassure and remind us of what was promised. The Covenant we enjoy is vastly superior to the old one and was extremely costly for God to bring it to pass. Therefore He has made it the job of the Holy Spirit to constantly remind believers of the amazing things that are included.

The Covenant enjoyed through Jesus was prophesied through the prophet Jeremiah hundreds of years before Christ (Jeremiah 31:31-34). It includes many things and in these verses we are reminded of that to which the Holy Spirit is sent to testify. First, God writes His righteousness and His faithfulness in our minds and upon our hearts. God's law is now a part of us, not something external to accuse us, but they are written by the Spirit of God on the inside of us (Psalm 40:6-10; Romans 8:4; Galatians 5:16). Secondly, God will not only forgive our sins but He will not remember them (Psalm 103:12; Jeremiah 31:34b; Hebrews 8:12; 10:17). God completely and permanently dealt with sin once for all through Jesus' sacrificial death on the cross (Hebrews 9:28; 10:10, 12, 14, 18; I Peter 3:18; I John 2:2). Because of it, by faith, we have been made holy and acceptable to God which is why God sends the Holy Spirit to confirm this to us, He doesn't want us to miss this amazing truth!

To use an old metaphor; the Holy Spirit is really the icing on the entire redemption cake! Not only are we saved, redeemed and restored through Jesus' precious blood, but the Holy Spirit constantly speaks these things to us so that we will have confidence in our relationship with God (Hebrews 4:16; 10:22). Jesus foretold that this would be His function, *"But the Counselor, the Holy Spirit, whom the Father will send in my name, will teach you all things and will remind you of everything I have said to you" (John 14:26)*. The Amplified Bible calls Him the Comforter, Counselor, Helper, Intercessor, Advocate, Strengthener and Standby. All are marvelous words to describe how He relates to us.

God thought that is was imperative that we be constantly reminded of our Covenant because the reason Jesus died was to bring it to pass. This is good news for us because it means we can find peace and rest through Jesus by confirmation of the Holy Spirit speaking these things to us, *"This then is how we know that we belong to the truth, and how we set our hearts at rest in his presence whenever our hearts condemn us. For God is greater than our hearts, and he knows everything. Dear friends, if our hearts do not condemn us, we have confidence before God" (I John 3:19-21)*.

Drawing Near to God With a Sincere Heart in Full Assurance of Faith

"Therefore, brothers, since we have confidence to enter the Most Holy Place by the blood of Jesus, by a new and living way opened for us through the curtain, that is, his body, and since we have a great priest over the house of God, let us draw near to God with a sincere heart in full assurance of faith, having our hearts sprinkled to cleanse us from a guilty conscience and having our bodies washed with pure water. Let us hold unswervingly to the hope we profess, for he who promised is faithful" (Hebrews 10:19-23)

These verses are a culmination of the entire book of Hebrews. Everything that has been said has been leading up to this point, we can draw near and approach God on the basis of faith in what Jesus did to make us acceptable, knowing that nothing stands in our way. This is a profound truth!

Reflecting on the entirety of Hebrews we see that Jesus is God's Son, an exact representation of the Father and far superior to angels (Hebrews 1). Secondly, we see that He was sent to destroy the power of sin and death and release us from slavery to it (Hebrews 2). Next, we see how vastly superior Jesus is to Moses (Hebrews 3) and by believing in Him we enter into the very Sabbath Rest that God promised His people (Hebrews 4). Next we see how Jesus was chosen by God to be our High Priest fashioned after the order of Melchizedek (Hebrews 5). After a short warning about falling away, the writer goes on to explain this priesthood, given on oath and how Jesus meets all of its requirements (Hebrews 6, 7). Next, the New Covenant is introduced and explained with Jesus at its epicenter (Hebrews 8). Chapter 9 compares and contrasts earthly tabernacle worship with Jesus' heavenly duties and shows how His perfect and Holy blood has ratified and guaranteed the New Covenant (Hebrews 9). Chapter 10 brings home the point that this sacrifice was only made once to forever seal the deal. It shows how Jesus' work on the cross was perfect and complete (Hebrews 10).

In light of all of these things, the main point now becomes the fact that we can have boldness and confidence to draw on what Jesus did and approach God fully assured that we are acceptable to Him. By faith we can come to Him in absolute conviction that we are not guilty of sin and we are not polluted by its effects. Because of Jesus we are righteous and holy.

The only requirement is that we come through the veil of His body, washed solely by His blood. Jesus on the night that He was betrayed spoke of this very thing, *"While they were eating, Jesus took bread, gave thanks and broke it, and gave it to his disciples, saying, "Take and eat; this is my body." Then he took the cup, gave thanks and offered it to them, saying, "Drink from it, all of you. This is my blood of the covenant, which is poured out for many for the forgiveness of sins. I tell you, I will not drink of this fruit of the vine from now on until that day when I drink it anew with you in my Father's kingdom"* (Matthew 26:26-29).

This was not the first time Jesus made mention that both His body and His blood was necessary to be brought into fellowship with God. He deliberately said it to the multitudes that were following Him looking for miracles. They were offended at the words He spoke so He took a hard stance declaring, *"Whoever eats my flesh and drinks my blood has eternal life, and I will raise him up at the last day. For my flesh is real food and my blood is real drink. Whoever eats my flesh and drinks my blood remains in me, and I in him"* (John 6:54-56). Many left Him that day and followed Him no longer. However, His point was that there is only one way to be accepted by God and that is through the body of Christ which was broken for us and through the blood of Christ, shed as atonement for us. This hasn't changed since Jesus spoke these words, *"I am the way and the truth and the life. No one comes to the Father except through me"* (John 14:6).

At the cross the veil in the temple that separated mankind from the Holy of Holies where God resides was torn in two from top to bottom in a divine act of God (Matthew 27:51; Mark 15:38; Luke 23:45). Jesus' body has become the veil where we can pass through in faith into the very presence of God the Father. This is an amazing truth! Jesus opened up a new and fresh way of approaching God. We now enter, not by the blood of bulls and goats but by His body and blood which cleanses and absolves us from all guilt associated with sin.

Because this is so, we are called to draw near to God in confidence and boldness. Jesus' changed the rules. *"So let us seize and hold fast and retain without wavering the hope we cherish and confess and our acknowledgement of it, for He Who promised is reliable (sure) and faithful to His word" (Hebrews 10:23 AMP).*

Assembling of the Saints to Encourage One Another

"And let us consider how we may spur one another on toward love and good deeds. Let us not give up meeting together, as some are in the habit of doing, but let us encourage one another—and all the more as you see the Day approaching" (Hebrews 10:24-25)

Jesus brings together men, women and children from all walks of life. All over the world there is a fellowship of believers that transcends time and distance having the commonality of Christ. The Church, His body of believers, is a truly marvelous thing and as such we have the responsibility to care for and stimulate one another toward love and good deeds by reminding ourselves of the amazing things Christ has done for us.

We do this by assembling with the saints. Not merely going to a church building, not just showing up once a week to check it off our list. But rather meeting with other like-minded believers, regularly, is the key to spiritual growth. When we come to share our lives and talk about the Lord, excitement builds and encouragement spills over onto one another. The effects are contagious.

The early Church understood this; the book of Acts is filled with many accounts where believers would gather daily giving themselves to prayer, breaking of bread and the disciples' teaching. *"They devoted themselves to the apostles' teaching and to the fellowship, to the breaking of bread and to prayer. Everyone was filled with awe, and many wonders and miraculous signs were done by the apostles. All the believers were together and had everything in common. Selling their possessions and goods, they gave to anyone as he had need. Every day they continued to meet together in the temple courts. They broke bread in their homes and ate together with glad and sincere hearts, praising God and enjoying the favor of all the people. And the Lord added to their number daily those who were being saved" (Acts 2:42-47).*

As you can see, a lot of things happened as a result. The assembly of believers had unity among each other, they saw many wonders and miracles, they continually sold their possessions so they would have the means to give when a need arose and their hearts were merry. They praised God continually because they were constantly reminded of what He had done for them. As a result the world saw what was happening and wanted it. People came running to the Lord to accept His wonderful gift of salvation as a result of the fellowship of believers and the things that happened when they met together.

This is what should happen when the saints get together. This is why it is important for us to come, stir each other up and encourage one another continually; growing through the Word and prayer. We do not have to go through life alone; we have millions of brothers and sisters in Christ Jesus. Our family is based in the finished work of Christ so it makes sense that we should continually remind ourselves of these truths. The time of Christ's return is approaching, so it is time for the Church to be the Church and to be prepared, encouraged and built up in love and unity. Returning to the example set by the early church. Not forgetting to assemble but doing so readily to encourage each other and grow in the knowledge of the grace of our Lord Jesus Christ.

No Other Sacrifice for Sin is Left, Only Judgment

"If we deliberately keep on sinning after we have received the knowledge of the truth, no sacrifice for sins is left, but only a fearful expectation of judgment and of raging fire that will consume the enemies of God" (Hebrews 10:26-27)

In today's world of political correctness, it is not popular to say that Jesus is the only way, but that doesn't change this truth which rings loud and clear; Jesus is the only way to get to heaven. Jesus is the only way for salvation. Jesus is the only way to be right with God.

This is good news for us because it simplifies something that the world tries to complicate. What we hear from many sources is that we must be good, we must follow the rules, we must attend a certain church and we must adhere to certain religious practices; all while keeping us busy with other things so we miss the Savior. God didn't want it to be complicated; He wanted it to be accomplished, so He sent Jesus to do what we could not.

Jesus was our sacrifice for sin. Not only is this so but the Scriptures also say *"He is the atoning sacrifice for our sins, and not only for ours but also for the sins of the whole world" (I John 2:2)*. Jesus died for all; even those who do not accept this wonderful message of grace have been forgiven and absolved from sin. He died to bring forgiveness to everyone, *"For Christ died for sins once for all, the righteous for the unrighteous, to bring you to God. He was put to death in the body but made alive by the Spirit" (I Peter 3:18)*. This is an amazing truth, all sins; past, present and future have been paid for and forgiven by Jesus!

Since this is an absolute truth we also know that there can be no other sacrifice for sin because the debt that sin left is gone and paid for. Jesus came, died and rose again. This chapter has been written and closed. There has been one sacrifice to atone for sin which is why *"Salvation is found in no one else, for there is no other name under heaven given to men by which we must be saved" (Acts 4:12).* If we reject that name and the person behind it who has provided the means for salvation, then there is no other option; only a fearful expectation of judgment.

Jesus came not to judge the world, but to save it (John 12:47). However, there is one who will judge. The judgment has nothing to do with sin. But rather, the judgment has to do with whether or not you have accepted the gospel message and believed in Jesus Christ as Savior. The answer to this question is the determining factor for Salvation. The Scriptures are very clear on this point, God loves us and did everything to reconcile us to Himself, but He has given us the choice whether or not we accept Jesus who paid the price of our forgiveness. If we reject Him, then there can be no other payment because there was, and is, only one sacrifice (the death of Jesus) which can atone for sin.

This is what this passage in Hebrews is saying; if we deliberately and willingly refuse Jesus, then this sin is the only thing that will not be forgiven and the only thing that will send us to hell. All other sins have been paid for, and there is no other sacrifice which can be made. There is then, only the fearful prospect and expectation of divine judgment against those who set themselves up in opposition to God.

But it doesn't have to be like this, *"For God so loved the world that he gave his one and only Son, that whoever believes in him shall not perish but have eternal life. For God did not send his Son into the world to condemn the world, but to save the world through him. Whoever believes in him is not condemned, but whoever does not believe stands condemned already because he has not believed in the name of God's one and only Son" (John 3:16-18).* What you do with Jesus is the determining factor for eternity. However, we already have the answer to the question. The answer is to believe in the name of the One and Only Son and by doing so you will find abundant life starting right now! Praise God for Jesus!

It is a Dreadful Thing to Fall into the Hands of the Living God

"Anyone who rejected the law of Moses died without mercy on the testimony of two or three witnesses. How much more severely do you think a man deserves to be punished who has trampled the Son of God under foot, who has treated as an unholy thing the blood of the covenant that sanctified him, and who has insulted the Spirit of grace? For we know him who said, "It is mine to avenge; I will repay," and again, "The Lord will judge his people." It is a dreadful thing to fall into the hands of the living God" (Hebrews 10:28-31)

I've only seen the movie *The Passion of the Christ* once. When the film was released I went to the theatre and I watched the horrific portrayal of the crucifixion of Jesus. It was a somber day. But in reality, I know the images of this movie, which are burned into my mind, do not even come close to what Jesus actually experienced; dying a criminal's death on the cross to redeem me. We cannot even begin to imagine what Jesus went through that day. Isaiah tells us; *"his appearance was so disfigured beyond that of any man and his form marred beyond human likeness" (Isaiah 52:14b)*. It is hard to comprehend the intense suffering our Savior endured.

Isaiah went on to tell us, in perhaps one of the most beautiful passages in scripture, that it was God's will that Jesus suffer so intensely because the result was the justification of many (Isaiah 53:10-12). He describes what Jesus went through that day. He was pierced, He was stricken and smitten by God, He was oppressed, He was afflicted, He was led like a lamb to the slaughter, He was cut off from the land of the living and He was assigned a grave with the wicked (Isaiah 53) and yet in spite of all these things *"He poured out his life unto death, and was numbered with the transgressors. For he bore the sin of many, and made intercession for the transgressors" (Isaiah 53:12b).* Jesus went through with this because it meant restoration for us.

In fact, Jesus died for everyone, for those who accept His grace and for those who willingly reject it. He eliminated any barrier in bringing us to God dying for all. Because of this, Jesus has inherited a name that far exceeds any name in existence and He owns a position for eternity far above any other (Philippians 2:9-11; Colossians 1:18; Hebrews 1:4; 2:8). So, imagine how dreadful it is to reject the name and person of Jesus Christ.

We see examples from the Law, anyone who rejected the law died without mercy. How much more severe is rejecting everything the law pointed to. Jesus' blood was given to cleanse mankind of sin and the guilt associated with it. How dreadful and unforgivable it is to spurn and consider this blood unholy. How outrageous it is to reject the only One who can save. It is a public humiliation of Jesus; it is like crucifying Him over and over again.

The Holy Spirit imparts grace to mankind on behalf of God because of Jesus. He is the one to speak these truths to our hearts and to invite and draw mankind toward this grace. Repeatedly rejecting and denying this grace is an insult in the face of Jesus. How dreadful it will be for those who reject Jesus and trample the Son of God underfoot.

This is why paying attention to the message of Jesus is so very important. He took the punishment reserved for us upon Himself and bore the marks we deserve on His body. He became sin so we could become righteous (II Corinthians 5:21). If there is only one thing in life that matters, it is this; to believe in the Lord Jesus Christ. By doing so, not only do we escape the wrath of rejecting Jesus, but we gain so much more. We gain eternal life wrapped up securely in our Savior. We experience mercy, grace and love in an endless and wonderful way. We experience restoration at the hand of Jesus in all things. He speaks peace and love over us and there is no fear in death. *"In this way, love is made complete among us so that we will have confidence on the day of judgment, because in this world we are like him. There is no fear in love. But perfect love drives out fear, because fear has to do with punishment. The one who fears is not made perfect in love" (I John 4:17-18).*

Better and Lasting
Possessions

"Remember those earlier days after you had received the light, when you stood your ground in a great contest in the face of suffering. Sometimes you were publicly exposed to insult and persecution; at other times you stood side by side with those who were so treated. You sympathized with those in prison and joyfully accepted the confiscation of your property, because you knew that you yourselves had better and lasting possessions" (Hebrews 10:32-34)

Jesus said in Mark 4 that persecution will come after someone receives the Word of God (Mark 4:17). The intent is to choke the seed from taking root and growing. If the seed can be snuffed out in the early stages then no crop will grow and flourish as result. However, Jesus also said in the Parable of the Sower of the Seed that when the Word is understood taking root, it will grow and the yield is thirty, sixty, one hundred times what was sown (Matthew 13:23; Mark 4:20; Luke 8:8).

Once the truth of God's Word is rooted in your life then persecution has a reverse effect. We can see this from our example of the early church. They were publicly exposed to insults and abuse. They were mistreated, laughed at and even killed. They were stripped of their property, their jobs and their means of support and yet they stood their ground in the face of such hardship. Not only is this so, but others joined them, standing side by side with those who were being treated in this way. Persecution served as a catalyst for their faith.

The reason these believers rejoiced was because they understood their reward and lasting possessions were vastly different than anything the world offers. The things they valued started changing as they saw the glory of God through suffering and hardship. James gives us this promise to cling to when trials come our way, *"Consider it pure joy, my brothers, whenever you face trials of many kinds, because you know that the testing of your faith develops perseverance. Perseverance must finish its work so that you may be mature and complete, not lacking anything"* (James 1:2-4). The promise is that we will always come through the fiery trials as pure gold.

The other reason these men and women could rejoice was that they bore the name of Christ. Peter tells us, *"Dear friends, do not be surprised at the painful trial you are suffering, as though something strange were happening to you. But rejoice that you participate in the sufferings of Christ, so that you may be overjoyed when his glory is revealed. If you are insulted because of the name of Christ, you are blessed, for the Spirit of glory and of God rests on you. If you suffer, it should not be as a murderer or thief or any other kind of criminal, or even as a meddler. However, if you suffer as a Christian, do not be ashamed, but praise God that you bear that name"* (I Peter 4:12-16). Persecution and suffering happens because of the Word and trusting in God, so when it comes, rejoice; because you know that it is not on your account, but on the account of God that you bear the glorious name of Jesus.

We are the recipients of such faith. We enjoy the benefits of the men and women who gave their lives to pass the Word of God to us. The centuries are riddled with stories of martyrdom and suffering. These great men and women now enjoy their very great rewards and lasting possessions in the heavenly places. Paul told the church at Corinth that they not only participated in his suffering but they also shared in the comfort he received as a result (II Corinthians 1:3-7). True to this idea, we also have received the immeasurable comfort and joy that has come as a result of the suffering and persecution that the early church faced and we are so very thankful for their sacrifice.

Do Not Throw Away Your Confidence - It Will Be Richly Rewarded

"So do not throw away your confidence; it will be richly rewarded. You need to persevere so that when you have done the will of God, you will receive what he has promised" (Hebrews 10:35-36)

Did you know that each one of us has a mission in life? God has a will concerning us. He has chosen something very special for each one of us, but it is up to us to carry it out. We learn what this will is, by renewing our minds to the Word of God and presenting ourselves as living sacrifices (Romans 12:1-2). After we know what this is, then we should pursue it at all costs because it carries with it the promise of a very great reward.

These verses, encouraging us to continue in the will of God, come on the heels of persecution. They early church had been persecuted, ridiculed and publicly humiliated, however the writer is reminding us to continue on, not throwing away the confidence we have in Christ; because this carries with it a great and glorious compensation of reward (Hebrews 10:35).

We are reminded that we will receive what God has promised us, even in the midst of painful trials and persecution. In fact if we are suffering in this way we can be confident that we are doing the will of God. Persecution comes because of the Word (Matthew 13:21; Mark 4:17; Luke 8:13). If we are walking according to His will for our lives, we can be assured that we will probably be persecuted for it. It happened then, it will happen now.

Paul experienced this everywhere he went. There was such opposition to the gospel that He was given a thorn in the flesh, a messenger of Satan to buffet him wherever he went. *"To keep me from becoming conceited because of these surpassingly great revelations, there was given me a thorn in my flesh, a messenger of Satan, to torment me. Three times I pleaded with the Lord to take it away from me. But he said to me, "My grace is sufficient for you, for my power is made perfect in weakness." Therefore I will boast all the more gladly about my weaknesses, so that Christ's power may rest on me. That is why, for Christ's sake, I delight in weaknesses, in insults, in hardships, in persecutions, in difficulties. For when I am weak, then I am strong" (II Corinthians 12:7-10).*

Satan tried his best to snuff out the gospel message from being preached, so he stirred up trouble and persecution everywhere Paul went. He constantly faced resistance to preaching the gospel message because it is the power of God (Romans 1:16). He was constantly under the fear of death; however he also had a promise from God that His grace was sufficient to overcome any opposition. Paul was reminded not to throw away his confidence in Christ because it came with a great reward. The reward Paul received was millions of believers coming to know Christ throughout the centuries because of his perseverance with the message he was sent to preach (Romans 1:1).

We like Paul, and countless others, need to persevere in the midst of trials and persecution so that we can complete the will of God for our lives. We need to rest in the confidence we have through faith in Jesus Christ who enables us to carry it out. We should disregard everything that hinders us and run the race set before us looking only to the glorious finish line (Hebrews 12:1-3). Then for the rest of eternity we will also enjoy to the fullest what God has promised us!

My Righteous Ones Will Live By Faith

"For in just a very little while, "He who is coming will come and will not delay. But my righteous one will live by faith. And if he shrinks back, I will not be pleased with him." But we are not of those who shrink back and are destroyed, but of those who believe and are saved" (Hebrews 10:37-39)

Faith pleases God, in fact Hebrews 11 records, *"without faith it is impossible to please God..."* This means that our faith is a baseline. The verse goes on to say, *"...because anyone who comes to him must believe that he exists and that he rewards those who earnestly seek him" (Hebrews 11:6)*. So it is no surprise that the Bible says that the righteous will live by faith.

We first come to God by faith. We place faith in what Jesus did for us to bring us into fellowship with God. Colossians tells us that in the same way we received Christ we are to continue living in Him (Colossians 2:6). We received Christ by faith so it makes sense that all of our lives we are to continue in faith believing God in all things.

So we learn an important truth in this passage, through faith we are not of those who shrink back and are destroyed throughout life, instead we are of those who believe and rise to any occasion because of what God is able to accomplish through us. Paul said that we are more than conquerors (Romans 8:37), nothing in life can stand in our way, *"For I am convinced that neither death nor life, neither angels nor demons, neither the present nor the future, nor any powers, neither height nor depth, nor anything else in all creation, will be able to separate us from the love of God that is in Christ Jesus our Lord" (Romans 8:38-39)*. His love enables us to be more than conquerors and to rise up in faith by believing what God has spoken to us.

We also have a promise that Christ is coming very soon. He will not delay, so as we wait for that glorious day, we are to live by faith knowing without a doubt that this day is quickly approaching. To prepare, this is how we can please God, by trusting Him in all things, By waiting patiently knowing that what He has said will come to pass and by continually standing in faith. Because *we are not of those who shrink back and are destroyed, but of those who believe and are saved"* (Hebrews 10:39).

hebrews 11.

THE FAITH
HALL OF FAME

Now Faith is Being Sure of What We Hope For

"Now faith is being sure of what we hope for and certain of what we do not see. This is what the ancients were commended for" (Hebrews 11:1-2)

In the natural realm, faith doesn't make sense. Because faith cannot be seen, understood or explained when situations beyond human control require its use. And yet faith is absolutely necessary for the believer. In fact, faith is the first and only thing required of us when we come to God (Ephesians 2:8-9). Later on in this chapter the writer draws attention to the fact that without faith we cannot please God, which means it is absolutely necessary (Hebrews 11:6).

Paul told the believers in Corinth, *"We live by faith, not by sight" (II Corinthians 5:7).* If this is the case, it is important to know what faith is, so that we can regulate and conduct ourselves in faith, not by what we see, taste, touch, hear or feel.

This passage in Hebrews is the mere definition of faith. It is being sure, certain and confident of the things we hope for. The King James Bibles tells us that faith is a substance. And the Amplified Bible puts it best when it calls faith the title deed of the things we hope for. If we have the title deed to something we own it.

The Amplified goes on to explain it this way, *"NOW FAITH is the assurance (the confirmation, the title deed) of the things [we] hope for, being the proof of things [we] do not see and the conviction of their reality [faith perceiving as real fact what is not revealed to the senses]" (Hebrews 11:1 AMP).* Faith is what assures and having faith is perceiving as real what is not yet evident in the natural realm. The ancients had it; otherwise they would not have seen nor done the things they did.

Faith is what carries you from point A to point B. You can hope for something but faith is the substance that moves you forward until you experience it. Take salvation for example. We receive this by faith. Being saved is not something that you can see, hear, smell, touch or feel. However, chances are if you've experienced it no one can talk you out of it because your faith is the substance that testifies to you that it is real and genuine. The hope of salvation hasn't been realized yet, in the sense that we still are on this earth, but faith is what assures us that salvation is a done deal and one day very soon the hope of salvation will be realized.

This same principal applies to all situations in the believer's life. This is why the writer declared at the end of Hebrews 10, *"But we are not of those who shrink back and are destroyed, but of those who believe and are saved"* *(Hebrews 10:39).* Why? Because we have faith! We have the title deed to the things that God has promised us. All we need to do is believe them until the hope of them is realized. *"This is what the ancients were commended for"* *(Hebrews 11:2).* They believed God when all seemed lost and obtained a good report.

By Faith We Understand that the Universe was Formed at God's Command

"By faith we understand that the universe was formed at God's command, so that what is seen was not made out of what was visible" (Hebrews 11:3)

By faith we understand that the universe was made by the spoken Word of God. However, faith also had an incredible role in the creation of the world. God spoke creation into existence when nothing was. This took faith on His part, He believed His Words would form the physical and it did.

Faith is a key element in how the kingdom of God works. God himself operates in this way. This is an important lesson for us, by it we see two amazing truths. First, as in our example from creation, faith has the power to bring what does not exist into existence. Secondly, we see that speaking in faith is what unlocks that power to bring it to pass (Romans 4:17). We can speak the Word of God with authority to any situation, being confident that it will change the circumstances and the outcome. It may seem odd, but that is why faith is required.

The previous verse describes faith as *"being sure of what we hope for and certain of what we do not see" (Hebrews 11:1)*. Meaning the substance behind faith cannot be seen or understood with the five senses, but there is a certainty to it. Just as in our example from creation, the substance supporting faith is the Word of God. When we have a Word, we have the means to get us to where our hope is realized.

God spoke the universe into existence by faith. He instructed His Word to go and produce, believing that it would happen and the rest is history. In the same way, we can have such confidence in the Word of God because we also have a wonderful promise concerning it, *"As the rain and the snow come down from heaven, and do not return to it without watering the earth and making it bud and flourish, so that it yields seed for the sower and bread for the eater, so is my word that goes out from my mouth: It will not return to me empty, but will accomplish what I desire and achieve the purpose for which I sent it"* (Isaiah 55:10-11).

By Faith Abel Offered God a Better Sacrifice

"By faith Abel offered God a better sacrifice than Cain did. By faith he was commended as a righteous man, when God spoke well of his offerings. And by faith he still speaks, even though he is dead" (Hebrews 11:4)

By reading the account of Cain and Abel in Genesis 4, it is easy to be confused about why Abel's sacrifice was accepted and Cain's was not. However, this passage in Hebrews clarifies it, telling us that Abel offered his sacrifice in faith, Cain on the other hand did not. The result is that God commended Abel as a righteous man and accepted his offering.

To understand this, we must first look back at Genesis 4. Although not much detail is given about the instructions God gave to them when bringing their sacrifices, we see that Cain brought the fruit of the ground to God and Abel brought an animal sacrifice. God looked favorably on Abel's sacrifice. When Cain's was rejected God said to him, *"Why are you angry? Why is your face downcast? If you do what is right, will you not be accepted? But if you do not do what is right, sin is crouching at your door; it desires to have you, but you must master it" (Genesis 4:6-7).* The first thing we see is that Cain did not do what was right, which is why he was rejected.

The reason was because he brought the toil of his labor to God as an offering. This was wrong because God had cursed the ground at the fall of mankind. *"To Adam he said, "Because you listened to your wife and ate from the tree about which I commanded you, 'You must not eat of it,' "Cursed is the ground because of you; through painful toil you will eat of it all the days of your life" (Genesis 3:17).* Cain brought to God what he grew from the cursed ground, this was approaching God in self-righteousness and on that basis we are never accepted. Isaiah tells us that all of our righteous acts are as filthy rags (Isaiah 64:6), not our unrighteousness but our righteousness. All of the things we do to be acceptable to God are as soiled dirty rags. This is why we are never accepted when we approach Him in this manner.

Abel, on the other hand, brought to God a covering that had been provided for him. Abel, by faith, accepted what God did and on that basis he was accepted. He took God's righteousness as a gift which made him acceptable. God was so pleased with Abel that He wrote about it in Hebrews 11 so we could still celebrate his faith.

This same truth rings loud and clear for us today. When we rely on what Jesus did for us to make us righteous, then we are always accepted. This takes faith, but that faith commends us as righteous before God and like Abel speaks a good word on our behalf.

By Faith Enoch Was Commended as One Who Pleased God

"By faith Enoch was taken from this life, so that he did not experience death; he could not be found, because God had taken him away. For before he was taken, he was commended as one who pleased God" (Hebrews 11:5)

Enoch is one of the most interesting records found in the Bible. Four short verses in Genesis describe his life. What makes it unique is that he is one of two men who didn't experience death. Instead God translated him to where He was because Enoch had a faith report that he pleased God.

According to the account found in Genesis, Enoch had a legacy of walking in close fellowship with God for three hundred years (Genesis 5:22). The Amplified Bible describes this relationship as habitual fellowship (Genesis 5:24 AMP). This means that they enjoyed intimacy and a fellowship that pleased and satisfied both God and man. From this relationship, Enoch for all time, has this testimony given by God that he pleased him. What marvelous faith Enoch had.

When I think about him being translated from this earth without experiencing death, I am reminded that God does the same thing with us. Colossians says, *"For he has rescued us from the dominion of darkness and brought us into the kingdom of the Son he loves" (Colossians 1:13).* The King James Bible says it this way, *"Who hath delivered us from the power of darkness, and hath translated us into the kingdom of his dear Son" (Colossians 1:13 KJV).*

The amazing thing that we can take away is that through Jesus, we like Enoch, experienced translation from death at the moment of salvation and were forever united with God. This of course takes place on a spiritual level; we are moved from the kingdom of darkness under the shadow of death into the kingdom of Jesus, and given eternal life. This happens by faith. Just as Enoch received a testimony that he pleased God, we too, by faith can obtain that very same report.

There is a great lesson to be learned from Enoch. The faith of Enoch made it into the Faith Hall of Fame for a reason. His faith pleased God obtaining a good report recorded for all future generations to have this example. This report came by habitual fellowship with His creator and walking with Him all the days of His life until he was no more because God had taken him home.

Without Faith it is Impossible to Please God

"And without faith it is impossible to please God, because anyone who comes to him must believe that he exists and that he rewards those who earnestly seek him" (Hebrews 11:6)

Faith is a must. Faith is the entrance point to a relationship with God. He interacts with us based on His grace, we respond in faith. Given the basis of this type of relationship we understand how important faith is to the believer. In fact, this passage boldly declares that without it, it is impossible to please God because the simple truth remains that we must believe that He is before we can come to Him.

If faith is the starting point, then it makes sense that faith is a key element for life. Throughout the Gospels, Jesus commented on people's faith. In most cases He asked and wondered where it was, saying *'you of little faith'* or *'where is your faith?'* On other occasions He marveled, as in the example of the centurion soldier (Matthew 8:5-13). When the centurion came to Jesus asking for help for his servant Jesus agreed to come with him. But in a marvelous display of faith he told Jesus to just say the word and it would be done; citing his understanding of authority and appropriating it. *"When Jesus heard this, he was astonished and said to those following him, "I tell you the truth, I have not found anyone in Israel with such great faith"* (Matthew 8:10). The centurion's faith made Jesus stop and marvel which is noteworthy. *"Then Jesus said to the centurion, "Go! It will be done just as you believed it would." And his servant was healed at that very hour"* (Matthew 8:13). The healing took place according to the faith of the solider and in the manner he asked for, Jesus just came into agreement with the faith that had been displayed.

If it is impossible to please God without faith, the opposite is also true; faith is what pleases God. As in our examples from the gospels, faith was important to Jesus, He looked for it and responded to it everywhere He went. So the underlying truth to draw from is that God responds to faith. It pleases Him, it moves Him to act and it is essential in the life of the believer.

Noah Became Heir of the Righteousness that Comes by Faith

"By faith Noah, when warned about things not yet seen, in holy fear built an ark to save his family. By his faith he condemned the world and became heir of the righteousness that comes by faith" (Hebrews 11:7)

It takes faith to build an ark. Only one man has ever needed this kind of faith. Even though Noah had never experienced the flooding that exists with earth covering amounts of water, he obeyed God when instructed to build the ark. He had only God's word to counter everything he knew and had previously experienced.

Noah was six hundred years old when the ark was finished and probably endured endless harassment by society during construction. Yet he did not waver in faith but carried out every detail as instructed. This is faith in action. Noah is a text book case of the definition of faith, *"Now faith is being sure of what we hope for and certain of what we do not see" (Hebrews 11:1).* He believed God when all indicators of reality pointed another direction.

Backing up to the beginning of this account we see that Noah had found favor in the eyes of the Lord, *"The LORD saw how great man's wickedness on the earth had become, and that every inclination of the thoughts of his heart was only evil all the time. The LORD was grieved that he had made man on the earth, and his heart was filled with pain. So the LORD said, "I will wipe mankind, whom I have created, from the face of the earth—men and animals, and creatures that move along the ground, and birds of the air—for I am grieved that I have made them." But Noah found favor in the eyes of the*

LORD. This is the account of Noah. Noah was a righteous man, blameless among the people of his time, and he walked with God" (Genesis 6:5-9).

Noah was righteous and blameless and had a long history of fellowshipping with God. His track record of seeing God true to His Word was all the reassurance he needed year after year while building the ark. With each board put in place Noah condemned the world of its wickedness choosing to believe God. Because of this he saved his family, livestock, animal species and future generations while obtaining the righteousness that only comes through faith.

Now we have a wonderful reminder of the covenant that God made with Noah, that He would never again flood the earth. A rainbow in the sky speaks of this one man's faith (Genesis 9:8-17). He overcame obstacles, faced public humiliation choosing to believed God. Because of it, the world was condemned of its wickedness. Noah inherited the righteousness that comes by faith. What an amazing example to encourage us in our journey!

By Faith Abraham Made His Home in the Promised Land

"By faith Abraham, when called to go to a place he would later receive as his inheritance, obeyed and went, even though he did not know where he was going. By faith he made his home in the promised land like a stranger in a foreign country; he lived in tents, as did Isaac and Jacob, who were heirs with him of the same promise. For he was looking forward to the city with foundations, whose architect and builder is God" (Hebrews 11:8-10)

Faith propels people to do strange things from the viewpoint of the world. I had a friend who left family and friends, and moved to Costa Rica to be a missionary because she heard God instruct her to go. She didn't have missionary support when she left, she just knew she was supposed to go. She was heavily criticized by those around her for taking such bold steps without a husband, financial support or long term accommodations. However, in an act a faith, she went. And God, true to His word supplied everything she needed, bringing her into a loving community of missionaries who shared the same vision of ministering to the people of Costa Rica.

Although this seems like an unusual story of faith, it is not unheard of. Abraham experienced the same thing. God came to Abraham and told him to leave his country, his people and his father's household to go to a land He would later show him. Then God gave Abraham a very great promise. *"I will make you into a great nation and I will bless you; I will make your name great, and you will be a blessing. I will bless those who bless you, and whoever curses you I will curse; and all peoples on earth will be blessed through you" (Genesis 12:2-3).* At this time Abraham was seventy-five years old and without an heir. However, he considered the promise of God and set out in faith to participate. He left seeking the land he would receive as an inheritance knowing that God would also give him a son in the process.

While on this earth, Abraham lived as a stranger, in a foreign country. What makes this account amazing is that he was waiting expectantly and confidently for God's promise to come to pass. Abraham used faith to perceive from a distance what would be instead of looking at his present situation. Verse 10 shines light on this, *"For he was looking forward to the city with foundations, whose architect and builder is God" (Hebrews 11:10)*. Abraham could see through the eyes of faith what God would do if he believed and obeyed. He chose to disregard the things of this world for the things of God.

Just as in the example from my missionary friend, this type of faith is unusual and makes people uncomfortable. However, the reward is too great to pass on. We must look toward the future in faith with spiritual eyes. Considering that God is always faithful to His promises. Like Abraham we must disregard the things of this world for a chance to follow God's instructions knowing that God always rewards faith (Hebrews 11:6).

By Faith Abraham Considered God Faithful to His Promise

"By faith Abraham, even though he was past age—and Sarah herself was barren—was enabled to become a father because he considered him faithful who had made the promise. And so from this one man, and he as good as dead, came descendants as numerous as the stars in the sky and as countless as the sand on the seashore" (Hebrews 11:11-12)

It would be easy to become discouraged and hopeless in a situation like this. Abraham and Sarah waited for years hoping to have a child only to grow old without an heir. The possibility of reproduction gone with each passing year. The history of trying to conceive over and over without success would be more than enough to dash any hope for the future.

Then the Lord appeared to Abraham telling him at the same time next year Sarah would have a son. Sarah laughed as she overheard the conversation but the Lord replied to her, *"Is anything too hard for the LORD? I will return to you at the appointed time next year and Sarah will have a son" (Genesis 18:14).* Confirming the Word He originally gave Abraham that he would be the father of many nations (Genesis 12:2-3; 15:4-5).

Faced with a decision to believe God for the impossible, both Abraham and Sarah took the steps of faith required to conceive. Because of faith, Sarah received the physical power to get pregnant although she was long past the ability to do so. The key lies in the fact that she considered God faithful who had promised them a son. She chose not to consider the circumstances surrounding the situation only the guarantor of the promise.

In the same way, Abraham disregarded the fact that he was one hundred years old and that Sarah had been barren and had long since passed the age of childbearing. Instead he considered God faithful to His word and able to bring it to pass. Romans 4 gives a marvelous picture of Abraham's faith, *"Against all hope, Abraham in hope believed and so became the father of many nations, just as it had been said to him, "So shall your offspring be." Without weakening in his faith, he faced the fact that his body was as good as dead—since he was about a hundred years old—and that Sarah's womb was also dead. Yet he did not waver through unbelief regarding the promise of God, but was strengthened in his faith and gave glory to God, being fully persuaded that God had power to do what he had promised"* (Romans 4:18-21).

When hope was gone, Abraham got supernatural hope to carry him through to where the promise was released. Throughout the process he started considering God, rather than the circumstance. As a result Abraham started praising God, giving Him glory, building himself up in faith, being fully persuaded that God would do what He said He would. Praising unlocked the faith needed to see the promise fulfilled. And because of it Abraham's faith was credited to him as righteousness (Genesis 15:6; Romans 4:22).

You and I have been blessed by the faith of Abraham and Sarah. Because they believed God and saw the promise fulfilled. Abraham became the father of many nations and the father of faith. Now all who trust in Jesus as their Savior have been credited with the same righteousness that Abraham received by faith (Romans 4:23-24). All because they choose to believe God when the circumstances were impossible.

These People Were Still Living by Faith When they Died

"All these people were still living by faith when they died. They did not receive the things promised; they only saw them and welcomed them from a distance. And they admitted that they were aliens and strangers on earth" (Hebrews 11:13)

Faith has the ability to see the invisible, the impossible and the improbable. Faith takes what doesn't make sense to the natural mind and becomes the substance that moves the invisible forward until it becomes reality. There are many things in God's kingdom that require faith. The Word is full of promises that only become reality when believed and mixed with faith.

Interestingly, all of these men and women previously mentioned in Hebrews 11 died in faith, waiting for their promises to come to pass. It is counter-intuitive to think that these weren't fulfilled because it didn't happen in their lifetimes. But the scriptures say that they saw and welcomed them from a distance. Because of it, God was not ashamed to be called their God (Hebrews 11:16).

For example, Abraham believed God when He told him that he would be the father of many nations and through his Seed the Messiah would come (Galatians 3:16). God also revealed to Abraham through the promise that the entire world would be blessed by his faith, showing that God would justify the Gentiles through that same type of faith (Galatians 3:8). These were amazing promises. Abraham understood the implications of this; which is why he believed God and set the example of being declared righteous by faith (Genesis 15:6; Romans 4:22-23). He saw through spiritual eyes what God was going to do and got on board with His plan.

However, in Abraham's lifetime, he only got the down payment of the promise. Isaac was the beginning of its fulfillment but what was promised reached so far into the future that Abraham died in faith looking forward to a time when all would be fulfilled. That takes faith, and faith is what pleases God (Hebrews 11:6).

The examples of faith in Hebrews 11, show that these great men and women understood they were temporary residents on earth. They looked forward to their true home in heaven with God. They greeted the reality of their promises from a distance knowing it would eventually come to pass whether they were alive to see it or not. The reason is that God had something better planned for us, *"These were all commended for their faith, yet none of them received what had been promised. God had planned something better for us so that only together with us would they be made perfect" (Hebrews 11:39-40).*

We are the beneficiaries of their faith. We have witnessed these promises unfold throughout the centuries so that we too can partake in the precious promises of God; be thankful that they had the audacity to walk in faith regardless of their impossible situations. No wonder they were commended for their faith that continually blesses humanity.

God is Not Ashamed to be Called Their God

"People who say such things show that they are looking for a country of their own. If they had been thinking of the country they had left, they would have had opportunity to return. Instead, they were longing for a better country—a heavenly one. Therefore God is not ashamed to be called their God, for he has prepared a city for them" (Hebrews 11:14-16)

What the world looks at as strange, God looks at with favor. As in the examples from the patriarchs, these men and women of faith gave up everything in pursuit of something better. They left family, comfort and familiarity to chase after the promise God. They looked forward in faith, never looking back, lest they give themselves the opportunity to return to what they left.

Because of this God was not ashamed to be called their God. In fact, He allowed the generations that followed to call these men of faith by His surname. Hence to be known and referred to as The God of Abraham, Isaac and Jacob (Exodus 3:6, 15; 4:5). This is amazing, that God aligned His name with these men because of their faith.

Admitting that they were strangers on earth freed them to pursue God by faith. Discounting the circumstances and what they left behind in hopes of a better life and a better future. And true to His word, God has prepared a city for them. They only needed to look forward in faith seeing what God had prepared so they would not become homesick and return to what they left.

In the same way, we too must look forward in faith to all that God has planned for us. We must disregard the pleasures of this world, in hopes of a better and brighter future. Just like Abraham, Isaac and Jacob; God is not ashamed to be called our God and He is preparing a wonderful future for us. All we need to do is continue in faith believing God will remain true to His Word and His promises.

By Faith Abraham
Offered Isaac as a Sacrifice

"By faith Abraham, when God tested him, offered Isaac as a sacrifice. He who had received the promises was about to sacrifice his one and only son, even though God had said to him, "It is through Isaac that your offspring will be reckoned." Abraham reasoned that God could raise the dead, and figuratively speaking, he did receive Isaac back from death" (Hebrews 11:17-19)

Abraham is called the father of faith for a reason. He acted in faith when the circumstances seemed to contradict the promise. He reasoned that God would remain faithful to His promises so he made up his mind to follow God's instructions no matter the cost.

Abraham had been promised these things by God. First, God promised him that He would make him into a great nation. Secondly, God was going to bless Abraham. Next, He was going to make his name great. Lastly, all nations and future generations on earth would be blessed through him (Genesis 12:2-3). God confirmed and reiterated this promise many times to Abraham. The only thing required on his part was to believe what God had told him. Abraham did, this is why righteousness was credited to him (Genesis 15:6).

Then when Abraham was ninety-nine years old the Lord once again appeared to him to confirm what was originally promised saying, *"I am God Almighty; walk before me and be blameless. I will confirm my covenant between me and you and will greatly increase your numbers." Abram fell facedown, and God said to him, "As for me, this is my covenant with you: You will be the father of many nations. No longer will you be called Abram; your name will be Abraham, for I have made you a father of many nations. I will make you very fruitful; I will make nations of you, and kings will come from you. I will establish my covenant as an everlasting covenant between me and you and your descendants after you for the generations to come, to be your God and the God of your descendants after you. The whole land of Canaan, where you are now an alien, I will give as an everlasting possession to you and your descendants after you; and I will be their God"* (Genesis 17:1b-8). That day God changed the names of both Abram and Sarai giving them new meaning to confirm that He considered this fulfilled. Then He gave Abraham the token of circumcision as an outward showing of the faith he inwardly had. Everything happened just as the Lord said it would, Sarah became pregnant and gave birth to Isaac, the long awaited promised son.

Because of this long history of believing God and seeing these promises fulfilled just as God said they would be, Abraham followed God's instruction to sacrifice his one and only son of promise. He reasoned that God was able to raise him up from death because the covenant still had things waiting to be fulfilled. It stated that the entire world would be blessed through Abraham and his Seed, meaning the Christ (Galatians 3:16). God made it very clear that this would come through Isaac not Ishmael (Genesis 17:21; 21:12).

This act of faith is a type and shadow of Christ. Abraham took his one and only son and willingly set out to sacrifice him. When God saw he was intent on obeying His instructions no matter the cost, He stopped Abraham saying, *"Do not lay a hand on the boy," he said. "Do not do anything to him. Now I know that you fear God, because you have not withheld from me your son, your only son"* (Genesis 22:12). Abraham reasoned that God would raise Isaac from the dead and figuratively speaking Abraham did receive him back from the dead.

God tested Abraham and while this testing of faith was still in progress the Lord saw the extent he was willing to go. Because of this, God spared Isaac but in his place willingly gave His one and only Son. Abraham truly blessed the entire world because he didn't withhold his son, so God didn't withhold His. Abraham's act of faith ensured the world of its blessing. That blessing was in the person of Jesus Christ who died to set us free. God showed the gospel beforehand to Abraham so he could see how his faith would bless the world (Galatians 3:8). This is why we celebrate the faith that Abraham had, because we too are included in these wonderful promises that were obtained by Abraham believing God and acting on faith!

By Faith Isaac
Blessed Jacob and Esau

"By faith Isaac blessed Jacob and Esau in regard
to their future" (Hebrews 11:20)

Isaac acted in faith by pronouncing blessings on both of his sons. He looked far into the future and spoke about what would be. Jacob received a favorable blessing (Genesis 27:27-29) while Esau received what he deserved (Genesis 27:39-40). Although Esau was the first born son, Jacob was the one who rightfully received the blessing as first born. Isaac, by faith, gave Jacob what was rightfully his.

When Rebekah was pregnant with twins, she inquired of the Lord because the babies jostled within her. Before the twins were born, the Lord had spoke concerning them. God told Rebekah, *"Two nations are in your womb, and two peoples from within you will be separated; one people will be stronger than the other, and the older will serve the younger" (Genesis 25:23).*

As life unfolded, Esau chose to sell his birthright as the firstborn son to Jacob for a bowl of stew. He came in famished from the field and agreed to sell it in exchange for food (Genesis 25:29-34). Hebrews 12:16 calls Esau godless and sacrilegious. Selling his birthright for a single meal shows how he disregarded and despised it. Then when it mattered, when the blessing was to be passed down, he wanted to regain his inheritance but was rejected.

When the time came and Isaac was going to bless Esau, Rebekah remembered what the Lord told her about the twins and encouraged Jacob, who rightfully possessed the birthright after Esau sold it to him, to obtain his father's blessing. Jacob prepared a meal, dressed as Esau and went before his father and Isaac blessed him (Genesis 27).

When Esau found out, there was pleading and many tears but Isaac replied to him, *"I have made him lord over you and have made all his relatives his servants, and I have sustained him with grain and new wine. So what can I possibly do for you, my son?" (Genesis 27:37)*. Isaac abided by his blessing. He did not go back on his word which confirmed the word the Lord spoke to Rebekah when pregnant with the twins. He also confirmed that the birthright rightfully belonged to Jacob.

Isaac then blessed Esau saying, *"Your dwelling will be away from the earth's richness, away from the dew of heaven above. You will live by the sword and you will serve your brother. But when you grow restless, you will throw his yoke from off your neck" (Genesis 27:39-40)*.

After this happened Esau was enraged and vowed to kill Jacob who fled at his mother's request. The amazing thing is that God then confirmed this blessing to Jacob by calling himself the God of Abraham and Isaac, then He confirmed an oath to Jacob similar to that which Abraham enjoyed, *"There above it stood the LORD, and he said: "I am the LORD, the God of your father Abraham and the God of Isaac. I will give you and your descendants the land on which you are lying. Your descendants will be like the dust of the earth, and you will spread out to the west and to the east, to the north and to the south. All peoples on earth will be blessed through you and your offspring. I am with you and will watch over you wherever you go, and I will bring you back to this land. I will not leave you until I have done what I have promised you" (Genesis 28:13-15)*. God confirmed that what Jacob did in obtaining his birthright was righteous.

By faith, Isaac looked into the future and pronounced blessing on both of his sons. To Jacob he pronounced blessing, favor and that the nations of the world would serve him (Genesis 27:27-29). To Esau he pronounced strife and hardship for generations to come (Genesis 27:39-40). And both came to pass just as he said (Malachi 1:3; Romans 9:13).

By Faith Jacob Blessed Joseph's Sons

"By faith Jacob, when he was dying, blessed each of Joseph's sons, and worshiped as he leaned on the top of his staff" (Hebrews 11:21)

When Jacob's time was near an end, he took aside Joseph's sons to bless them. He had claimed Joseph's first born sons, Ephraim and Manasseh, as his own. As was the custom, when Joseph presented them before Jacob, he placed Manasseh, his first born, toward his right hand and Ephraim towards his left. But Jacob in faith choose Ephraim, though he was younger, to inherit the blessing.

"Then he blessed Joseph and said, "May the God before whom my fathers Abraham and Isaac walked, the God who has been my shepherd all my life to this day, the Angel who has delivered me from all harm —may he bless these boys. May they be called by my name and the names of my fathers Abraham and Isaac, and may they increase greatly upon the earth" (Genesis 48:15-16).

At hearing this and seeing that Jacob had placed his right hand on Ephraim's head, Joseph was displeased. Trying to correct it, Joseph told him to put his right hand on his firstborn. Jacob confirmed that Manasseh would also be a great people, but in faith, he pronounced his blessing on Ephraim.

Throughout Israel's history, the tribe of Ephraim flourished. From the rule of the Judges onward, this tribe became synonymous with Israel as it was the largest of the ten northern tribes. This was prophesied by Jacob, showing divine inspiration by choosing the younger son over the older. Moses also blessed this tribe in a similar manner. *"About Joseph he said: "May the LORD bless his land with the precious dew from heaven above and with the deep waters that lie below; with the best the sun brings forth and the finest the moon can yield; with the choicest gifts of the ancient mountains and the fruitfulness of the everlasting hills; with the best gifts of the earth and its fullness and the favor of him who dwelt in the burning bush. Let all these rest on the head of Joseph, on the brow of the prince among his brothers. In majesty he is like a firstborn bull; his horns are the horns of a wild ox. With them he will gore the nations, even those at the ends of the earth. Such are the ten thousands of Ephraim; such are the thousands of Manasseh" (Deuteronomy 33:13-17).*

Reuben, Jacob's firstborn son forfeited his birthright by sleeping with Bilhah, his father's concubine (Genesis 35:22). By Jacob adopting Joseph's two sons as his own and giving them a portion, he basically gave Joseph the double portion belonging to the first born son, which would have been Reuben. After that, Judah, another son, became tribal leader in Reuben's place (Genesis 49:8-10). He also inherited a wonderful blessing that the Messiah would come through his line (Genesis 49:10).

All of these things happened by faith and Jacob pronounced his blessing under the divine inspiration of God. He looked far into the future and worshiped the Lord in anticipation of bringing it all to pass, just as it had been spoken.

By Faith Joseph Spoke About the Exodus

"By faith Joseph, when his end was near, spoke about the exodus of the Israelites from Egypt and gave instructions about his bones" (Hebrews 11:22)

Speaking something about the future takes faith, Joseph is a great example of this. When the end of his life was drawing near he remembered the promise God made to Abraham about the land he was to inherit and gave instructions for the Israelites to leave Egypt in pursuit of it.

"Then Joseph said to his brothers, "I am about to die. But God will surely come to your aid and take you up out of this land to the land he promised on oath to Abraham, Isaac and Jacob." And Joseph made the sons of Israel swear an oath and said, "God will surely come to your aid, and then you must carry my bones up from this place" (Genesis 50:24-25).

Whether or not Joseph understood the implications of these instructions doesn't really matter, Joseph spoke them in faith, participating in the plan of God. Over four hundred years later this mass exodus took place just as Joseph prophesied.

Interestingly, Moses is the one who completed Joseph's instructions, *"Moses took the bones of Joseph with him because Joseph had made the sons of Israel swear an oath. He had said, "God will surely come to your aid, and then you must carry my bones up with you from this place" (Exodus 13:19).*

This originated by the faith of one godly man who had the courage to speak in faith, so future generations would know what they were supposed to do. Joseph reminded the children of Israel of God's promise and encouraged them to pursue it even when it seemed impossible because of their captivity.

By Faith Moses' Parents Hid Him for Three Months

"By faith Moses' parents hid him for three months after he was born, because they saw he was no ordinary child, and they were not afraid of the king's edict" (Hebrews 11:23)

It takes faith to ignore and disregard an edict of the king to do what is right. As the Israelites flourished in Egypt the Egyptians became increasingly aware of them, setting out to rule and oppress them. At first the king instructed the midwives to kill each baby that was born a boy. *"The king of Egypt said to the Hebrew midwives, whose names were Shiphrah and Puah, "When you help the Hebrew women in childbirth and observe them on the delivery stool, if it is a boy, kill him; but if it is a girl, let her live" (Exodus 1:15-16).*

However, the midwives feared God and did not do what the king instructed. When confronted by the king the women replied, *"Hebrew women are not like Egyptian women; they are vigorous and give birth before the midwives arrive" (Exodus 1:19).* God showed favor to the midwives giving them families of their own. After this, the king stopped giving mere suggestions and ordered the people, *"Every boy that is born you must throw into the Nile, but let every girl live" (Exodus 1:22).*

When Moses' parents became pregnant, giving birth to a son, his mother hid him away for many months until it was no longer possible to do so. Then she coated a papyrus basket in tar and set it afloat on the Nile. She would not bow to the king's order and kill her son. By faith, she provided a means to save him by placing him securely in the same waters that were meant to kill him.

As his sister kept watch over the basket, Pharaoh's daughter found the babe floating on the river and drew him out. She had compassion on him knowing he was a Hebrew child. Moses' sister was sent to fetch his real mother so she could continue nursing him. *"When the child grew older, she took him to Pharaoh's daughter and he became her son. She named him Moses, saying, "I drew him out of the water" (Exodus 2:10).*

By faith Moses' parents disregarded their lives to save their son who would grow up to deliver his people from slavery. The Nile was meant to be the tool to kill him, but God used that very thing to be the means for his deliverance. Even the meaning of his name reflects the miracle that occurred because God was faithful to His promise of sending a deliverer to the Israelites.

When we step out in faith, God will always meet us to carry it through. He will use the very things intended for harm to save us. Like Moses' parents, we too can participate in His mighty works by being sensitive to His leading in our lives.

By Faith Moses Refused to be Known as the Son of Pharaoh's Daughter

"By faith Moses, when he had grown up, refused to be known as the son of Pharaoh's daughter. He chose to be mistreated along with the people of God rather than to enjoy the pleasures of sin for a short time. He regarded disgrace for the sake of Christ as of greater value than the treasures of Egypt, because he was looking ahead to his reward" (Hebrews 11:24-26)

God will always reveal himself to those whose hearts are sensitive and looking for Him. In fact, God made a habit of revealing to the Old Testament patriarchs His plan of salvation through the promised Messiah. When Moses got a glimpse of this promise, the scriptures record that he chose to be mistreated with the people of God rather than enjoy his position among the Egyptians. He considered disgrace for the sake of Christ of far greater value. This shows that he was looking forward in faith to something far greater than the pleasures of this life.

To the outside world, this seems absurd. He was rescued by the daughter of Pharaoh as a baby, raised under Pharaoh's influence, wealth and position. In every sense of the word, he had it all. He had power, authority, riches and family connections. But this doesn't compare or hold a candle to what God offers. Moses willingly gave it all up to be associated with the mistreated people of Israel and for the sake of Christ.

This is amazing, this shows that Christ Jesus is and will always be the pinnacle of history. His work on the cross was so wonderful that Moses looked forward to it and it changed the course of his life and what he considered valuable. The world and all its splendor didn't compare to the riches of glory.

God, true to His wonderful nature fulfilled His promise to the people of Israel in Moses' lifetime. He saw firsthand the marvelous works of God in bringing the people out of bondage and into the promised land. *"During that long period, the king of Egypt died. The Israelites groaned in their slavery and cried out, and their cry for help because of their slavery went up to God. God heard their groaning and he remembered his covenant with Abraham, with Isaac and with Jacob. So God looked on the Israelites and was concerned about them" (Exodus 2:23-25).* He even used Moses as the means to bring it all to pass.

The Exodus of the Israelites from Egypt is a wonderful type and shadow of the deliverance from bondage of sin and death that Christ Jesus frees us from. Moses looked far into the future and saw what would be, which is why he disregarded everything for the sake of Christ. Faith was the substance that brought him through until his reward. Today we celebrate his faith as recorded in the Hebrews Hall of Fame and are thankful for his foresight in trusting God to fulfill His wonderful promises.

By Faith Moses
Kept the Passover

"By faith he left Egypt, not fearing the king's anger; he persevered because he saw him who is invisible. By faith he kept the Passover and the sprinkling of blood, so that the destroyer of the firstborn would not touch the firstborn of Israel" (Hebrews 11:27-28)

Moses lived a life propagated by faith in an unseen God. This faith was the means to see what was invisible and hidden to others. In return, God revealed Himself constantly to Moses making provision for him. Because Moses had faith, he left Egypt undismayed by the wrath of Pharaoh who was trying to kill him (Exodus 2:15). Instead he set his face steadily toward Him who is invisible disregarding everything else.

Because of this lifestyle of faith, Moses oversaw and instructed the people of Israel to carry out the Passover. This would be the breaking point for Pharaoh but a glorious triumph for Moses. The angel of the Lord was going to pass through the land and strike down the firstborn, both men and animals, it was a sign of judgment on Egypt (Exodus 12:12). However, God instructed the Israelites to slaughter a Passover lamb and mark the doorposts of their homes with the blood. The blood was a sign for them, when the Lord saw the blood the destroyer would pass over that house and everyone inside would be safe (Exodus 12:13). Moses, by faith, relayed this message to the Israelites and the entire nation did what Moses instructed (Exodus 12:28).

Because of this marvelous act of faith, when nothing like this had ever taken place before, the entire nation of Israel was spared and they learned to trust in God. Egypt was not as fortunate. The Bible records, *"At midnight the LORD struck down all the firstborn in Egypt, from the firstborn of Pharaoh, who sat on the throne, to the firstborn of the prisoner, who was in the dungeon, and the firstborn of all the livestock as well. Pharaoh and all his officials and all the Egyptians got up during the night, and there was loud wailing in Egypt, for there was not a house without someone dead" (Exodus 12:29-30).*

As a result, Pharaoh summoned Moses and Aaron during the night and told them to leave taking with them the entire nation, their families and all their livestock. Amazingly, the Lord made the Egyptians favorably disposed towards the Israelites as well and they gave them articles of silver, gold and clothing. In fact, they plundered Egypt (Exodus 12:35-36). They took with them the spoils and wealth of Egypt, just recompense for hundreds of years of hard labor.

By faith, Moses kept the Passover and saw the deliverance of his people in a mighty act of God. Simple trust and confidence in God was all it took to bring them out. And God proved He is always faithful to His Word.

By Faith the People Passed Through the Red Sea on Dry Land

"By faith the people passed through the Red Sea as on dry land; but when the Egyptians tried to do so, they were drowned" (Hebrews 11:29)

It takes faith to walk into the midst of the sea with water piled high to both your left and right side trusting that you will make it safely across. However, this is exactly what the Israelites did as they fled from the Egyptians. God demonstrated His power both to Israel and the nation of Egypt as He fully delivered His children from their captors.

As they fled, the Israelites looked back to see the Egyptians pursuing them. Crying out against Moses for bringing them to a place of sure death, Moses responded in faith *"Do not be afraid. Stand firm and you will see the deliverance the LORD will bring you today. The Egyptians you see today you will never see again. The LORD will fight for you; you need only to be still" (Exodus 14:13-14).* He spoke in faith that the Lord would deliver his people before he knew what the plan for deliverance was.

The account of what happened next was amazing, *"Then the LORD said to Moses, "Why are you crying out to me? Tell the Israelites to move on. Raise your staff and stretch out your hand over the sea to divide the water so that the Israelites can go through the sea on dry ground. I will harden the hearts of the Egyptians so that they will go in after them. And I will gain glory through Pharaoh and all his army, through his chariots and his horsemen. The Egyptians will know that I am the LORD when I gain glory through Pharaoh, his chariots and his horsemen" (Exodus 14:15-18).*

The Lord responded to Moses faith and delivered His people as promised. Moses acted in faith by raising his staff and stretching out his hand over the sea and in return God moved the waters creating an escape path of dry ground. The angel of God blocked the way of the Egyptians so that the Israelites could escape. After the entire nation was safely across, the Egyptians pursued, only to be drowned as the waters returned to their natural place. God's power and glory was displayed as He delivered His people and fulfilled His Word.

Faith is what propelled Moses to lead the people out of Egypt and faith is what sustained them through their escape. God always responds to the faith of His children. *"As Scripture says, "Anyone who believes in him will never be put to shame" (Romans 10:11).*

By Faith the Walls
of Jericho Fell

"By faith the walls of Jericho fell, after the people had
marched around them for seven days" (Hebrews 11:30)

This account of defeat of Jericho truly belongs in the Hebrews Hall of Fame.
This was a crowning moment for Israel as they trusted God to make good
on His promise to them. After wandering the desert for forty years, due
to their unbelief, the first mission in the promised land of Canaan was to
conquer Jericho, a fortified city whose walls were thick and impenetrable.

Previously Joshua had sent two spies into Jericho to scope out the city and
their report was vastly different than the report given back to Moses the
first time spying out the promised land. Instead of doubt, dissension and
unbelief, the spies told the people, *"The LORD has surely given the whole
land into our hands; all the people are melting in fear because of us" (Joshua
2:24).*

As they prepared to defeat the city, instructions were given about how to
do it. The entire army was to march around the city every day for six days.
On the seventh day they were to march around the city seven times. Then
the priests were to blow their trumpets while the people shouted and the
walls would fall down for them to enter and fight. The Ark of the Covenant
would go before them to remind them of their covenant with God.

Joshua also gave further instructions, *"Joshua had commanded the people,
"Do not give a war cry, do not raise your voices, do not say a word until the day
I tell you to shout. Then shout!" (Joshua 6:10).* This was wisdom on Joshua's
part after witnessing the repercussions on the entire nation of Israel, caused
by the ten spies who had made negative reports. (Numbers 13:26-14:4).
The people of Israel had allowed these negative words to talk them out of

God's promise and His best for them. As a result they ended up wandering the desert for forty years until that entire generation died.

Since the idea of marching around the city day after day, believing at the end, the walls would cave in to deliver it into your hands takes faith, Joshua was helping them along forbidding them to speak any doubt. In fact, each day it probably got harder and harder to march around the city, I'm sure there were people camped on the walls shouting insults which only got worse with each passing day. I'm sure it would have been easy for the Israelites to talk themselves out of the victory even if only one person started voicing doubts. Instead they remained silent which allowed them to walk out their faith in what God had instructed them to do.

The result was complete and total victory. On the seventh day, they marched around the city seven times, blew the trumpets and shouted their war cry as they entered and defeated Jericho, burning it to the ground. They devoted the city to the Lord and destroyed with the sword every living thing, just as they were instructed. Only Rahab and the family that was with her was saved.

By faith the walls of Jericho fell and the people of Israel enjoyed great success. They took God at His promise and carried out His instructions allowing God to do exactly what He promised He would do. What a great lesson in faith for all future generations to study and examine.

By Faith the Prostitute Rahab was Redeemed

"By faith the prostitute Rahab, because she welcomed the spies, was not killed with those who were disobedient" (Hebrews 11:31)

Rahab had an understanding of God's character; an understanding that many of His covenant people lacked. As terror spread throughout the land, because of the Israelites camped at the Jordan awaiting entrance into their promised land, Rahab made a deal with the spies hidden in her house and God honored it. The account of Rahab's faith is an amazing story of redemption.

When Joshua sent spies into the land to bring back a report, they stopped at Jericho entering into Rahab's house. As a prostitute, her house gave them opportunity to blend in. After hiding them on the roof, she redirected the king's servants, who were looking for them, into the countryside on a wild goose chase. She reveals to the spies that the entire land was shaking with fear because their God's fame and the mighty works had preceded them for decades (Joshua 2:9-11).

Rahab's next move was amazing, she asked the spies to exchange her kindness for a sign that she and her family would be spared when Jericho was defeated (Joshua 2:12-13). Agreeing to her terms, they instructed her to keep the scarlet cord, on which they escaped in the window. Assuring that everyone remaining inside would be spared (Joshua 2:17-20).

What is interesting about this, is that Rahab made this deal based solely on God's grace. She was from Jericho, she was a harlot, she had no right to ask anything. Secondly, she put herself in grave danger by helping the spies and then remaining in the city surrounded by enemies who could turn on her if they knew her part in helping the Israelites. And yet, her token of this agreement and her life line was a scarlet cord hanging in plain view. This is a marvelous picture of redemption. She put her faith in the grace of God and God provided a way out giving her a reminder by the scarlet, blood-colored cord, ever present before her; reassuring her redemption was drawing nigh.

As the city fell, Joshua gave the spies the honor of bringing Rahab, her family and all her possessions out from the midst of the destruction and into the Israelite community (Joshua 6:22-25). She trusted God to save her because she had insight into God's character trusting solely in His goodness and His grace. God responded to her faith and forever commemorated her in the lineage of the Messiah, Jesus Christ (Matthew 1:5). Her story is one of redemption and restoration and will forever be celebrated in the Hebrews Hall of Fame.

The World Was Not Worthy of Them

"And what more shall I say? I do not have time to tell about Gideon, Barak, Samson, Jephthah, David, Samuel and the prophets, who through faith conquered kingdoms, administered justice, and gained what was promised; who shut the mouths of lions, quenched the fury of the flames, and escaped the edge of the sword; whose weakness was turned to strength; and who became powerful in battle and routed foreign armies. Women received back their dead, raised to life again. Others were tortured and refused to be released, so that they might gain a better resurrection. Some faced jeers and flogging, while still others were chained and put in prison. They were stoned; they were sawed in two; they were put to death by the sword. They went about in sheepskins and goatskins, destitute, persecuted and mistreated— the world was not worthy of them. They wandered in deserts and mountains, and in caves and holes in the ground" (Hebrews 11:32-38)

Faith has always been the defining characteristic of God's people. Throughout the entire chapter of Hebrews 11, we see example after example of faith. Circumstances grim, chances for success low and yet, God's people always flourish because of faith and God's promise to respond to it. Faith is so important to the believer that Paul told the Corinthian church, *"We live by faith, not by sight" (II Corinthians 5:7).* The Amplified Bible describes it this way, *"For we walk by faith [we regulate our lives and conduct ourselves by our conviction or belief respecting man's relationship to God and divine things, with trust and holy fervor; thus we walk] not by sight or appearance"* *(II Corinthians 5:7 AMP).*

In every example given, faith was a lifestyle, there was no going back to live a normal life. Faith made the difference from ordinary into extraordinary, although in the natural they faced torment, beatings, prison, mutilation and death, wandering in the deserts, mountains and living in caves. However, the scripture says that the world was not worthy of them. Like Enoch, they received a good report that God was pleased with them and it is still on record today, centuries after their experiences.

These examples were given to encourage and give us hope. Throughout the entirety of the scriptures we see countless examples of the men and women of faith. This was written for us, Paul said, *"For everything that was written in the past was written to teach us, so that through endurance and the encouragement of the Scriptures we might have hope" (Romans 15:4)*. Since faith is the substance of things hoped for (Hebrews 11:1), the scriptures were given to give us a place to aim, hope.

No wonder the world was not worthy of the countless individuals that decided to trust God when all else seemed hopeless. They have received a good report and have run their race so that we might draw encouragement from their example of faith. Therefore, *"Let us not become weary in doing good, for at the proper time we will reap a harvest if we do not give up" (Galatians 6:9)*.

God Had Planned Something Better for Us

"These were all commended for their faith, yet none of them received what had been promised. God had planned something better for us so that only together with us would they be made perfect" (Hebrews 11:39-40)

To die in faith, believing God until the very end was a privilege that the patriarchs shared. Their ultimate promise was the Messiah and they looked forward in faith until the time of Jesus. God had planned this for us, so along with these heroes of faith we would be the recipients of this promise. David saw what New Testament believers would have and called us blessed and highly favored (Psalm 32:1-2). We now live in the time they saw from a distance. God truly had something better planned for us!

Every example of faith given, is to solidify the message of mercy and redemption in the book of Hebrews. Jesus' sacrifice for us, made us righteous, holy and cleansed from the guilt of sin. He resides, seated on His throne in heaven, as our High Priest guaranteeing this right standing with God. His blood has cleansed us and speaks a powerful word of righteousness on our behalf. Because of this we have confidence to live a dramatic faith-filled existence as the writer notes in chapter 10, *"we are not of those who shrink back and are destroyed, but of those who believe and are saved" (Hebrews 10:39).*

Those listed in Hebrews 11 understood this and yet they did not receive what had been promised. However we have, which is why we live and walk by faith (II Corinthians 5:7). This is what the ancients were commended for, it is what pleases God and it is what ensures and makes readily available the sweet and precious promises given to us in the Scriptures. Faith is how the righteous live (Habakkuk 2:4; Hebrews 10:38). Together with the patriarchs, we have now been made perfect by the blood of Jesus and we have received the blessings of their faith. What an amazing truth!

hebrews 12.

JESUS IS

OUR EXAMPLE

Fixing Our Eyes on Jesus

"Therefore, since we are surrounded by such a great cloud of witnesses, let us throw off everything that hinders and the sin that so easily entangles, and let us run with perseverance the race marked out for us. Let us fix our eyes on Jesus, the author and perfecter of our faith, who for the joy set before him endured the cross, scorning its shame, and sat down at the right hand of the throne of God. Consider him who endured such opposition from sinful men, so that you will not grow weary and lose heart" (Hebrews 12:1-3)

No matter what circumstances life brings, this passage of scripture is the remedy. Whatever trials come your way, this is the key to success in the middle of it. We even have an entire chapter of faith examples preceding this to encourage us. So whatever comes, if we fix our eyes on Jesus and consider what He endured while here on earth, we will never lose heart.

Every time I read this, I picture countless men and women lining the streets of heaven cheering for the saints still in the race. We are surrounded by a great cloud of witnesses who have borne testimony to the truth and have finished their course in this world. Learning from their examples, the writer encourages us to run with patient endurance the race marked for us.

He mentions two things to get rid of, so we can run well. First, he says to strip off and throw aside everything that weighs us down, hinders or encumbers us. This could be fear, this could be excuses, it could be a lot of things. This is unnecessary weight and we are to throw it aside and leave it. Secondly, we are also to remove sin that so readily entangles us. The Greek word here is *hamartia,* in which the first definition means *'to be without a share in'* as well as *'to miss the mark, to err, to be mistaken'*. Given the context of faith examples in this passage, the writer is talking about unbelief. We are to get rid of any unbelief as it clings and entangles and it hinders us from running well. Remember, faith pleases God (Hebrews 11:6) and it is impossible to do the things of God without faith. So to run our race, we need to get rid of unbelief so we can run with patient endurance, steadily and consistently making progress.

In the middle of life, it is easy to get distracted and off course. So we must always look to Jesus and focus on Him. The Amplified Bible paints a wonderful picture of this, *"Looking away [from all that will distract] to Jesus, Who is the Leader and the Source of our faith [giving the first incentive for our belief] and is also its Finisher [bringing it to maturity and perfection]. He, for the joy [of obtaining the prize] that was set before Him, endured the cross, despising and ignoring the shame, and is now seated at the right hand of the throne of God" (Hebrews 12:2 AMP)*. We have an amazing example in Jesus, who endured the unimaginable to obtain the prize of redemption. He looked forward with joy to the cross because He knew it meant restoration for mankind. He disregarded the shame of dying a criminal's death because the outcome far surpassed it. We are to consider this in comparison to our trials so that we do not grow weary, become exhausted or lose heart.

When we focus on the example set by Jesus and fix our eyes steadfastly on Him, then we will have great encouragement to faithfully continue moving forward with our mission in life. We should focus on the race set before us, until we run through the glorious finish line. We must consider Jesus, who endured opposition and bitter hostility and yet finished what He was called to do. So that we too, will continue moving forward with great joy and steadfastness.

Endure Hardship as Discipline; God is Treating You as Sons

"In your struggle against sin, you have not yet resisted to the point
of shedding your blood. And you have forgotten that word of
encouragement that addresses you as sons: "My son, do not
make light of the Lord's discipline, and do not lose heart when
he rebukes you, because the Lord disciplines those he loves,
and he punishes everyone he accepts as a son." Endure hardship
as discipline; God is treating you as sons. For what son is not
disciplined by his father? If you are not disciplined (and everyone
undergoes discipline), then you are illegitimate children and not true
sons. Moreover, we have all had human fathers who disciplined
us and we respected them for it. How much more should we
submit to the Father of our spirits and live!" (Hebrews 12:4-9)

At one point in my life I was struggling with a situation at work. I felt that
I had been treated unfairly. Everything I had worked for was taken away,
renamed and given to another who had joined our team under interesting
circumstances. To make matters worse, I felt that no one understood my
position or validated the feelings of betrayal I had toward the company,
toward this individual and toward my boss. It was a tumultuous time in my
life both personally and professionally. I greatly struggled over the whole
ordeal and after months, things did not get better, only worse.

One day, I went for a walk. While I walked I listened to scripture, it was
Jesus' Sermon on the Mount. The words spoken were as relevant that day
as the day He gave them. As I walked, His words burned holes in my chest.
Each sentence spoken seemed to weigh a thousand pounds. At the end I
was crying and I knew what I had to do. The Lord spoke into my heart

that I needed to seek forgiveness from my boss, even though to me, I was the one who had been wronged. The Lord dealt very sternly with me, but as I responded in obedience He gave me the grace to go to my boss, ask forgiveness and then healing began.

After humbling myself, both my professional and personal life got better and I learned an important lesson. The Lord desires the finished product to be pure and refined. Although trials and the circumstances of life do not mean that the Lord causes them, He can and does use them to perfect us. Just as the writer notes in this passage in Hebrews, we should view hardship as discipline which validates our status as God's sons and daughters.

God will speak truth to us in the midst of all circumstances in life. Sometimes, it is painful to hear but the outcome far outweighs the stretching and pain we experience in the midst. As in my example, the primary way God corrects us is through His word. Paul said, *"All Scripture is God-breathed and is useful for teaching, rebuking, correcting and training in righteousness, so that the man of God may be thoroughly equipped for every good work" (II Timothy 3:16-17).* David observed something similar in Psalm 94, *"Blessed is the man you discipline, O LORD, the man you teach from your law" (Psalm 94:12).*

The Word is the tool He uses to break the power of sin, pull down strongholds, correct us and train us in the way we should go. Just as our earthly fathers disciplined us in our youth so that we would turn out as good responsible adults, God also disciplines and refines us so that we are fully equipped and trained in righteousness. This is the perspective we need in the midst of all of life's circumstances.

Discipline Produces Holiness, Righteousness and Peace

"Our fathers disciplined us for a little while as they thought best; but God disciplines us for our good, that we may share in his holiness. No discipline seems pleasant at the time, but painful. Later on, however, it produces a harvest of righteousness and peace for those who have been trained by it. Therefore, strengthen your feeble arms and weak knees. "Make level paths for your feet," so that the lame may not be disabled, but rather healed" (Hebrews 12:10-13)

Christ's goal is to present His glorious Church to God, pure, holy and blameless. In every sense of the word this was accomplished on the cross. However, humanity being made up of a spirit, a soul and a body (I Thessalonians 5:23), and still being one-third flesh in our soulish realm, will struggle in life and need correction. Just as a father disciplines his children, God will discipline us so that we will share in His holiness.

A few verses before, the writer said to endure hardship as discipline (Hebrews 12:7). Although painful, the results of correction far outweigh the process of discipline. On the other side we come through refined, purified, tried and tested. The goal is to train us in righteousness, peace and holiness.

Since this process is expected and proves our status as heirs, it is important to understand how God will discipline. Paul told Timothy that the Word is useful for correcting and training, *"All Scripture is God-breathed and is useful for teaching, rebuking, correcting and training in righteousness, so that the man of God may be thoroughly equipped for every good work" (II Timothy 3:16-17).* God speaks and trains us through His Word. Everything needed for life and godliness comes through the knowledge of Him (II Peter 1:3-4), so it only makes sense that this knowledge, through the Word, will train and correct us in the way we should go.

Paul confirmed this to the church at Ephesus, *"Husbands, love your wives, just as Christ loved the church and gave himself up for her to make her holy, cleansing her by the washing with water through the word, and to present her to himself as a radiant church, without stain or wrinkle or any other blemish, but holy and blameless"* (Ephesians 5:25-27).

Keeping this perspective in mind should allow us to be sensitive to the Lord's leading in all things. Our responsibility is to heed His Word and repent, which just means turning and going the other way. When this happens we allow righteousness, peace and holiness to dictate our lives which is the desired outcome of discipline. Just as He told the church of Laodicea, *"Those whom I love I rebuke and discipline. So be earnest, and repent. Here I am! I stand at the door and knock. If anyone hears my voice and opens the door, I will come in and eat with him, and he with me. To him who overcomes, I will give the right to sit with me on my throne, just as I overcame and sat down with my Father on his throne. He who has an ear, let him hear what the Spirit says to the churches"* (Revelation 3:19-22).

Holiness is the Byproduct of Relationship

"Make every effort to live in peace with all men and to be holy; without holiness no one will see the Lord" (Hebrews 12:14)

In following the example set by the Lord Jesus, we are to toss off everything that hinders us and look to Him as an example of perseverance and faith (Hebrews 12:1-3). One way to accomplish this is to live at peace with others and to pursue holiness.

Holiness can be defined in two ways. First holiness means consecration and purification, it is the result of being set apart to God (I Corinthians 1:30; II Thessalonians 2:13; I Peter 1:2). This happens when we enter into a relationship with God by faith in Jesus (Acts 26:18; I Corinthians 6:11).

Paul said in Romans, *"But now that you have been set free from sin and have become slaves to God, the benefit you reap leads to holiness, and the result is eternal life" (Romans 6:22).* Holiness is a byproduct of our union with Christ, it is the reward of that union. It is not through natural means that we possess this. Holiness comes as a gift through Christ Jesus.

Secondly, holiness is also the effect of being consecrated or being set apart. It is sanctification of our heart and its what becomes evident in our daily lives through union with God. It is the outgrowth of leaving behind old desires and pursuing the things of God. Sanctification is a process for the believer (Romans 6:19, 22; I Thessalonians 4:3-4, 7; Hebrews 12:14).

In the New Testament, the process of sanctification or holiness can be understood in these ways, first it is God's will for the believer (I Thessalonians 4:3). Secondly, it is learned by God and taught by His Word (Psalm 17:4; 119:9; John 17:17-19). Next, the Holy Spirit is the agent in sanctification

redemption.

(Romans 15:16; I Corinthians 6:11; II Thessalonians 2:13; I Peter 1:2). And lastly, holiness must be pursued by the believer (Hebrews 12:14). We are to be built up by obedience to the Word following the example of Christ Jesus according to the Holy Spirit who enables this change to happen.

Relationship with Christ and attention to His Word will birth holiness into the natural realm. He has already provided this by faith in Him, as we were given everything needed to live as Christ in this world (Galatians 5:22-25; I John 4:17). This is why, as believers, we must pursue holiness; letting His truth and life-giving Spirit change us from the inside out. Letting what is on the inside of us match what the world sees, a life set apart, sanctified and holy. Without it, others will not see the Lord working in us.

This is an amazing truth! God has sanctified us and set us apart. He has given us everything we need to live a holy life. We respond by pursuing holiness in every aspect of our walk with Him. By His Word and by His Spirit we are changed and everyone around will experience the result of our sanctification!

Cutting Down the Bitter Root with Grace

"See to it that no one misses the grace of God and that no bitter root grows up to cause trouble and defile many" (Hebrews 12:15)

Grace does not stop being extended to mankind once they are born again. The opposite is actually true; through Jesus we receive grace upon grace (John 1:16). God's grace is continually influencing us as believers. His grace is the anchor that keeps us turned and focused on Christ, growing in faith, growing in the knowledge of God and it is what continually strengthens us in His love. Remaining steadfast in that grace protects us from harm.

One of the admonishments from the writer of Hebrews is to be on the lookout for one another; encouraging each other to remain secure in the state of grace, God's unmerited favor and spiritual blessing. Grace protects our heart from allowing bitterness from situations and experiences to creep in and wreak havoc. The attitude of bitterness is likened to a bitter root that grows and produces fruit of its kind.

It is interesting that bitterness will not only affect your own life but this verse explains that when it grows it will cause trouble by defiling many. By definition defilement means to stain, to soil, to sully or to contaminate. Bitterness can overflow and take root in others very easily when unchecked and released. This is why we must pay attention to the grace of God. His grace covers a multitude of sins. His grace has the power to wash over resentment, hurt and misunderstandings so bitterness has no place to grow. His grace can replace hurt with healing, which is exactly what it will do when we let it.

In the previous verse, we are encouraged to live at peace and be holy, this verse provides a practical way in which to do this; we are to remain steadfast

redemption.

in God's grace allowing it to dictate our reaction to all situations. God's grace is what transforms us continually into the men and women He has called us to be.

Beware of Sexual Immorality

"See that no one is sexually immoral, or is godless like Esau, who for a single meal sold his inheritance rights as the oldest son. Afterward, as you know, when he wanted to inherit this blessing, he was rejected. He could bring about no change of mind, though he sought the blessing with tears" (Hebrews 12:16-17)

Did you know that faith in Jesus brings you into an elite group of royal priests (I Peter 2:5)? Jesus bestows His righteousness to you the moment you believe (Romans 3:21-22; II Corinthians 5:21). The result is that God looks at you in the same way, with the same love, as He looks at His Son Jesus (John 17:22-23; I John 4:17). This is incredible! Not only are we redeemed and saved from wrath and judgment but we are given the rights of sons and daughters of the Most High God (Romans 8:15) and entitled to an inheritance that can never perish, spoil or fade (Romans 8:17; I Peter 1:4).

This change happens at the moment we believe and it makes us entirely different than we once were, (II Corinthians 5:17). We no longer belong to the rank of sinners; instead we belong to God as a holy and righteous people. Therefore, it is important for us to act as who we are, not what we were.

Previously, the writer of Hebrews instructed us to be holy by pursuing holiness and acting on the Word of God which gives instruction (Hebrews 12:14). Now, the charge in this verse is geared specifically toward our sexual nature. As believers we are to abstain from sexual sin, because it is God's will that we are holy (I Thessalonians 4:3; I Peter 1:16).

Paul wrote specifically about this, *"Flee from sexual immorality. All other sins a man commits are outside his body, but he who sins sexually sins against his own body. Do you not know that your body is a temple of the Holy Spirit, who is in you, whom you have received from God? You are not your own; you were bought at a price. Therefore honor God with your body" (I Corinthians 6:18-20).* The reason the sin is committed against your own body is in the previous verse, *"But he who unites himself with the Lord is one with him in spirit" (I Corinthians 6:17).*

To help us understand this, the writer uses the example of Esau, who by tradition, rightfully owned the birthright as the oldest son. In his lust for the physical, Esau traded this incredible blessing for a bowl of stew (Genesis 25:29-34). The Bible calls him godless and sacrilegious because of this (Hebrews 12:16-17). He despised and disdained the family blessing for that which was temporary. Afterwards, Isaac honored this transaction and Jacob received the blessing as rightful heir, regardless of the tears and protest of Esau (Genesis 27:27-29, 38; Hebrews 11:20).

In the same way, we are not to trade a holy relationship, defile the marriage covenant for temporary gratification of the body. God has given sex as a special thing between a husband and wife. He has given it to us, to bless us and uses the marriage relationship to illustrate His covenant with us (Ephesians 5:25-32). Which is why, as believers we are to protect this from defilement and honor it our entire lives. God desires so much more for us that what is temporary; *"So we fix our eyes not on what is seen, but on what is unseen. For what is seen is temporary, but what is unseen is eternal" (II Corinthians 4:18).*

You Have Come to God and Jesus the Mediator of a New Covenant

"You have not come to a mountain that can be touched and that is burning with fire; to darkness, gloom and storm; to a trumpet blast or to such a voice speaking words that those who heard it begged that no further word be spoken to them, because they could not bear what was commanded: "If even an animal touches the mountain, it must be stoned." The sight was so terrifying that Moses said, "I am trembling with fear. But you have come to Mount Zion, to the heavenly Jerusalem, the city of the living God. You have come to thousands upon thousands of angels in joyful assembly, to the church of the firstborn, whose names are written in heaven. You have come to God, the judge of all men, to the spirits of righteous men made perfect, to Jesus the mediator of a new covenant, and to the sprinkled blood that speaks a better word than the blood of Abel" (Hebrews 12:18-24)

God's desire has always been to create a people for himself. As He assembled the Israelites together at Mount Sinai to give them the law, He told them that if they obeyed His decrees and kept His covenant they would be for Him, a kingdom of priests and a holy nation (Exodus 19:6). They were to be His people, a treasured possession (Exodus 19:5).

At this time, the Lord had Moses assemble the entire nation to speak directly to them from a cloud so the people would hear Him and put their trust in Him (Exodus 19:9). However they were strictly warned not to touch the mountain or they would be killed (Exodus 19:12). The people washed and consecrated themselves as Moses led them out, to meet face to face with God (Exodus 19:14, 17).

The whole sight was terrifying (Exodus 19:18-19; 20:18-21; Deuteronomy 4:11-12; 5:4-5, 22-27). God gave the Ten Commandments to the entire nation of Israel and afterwards they begged Moses to speak directly to God on their behalf. *"When the people saw the thunder and lightning and heard the trumpet and saw the mountain in smoke, they trembled with fear. They stayed at a distance and said to Moses, "Speak to us yourself and we will listen. But do not have God speak to us or we will die" (Exodus 20:18-19).* They wanted Moses to mediate for them, it was such a terrifying experience that they did not want to hear directly from God because they were afraid. They told Moses *"Go near and listen to all that the Lord our God says. Then tell us whatever the Lord our God tells you. We will listen and obey" (Deuteronomy 5:27).*

This was how it was under the Old Covenant. God's awesomeness was magnificent but also terrifying. Because of this, the Israelites did not wish to approach God individually, they chose to let Moses speak to God on their behalf. However, we as New Testament believers have not come to a mountain burning with fire and to a sight so terrifying that we run and hide. Instead we come to Mount Zion to the city of the living God and the perfect mediator Jesus Christ (I Timothy 2:5).

In fact, this illustration is a perfect summary of Hebrews and the differences between the Old and New Covenants. This entire book is focused solely on Jesus Christ and the change He has made in how we approach God now that we are holy and righteous.

Unlike the Israelites who trembled at the sight and sound of God, we can boldly approach His throne and always receive grace and acceptance (Hebrews 4:16; 10:19-23). If Abel's blood poured out on the ground cried out to God for vengeance (Genesis 4:10), Jesus' blood poured out on the mercy seat continually speaks for grace upon grace (Zechariah 4:7; John 1:16; Hebrews 9:12, 14-15).

In light of this, we should have no fear or trepidation in coming to God the Father for anything. We should take a biblical view of what Jesus has done for us and run to Him knowing we are accepted and loved and God considers us holy and righteous. He holds us in high regard as sons and daughters. Therefore, *"Let us then approach the throne of grace with confidence, so that we may receive mercy and find grace to help us in our time of need" (Hebrews 4:16).*

So That What Cannot Be Shaken May Remain

"See to it that you do not refuse him who speaks. If they did not escape when they refused him who warned them on earth, how much less will we, if we turn away from him who warns us from heaven? At that time his voice shook the earth, but now he has promised, "Once more I will shake not only the earth but also the heavens." The words "once more" indicate the removing of what can be shaken —that is, created things—so that what cannot be shaken may remain" (Hebrews 12:25-27)

Unlike the Israelites who trembled with fear as God spoke to them from the earthly mountain, we speak directly to God, which is why it is very important to pay attention to the message. If the Israelites did not escape when God spoke to them from earth, how will we escape if we ignore what is spoken to us from His heavenly position?

At that time, His voice shook the earth and now, once again, the promise is that everything that can be shaken will be. In the end, everything created will be removed. *"But the day of the Lord will come like a thief. The heavens will disappear with a roar; the elements will be destroyed by fire, and the earth and everything in it will be laid bare. Since everything will be destroyed in this way, what kind of people ought you to be? You ought to live holy and godly lives as you look forward to the day of God and speed its coming. That day will bring about the destruction of the heavens by fire, and the elements will melt in the heat. But in keeping with his promise we are looking forward to a new heaven and a new earth, the home of righteousness" (II Peter 3:10-13).*

Everything created will be destroyed in this way in order that what cannot be shaken may remain for eternity. As believers we have been given a kingdom that cannot be shaken or removed (Ephesians 1:13-14; Hebrews

12:28). Which is why we must pay attention to what God is speaking to us; so that the things in our lives that need to be removed can be, now.

His desire has always been to create a holy and righteous people for Himself (Exodus 19:5-6; I Peter 2:9-10). Entering into this community was accomplished by Jesus and we enter into this standing by faith. We have been given the Holy Spirit as a guide and helpmate to show us the Father and to remind us of what He said.

Jesus, when preparing the disciples for the things that would come, gave instruction about the Holy Spirit (John 16). He made it very clear what His role would be in the believer's life. *"But when he, the Spirit of truth, comes, he will guide you into all truth. He will not speak on his own; he will speak only what he hears, and he will tell you what is yet to come. He will bring glory to me by taking from what is mine and making it known to you. All that belongs to the Father is mine. That is why I said the Spirit will take from what is mine and make it known to you" (John 16:13-15).* His function is to relay God's message to us and to make known God's will for our lives.

The more we heed the voice and direction of God in our lives, the more the strongholds and struggles of this world wash away so we will be the people that God has invited us to be. We have been called into a life of transformation (II Corinthians 5:17) which is why we must pay attention to the words spoken to us each day. Throughout this process we will find grace to help us and as change happens what remains, will last for eternity to the praise and glory of God. *"Therefore, since we are receiving a kingdom that cannot be shaken, let us be thankful, and so worship God acceptably with reverence and awe, for our "God is a consuming fire" (Hebrews 12:28-29).*

Our God is a Consuming Fire

"Therefore, since we are receiving a kingdom that cannot be shaken, let us be thankful, and so worship God acceptably with reverence and awe, for our "God is a consuming fire" (Hebrews 12:28-29)

In the end, when it all comes down to it, the only things that remain are you and God. The things of this life will pass away and be forgotten. The desires and troubles of this world will no longer exist and what was, will no longer be. In light of this what kind of people should we be?

Since we are receiving a kingdom that cannot be shaken or removed, we should be a grateful people who worship God because of the great and mighty things He has done for us. While we look forward to eternity, we do not need to wait for it to experience the abundant, intimate life promised. Through Christ Jesus we have already begun eternal life (John 17:3).

This is the perspective we should have each and every day of our lives, not focusing on the cares of this world, but focusing on the kingdom which cannot be shaken, because it is what will remain when all is said and done. God is a jealous God (Deuteronomy 4:23-24) and He desires intimacy with us. We should actively worship Him, being thankful for all He has done, making our lives count on the basis of what Jesus has done for us.

"Through Jesus, therefore, let us continually offer to God a sacrifice of praise— the fruit of lips that confess his name. And do not forget to do good and to share with others, for with such sacrifices God is pleased" (Hebrews 13:15-16).

hebrews 13.

THE CHANGELESS
CHRIST

Keep On Loving Each Other as Brothers

"Keep on loving each other as brothers. Do not forget to entertain strangers, for by so doing some people have entertained angels without knowing it" (Hebrews 13:1-2)

Loving our brethren is the mark of a true believer. In fact this is so important that many of the New Testament writers gave instructions on this very thing. Paul said, *"Love must be sincere. Hate what is evil; cling to what is good. Be devoted to one another in brotherly love. Honor one another above yourselves" (Romans 12:9-10)*. He went on to say, *"Share with God's people who are in need. Practice hospitality" (Romans 12:13)*. The Apostle John also mentioned this several times throughout all his writings. Perhaps I John 4:7 says it best, *"Dear friends, let us love one another, for love comes from God. Everyone who loves has been born of God and knows God" (I John 4:7)*.

This is important because loving each other, considering others before one's self summarizes the heart of God. When asked which commandment was the greatest *"Jesus replied: "Love the Lord your God with all your heart and with all your soul and with all your mind.' This is the first and greatest commandment. And the second is like it: 'Love your neighbor as yourself.' All the Law and the Prophets hang on these two commandments" (Matthew 22:37-40)*. It is amazing that once the first is achieved and practiced, the second happens as a result. God is love (I John 4:8), therefore abiding in that love will overflow into our own lives, affect our own relationships and it is what makes us complete (I John 4:11-12). Which is why Paul said, *"The entire law is summed up in a single command: "Love your neighbor as yourself" (Galatians 5:14)*.

If we practice loving our brothers, not forgetting to entertain strangers, then we are caring for God's people and being good stewards of what He has entrusted to us. As in the examples of Abraham and Lot from the book of Genesis we are encouraged by the fact that God gives us opportunities to care for people in need and represent His loving kindness to them (Genesis 18:1-8; 19:1-3). Because of their hospitality both Abraham and Lot entertained angels. The result for Abraham was word that Sarah would conceive within the year. Because of Lot's actions, he and his family were delivered from Sodom before it was destroyed. Both received blessings from their generosity.

Jesus also referred to this when teaching, *"Then the King will say to those on his right, 'Come, you who are blessed by my Father; take your inheritance, the kingdom prepared for you since the creation of the world. For I was hungry and you gave me something to eat, I was thirsty and you gave me something to drink, I was a stranger and you invited me in, I needed clothes and you clothed me, I was sick and you looked after me, I was in prison and you came to visit me.' "Then the righteous will answer him, 'Lord, when did we see you hungry and feed you, or thirsty and give you something to drink? When did we see you a stranger and invite you in, or needing clothes and clothe you? When did we see you sick or in prison and go to visit you?' "The King will reply, 'I tell you the truth, whatever you did for one of the least of these brothers of mine, you did for me'"* (Matthew 25:34-40). What a beautiful reminder that everything we do, we do for the Lord.

"Dear friends, since God so loved us, we also ought to love one another. No one has ever seen God; but if we love one another, God lives in us and his love is made complete in us" (I John 4:11-12).

Remember Those Who are Mistreated as if You Were Suffering

"Remember those in prison as if you were their fellow prisoners, and those who are mistreated as if you yourselves were suffering" (Hebrews 13:3)

All over the world intense persecution happens because of Christ. Jesus himself said, *"I have told you these things, so that in me you may have peace. In this world you will have trouble. But take heart! I have overcome the world"* *(John 16:33).* He did not want us to be unprepared that bearing His name will bring trouble, persecution and hardship.

Just as in the days of the apostles, all over the world, our brothers and sisters in Christ are locked up and tortured because they stand for Him. Many bear death sentences simply because they follow Christ. Many risk their lives and their families to meet, read a Bible if they can get one and encourage one another. Women are burned in the streets, men are locked up in prison and children suffer atrocities at the hands of others.

What should our godly response be? We need to stand together with these precious people praying for their strength and endurance. We need to give our resources when opportunities arise. We need to unite our voice together in outrage at their treatment demanding change! We need to bear with their suffering as if it were us that were suffering. The Church needs to act on their behalf.

These are the people who will stand before the Throne of God crying out for the Lamb to avenge their blood (Revelation 6:9-11). They are given a long flowing and festive robe to wear honoring them for their sacrifice and asked to wait a little longer until the full number comes in (Revelation 6:11 AMP). This scene from scripture is very powerful, these individuals are very precious in the sight of the Lord. So we too must remember their suffering and act with conviction for those who cannot act for themselves.

I encourage you to remember our brothers and sisters in Christ who suffer tremendously because they bear the blessed name of our savior. Remember to pray and stand with them knowing that Jesus has overcome the world and in the end will right every wrong!

Marriage Should Be Honored By All

"Marriage should be honored by all, and the marriage bed kept pure, for God will judge the adulterer and all the sexually immoral" (Hebrews 13:4)

God created marriage. In fact, marriage existed in the perfect paradise of the garden. It was instituted from the very beginning to bless us. Paul gives further insight into this wonderful covenant in the book of Ephesians. The main point for his encouragement on marriage is to illustrate the type of relationship that we have with Christ as His bride. He uses the relationship between a husband and wife so we can understand the intimacy that we can experience with the Lord.

"For this reason a man will leave his father and mother and be united to his wife, and the two will become one flesh." This is a profound mystery—but I am talking about Christ and the church. (Ephesians 5:31-32).

When we are united with Christ we become one with him. We are his bride, we are his wife. We belong to Him. This truly is a profound mystery! This is why we must continually honor our earthly marriages as well, because they are also holy unions. It is a covenant relationship which means that God blesses it and puts His stamp of approval on it. We are to take this commitment very seriously and honor it above all. We should remain faithful to our spouses in both word and deed.

God considers marriage especially dear and holds it in high esteem which is why He blesses this union with children through intimacy. So we too must consider this relationship worthy of great price and continually honor and nurture it. Next to our relationship with God we must honor our marriage above all.

redemption.

Paul gives further insight on how to do this, *"However, each one of you also must love his wife as he loves himself, and the wife must respect her husband" (Ephesians 5:33).* Love and respect is the secret to experiencing a happy marriage. Amazingly this attitude will also overflow and bless your union with the Lord as well. Marriage is a great illustration of our relationship with the Lord which is why it is to be greatly honored above all else.

Keep Yourself Free From the Love of Money and Be Content

"Keep your lives free from the love of money and be content with what you have, because God has said, "Never will I leave you; never will I forsake you." So we say with confidence, "The Lord is my helper; I will not be afraid. What can man do to me?" (Hebrews 13:5-6)

I went through a period in life where I was obsessed with material possession. I worked a lot and spent everything I had on clothes, shoes and purses. While it is not wrong to own nice things, trouble arises when our focus switches from heavenly things to materialism. After a while I realized that this was not the path for me, so I wrote this verse on a notecard and put it in my wallet. Every time I opened it to purchase something I had to come face to face with this truth, *"Keep your lives free from the love of money and be content with what you have, because God has said, "Never will I leave you; never will I forsake you" (Hebrews 13:5).*

This worked for me. Sometimes I would re-evaluate whether I really needed it or just wanted it. Sometimes, I would remember that there were more important things to spend my time and money on. But most often, it would make me angry because I wanted to continue shopping and buy things. However, through this process I always had to acknowledge this simple truth, and it continued to make an impact.

God has promised to never leave us. The Amplified Bible records it this way, *"Let your character or moral disposition be free from love of money [including greed, avarice, lust, and craving for earthly possessions] and be satisfied with your present [circumstances and with what you have]; for He [God] Himself has said, I will not in any way fail you nor give you up nor leave you without support. [I will] not, [I will] not, [I will] not in any degree leave you helpless nor forsake nor let [you] down (relax My hold on you)! [Assuredly not!]"* (Hebrews 13:5 AMP). Pay special attention to the fact that He says three times, "I will not, I will not, I will not!" In the passage, three negatives precede the verb, this is added so that we can understand God's resolve in this matter. He will not in any circumstance leave us helpless or let us down.

So what should our response be? The writer of Hebrews gives us the answer in the next verse, *"So we take comfort and are encouraged and confidently and boldly say, The Lord is my Helper; I will not be seized with alarm [I will not fear or dread or be terrified]. What can man do to me?" (Hebrews 13:6 AMP).* We use the truth of God's unfailing love and grace to combat the desires for worldly possessions.

Wealth is not a bad thing as long as we have a healthy godly perspective of it. We are to keep our lives free from the love of money, always realizing that it is God who takes care of us and provides for our needs. Knowing this will give us the right perspective concerning money. We are to use it not to love it. We are God's stewards of it and through us He can use it to bless and care for others which is greater by far than any worldly possession.

Remember Your Leaders
and Imitate their Faith

"Remember your leaders, who spoke the word of
God to you. Consider the outcome of their way of
life and imitate their faith" (Hebrews 13:7)

Growing up, there was a lady in our church who took the time to disciple me. She invited several of the youth age girls into her home on a weekly basis where she spent time with us in the Word and in prayer. It was a special time as her love for Jesus was unmistakable. The impact that this dear lady made on me has affected my entire life because I learned how, from an early age to spend time with the Lord.

Since then, the Lord has sent a few others to come beside and mentor me in the Word. Showing, teaching and explaining His truths until they've taken hold. These precious people have spoken truth into my life in a way that cannot be measured. As such, this pattern has propagated as I, in turn have also discipled young friends, teaching them from the Word and showing them who the Lord is as they start to grow in their faith.

The people who teach the Word of God to us are very dear so we should honor them and imitate their faith. We should consider their lives, how they live and do our best to emulate them. Paul also gave similar instruction about this, *"Join with others in following my example, brothers, and take note of those who live according to the pattern we gave you" (Philippians 3:17).* The Word of God is life-changing so it makes sense that those who spend a lot of time in it will think and act differently. We are to live according to that pattern.

Amazingly, the Lord will always send people to us to encourage and build us up in our faith as we grow in the grace and knowledge of God. We are never left to our own; He will surround us by a fellowship of believers. We can use their example of faith and obedience to pattern our lives after. The result will be unity just as Paul encouraged the Philippians, *"Whatever happens, conduct yourselves in a manner worthy of the gospel of Christ. Then, whether I come and see you or only hear about you in my absence, I will know that you stand firm in one spirit, contending as one man for the faith of the gospel"* (Philippians 1:27). Not only will we imitate the faith of those who went before us, our lives will be worthy of the gospel that saved and redeemed us!

Jesus Christ is the Same Yesterday, Today and Forever

"Jesus Christ is the same yesterday and today and forever" (Hebrews 13:8)

If there was ever a scripture to draw encouragement from, this would be it. *"Jesus Christ is the same yesterday and today and forever" (Hebrews 13:8)*. This is a foundational truth written in heaven, Jesus does not change. He will not recant His words. He will not revoke His offer of unconditional love and grace. As the world gets increasingly worse, Jesus is the anchor that keeps us safe until the end.

In fact, one of the main points in the book of Hebrews is that Jesus is the guarantor of God's promise of redemption. Chapter 6 speaks volumes about this, *"Because God wanted to make the unchanging nature of his purpose very clear to the heirs of what was promised, he confirmed it with an oath. God did this so that, by two unchangeable things in which it is impossible for God to lie, we who have fled to take hold of the hope offered to us may be greatly encouraged. We have this hope as an anchor for the soul, firm and secure. It enters the inner sanctuary behind the curtain, where Jesus, who went before us, has entered on our behalf. He has become a high priest forever, in the order of Melchizedek" (Hebrews 6:17-20)*.

God secured our redemption by an oath; swearing by Himself to make it absolutely certain (Hebrews 6:13-14). Jesus ratified this oath by His blood shed on the cross (Matthew 26:28; I Corinthians 11:25; Hebrews 6:16-20; 7:21-22; 13:20). Now we are reminded that Jesus never changes, He will be the same throughout the ages. This is an encouraging word for us whose entire faith and hope rest on Him.

Scripture tells us over and over that God will not change His mind, *"I the Lord do not change" (Malachi 3:6a)*. James also spoke of this, *"Every good and perfect gift is from above, coming down from the Father of the heavenly lights, who does not change like shifting shadows" (James 1:17)*. He does this to make His intentions very clear to us so we can rest in those promises. In fact, in Numbers 23, when Balaam was paid to curse Israel, God did not allow it, instead He pronounced a blessing on them through the oracle and this was part of it, *"God is not a man, that he should lie, nor a son of man, that he should change his mind. Does he speak and then not act? Does he promise and not fulfill?" (Numbers 23:19)*. What was meant to harm them, turned out as an encouraging word to them because God wanted them to know He will not change.

In the same way, we can let this truth penetrate deep into every thought process we own. Jesus is the same, He will not change. He will not recant His Word. He will always prove Himself faithful from beginning to end with every moment in between testifying to it. *"Jesus Christ is the same yesterday and today and forever" (Hebrews 13:8)*, what an amazing truth!

It is Good For Our Hearts to be Strengthened by Grace

"Do not be carried away by all kinds of strange teachings. It is good for our hearts to be strengthened by grace, not by ceremonial foods, which are of no value to those who eat them. We have an altar from which those who minister at the tabernacle have no right to eat" (Hebrews 13:9-10)

A few years ago a couple came to our church, started getting involved and after a while started sharing with others that Christians were supposed to live like Jesus lived, a mixture of grace and Jewish rituals and customs. They started teaching that since Jesus lived that way, we too were supposed to. Needless to say, this teaching caused problems as it confused people and caused conflict within the church body.

They avoided the leadership team every Sunday and when they were finally confronted to address the situation, they left quickly and never returned. This same thing has happened over and over throughout the centuries. In fact this is the exact teaching that bewitched the church at Galatia shortly after Paul had moved on from the church (Galatians 3).

This is why we are to remain strengthened and steadfast in grace, because understanding grace combats strange doctrine such as this. John said, *"From the fullness of his grace we have all received one blessing after another. For the law was given through Moses; grace and truth came through Jesus Christ" (John 1:16-17).* Jesus came with the message of grace, God's unmerited favor and spiritual blessing heaped on us through Him. The grace message says that what we cannot do, God did through Jesus. He has reconciled us back to the Father so that we may know and experience Him. In fact, there is not one thing that we can add to what Jesus did, so why try?

When we are established in grace then this truth combats anything contrary to it. If someone tells us we must live holy by keeping the law, then the grace of God shows us that He has already made us holy as we are fashioned after Him in righteousness and holiness (Ephesians 4:24). If someone tells us that we must adhere to Jewish dietary laws, then the grace of God shows us that the kingdom of God is not a matter of eating and drinking, but of righteousness, joy and peace (Romans 14:17). If someone tells us that we must keep the Sabbath then the grace of God shows us that the true Sabbath Rest for the people of God is in Jesus Christ (Colossians 2:16-17; Hebrews 4:9-11). Grace is able to keep us in the truth.

In the final exhortations from Hebrews we see this amazing truth; grace is what strengthens and encourages us throughout this life. We begin by grace and we end in grace, it is a constant that will never change. Amazingly, this grace received by faith gives us privileges that those under the Old Covenant never had right to. Just as these verses say, *"We have an altar from which those who minister at the tabernacle have no right to eat" (Hebrews 13:10).*

We Are Looking for a City that is to Come

"The high priest carries the blood of animals into the Most Holy Place as a sin offering, but the bodies are burned outside the camp. And so Jesus also suffered outside the city gate to make the people holy through his own blood. Let us, then, go to him outside the camp, bearing the disgrace he bore. For here we do not have an enduring city, but we are looking for the city that is to come" (Hebrews 13:11-14)

Jesus was the lamb of God's appointment (I Peter 1:19-20; Revelation 13:8). He was sent as the atoning sacrifice for the sins of the entire world (I John 2:2). He came to His own people, His own kind and was rejected and despised by them (John 1:11; Acts 4:11; I Peter 2:6-8). However, His blood was given just the same. It was given to make peace and bring us back into fellowship with God.

While all of this was taking place in the heavenly realm (Hebrews 9:11-12), Jesus' body was carried outside of the Levitical sacrificial system, taken to calvary and crucified; fulfilling scripture saying that it must be done this way (Leviticus 16:27). He bore the shame and disgrace reserved for criminals, murderers and thieves.

This shows that Jesus was the true fulfillment of everything the sacrificial system pointed to (Hebrews 10:1-5). Because of this, we should constantly consider Jesus, and disregard anything that keeps us from Him (Hebrews 3:1; 12:2). Just as He did, we should go outside of the norm, willing to accept abuse, shame and ridicule by others because of our associating with Jesus. Why? Because this is not our home, we are looking forward to a city and a permanent home that is to come.

The previous verses give instruction on how to stay steadfast, *"Do not be carried away by all kinds of strange teachings. It is good for our hearts to be strengthened by grace, not by ceremonial foods, which are of no value to those who eat them. We have an altar from which those who minister at the tabernacle have no right to eat" (Hebrews 13:9-10).*

Through His grace we have received so much more that those who serve according to the illustration of Christ received. If we continue, steadfast and strengthened in grace, reminding ourselves over and over what Jesus did for us, then we will not be carried away by other things. This grace will also produce a passion and desire for us to follow wholeheartedly after Christ Jesus even in the midst of persecution and disgrace.

Let Us Continually Offer to God a Sacrifice of Praise

"Through Jesus, therefore, let us continually offer to God a sacrifice of praise—the fruit of lips that confess his name. And do not forget to do good and to share with others, for with such sacrifices God is pleased" (Hebrews 13:15-16)

I remember a time when at the beginning of our Sunday service the congregation members were invited to stand and share a testimony from the week. We took five minutes each Sunday to do this and it was always encouraging. Everyone always shared praise reports of what the Lord had been doing in their lives that week. When you see Him working in each and every detail and moment of life then it is impossible not to praise Him.

As this letter to the Hebrews winds down we are reminded to continually offer God sacrifices of praise. One of the offerings the Israelites brought to the Lord was the fellowship offering also known as the peace offering (Leviticus 7:11-21). The fellowship offering was an expression of thankfulness, it came from a grateful heart. The person, would bring the offering to the Lord as a token of gratitude. This is why the writer ties our praise back to this offering reminding us that we are to continually offer this type of sacrifice. However, our offering comes in word form, from lips and hearts that praise and confess His name.

Isaiah prophesied, *"Peace, peace, to him who is far off [both Jew and Gentile] and to him who is near! says the Lord; I create the fruit of his lips, and I will heal him [make his lips blossom anew with speech in thankful praise]" (Isaiah 57:19 AMP)*. Isaiah foretold of this very idea; once you have been healed, restored and redeemed by Jesus, then the words you speak will be laced with thanksgiving and bless the Lord.

This type of praise offering comes naturally when we realize the wonderful things God has done for us. As in the example from our church service, we always had people willing to share and praise the Lord. It brought both encouragement and reminded others of what He had done for them as well. The result in return was that others were willing to go out, share and help others in need when the opportunity arose. This in return also brought glory to God and pleased him.

Praising the Lord should be at the forefront of our hearts and minds. We should continually make an effort to praise Him being thankful for the ways in which He works. The way to bless the Lord is by praising Him.

Obey Your Leaders and Submit to their Authority

"Obey your leaders and submit to their authority. They keep watch over you as men who must give an account. Obey them so that their work will be a joy, not a burden, for that would be of no advantage to you" (Hebrews 13:17)

Did you know that one of the functions of our spiritual leaders is to persuade us with the truth? They are to teach and show us the truth from God's word so that we will listen, yield to it and obey it.

The word used for obey in this passage of scripture is peithō. This means to persuade or convince one to believe by the words spoken. This word occurs sixty-three times in the New Testament and many times it is translated as trusted, persuaded or convinced. Most of this occurs in the book of Acts when the people believed after they had been persuaded by the message spoken.

In the same way we are to trust and be convinced by the teaching and persuasion of our leaders. It is their job to teach the Word of God to us with authority and power, then we are to receive it, be convinced by it and yield to it. In this way, these truths become evident in our lives and in return bring joy to our leaders when they see change occur.

This is one of the main reasons we are to hold them in high regard, because they are commissioned to teach and persuade us by the Word of God. This is why we are to look to them as examples; *"Remember your leaders, who spoke the word of God to you. Consider the outcome of their way of life and imitate their faith" (Hebrews 13:7).* And why we are to respect them; *"Now we ask you, brothers, to respect those who work hard among you, who are over you in the Lord and who admonish you. Hold them in the highest regard in*

redemption.

love because of their work. Live in peace with each other" (1 Thessalonians 5:12-13).

By receiving the Word of God taught to us by our leaders and elders we are submitting to their authority and making their job a joy which is why we are reminded to obey in this. God has ordained leaders in the church to teach and help bring us into maturity as well as to give us an example to live by.

Pray for Us

"Pray for us. We are sure that we have a clear conscience and desire to live honorably in every way. I particularly urge you to pray so that I may be restored to you soon" (Hebrews 13:18-19)

As the book of Hebrews is winding down, the writer is giving final instructions. He starts off chapter 13 with wonderful reminders for those who read it.

Keep on loving each other (vs. 1)
Remember those in prison (vs. 3)
Honor your marriage (vs. 4)
Be content (vs. 5)
Remember and imitate your leaders (vs. 7)
Be strengthened by grace (vs. 9)
Continually praise God (vs. 15)
Obey your leaders (vs. 17)

And now he reminds them to pray specifically for them as they finish their course. He was convinced that he had a good and clear conscience and was living honorably. However he desired to come and visit the people he had addressed in this letter. In closing he instructs them to pray that he will be restored very soon.

No doubt the writer held these people in high regard. He carefully and skillfully explained Jesus' role in our redemption from beginning to end. So of course he desired to come to them personally to see how they were getting along. Amazingly he asked these precious people to join with him in prayer until this came to pass. As believers, we have the wonderful right and privilege to come before the Father to ask and receive. What a great final reminder from this writer, the reminder to pray and ask God for things we desire.

To Jesus Christ Be the Glory for Ever and Ever

"May the God of peace, who through the blood of the
eternal covenant brought back from the dead our Lord
Jesus, that great Shepherd of the sheep, equip you with
everything good for doing his will, and may he work in us
what is pleasing to him, through Jesus Christ, to whom be
glory for ever and ever. Amen" (Hebrews 13:20-21)

This is a perfect example of both grace and knowledge in action. Once we understand what was given to us through the blood of the eternal covenant we are free to be everything that God designed us to be.

In fact, we are to use this knowledge to strengthen, complete and equip us for doing God's will. Amazingly, it is also Him working in and through us to accomplish this will. Not only is this so, but it also pleases and brings glory to God when we participate in the role and the mission that God has designed for us.

All of this is possible because of Jesus and His role in our salvation & sanctification and His role as our High Priest. Jesus is the one who deserves glory, honor and praise for all eternity because of the great and mighty things He has done for us.

"Now to him who is able to do immeasurably more than all we ask or imagine, according to his power that is at work within us, to him be glory in the church and in Christ Jesus throughout all generations, for ever and ever! Amen" (Ephesians 3:20-22).

Grace Be With You All

"Brothers, I urge you to bear with my word of exhortation, for I have written you only a short letter. I want you to know that our brother Timothy has been released. If he arrives soon, I will come with him to see you. Greet all your leaders and all God's people. Those from Italy send you their greetings. Grace be with you all" (Hebrews 13:22-25)

At the close of this marvelous letter to the Hebrews we are reminded to bear these words of exhortation. We are to pay close attention and remind ourselves of these marvelous truths. The entire book is about Jesus and how He is the guarantee of a new and better covenant.

Throughout the letter the author walks us through the fundamental principles of Christ's superiority, His role in our salvation, His role as our eternal High Priest and how His perfect sacrifice guarantees our redemption. This book ends with a call to continue in faith citing examples from the patriarchs that went before us. We are reminded to look to Jesus as our example so we do not grow weary in this life. What an amazing story of God's love that reaches past our circumstances bringing us to Him.

A few final words from the writer about the welfare of Timothy and His desire to come and visit these precious people in person. Then he closes with a charge to remain in grace. *"Grace (God's favor and spiritual blessing) be with you all. Amen (so be it)" (Hebrews 13:25 AMP)*.

And now I commend you to His gospel of grace, that you may be rooted and established in it. To God be the glory both now and forever, amen!

Summary of Hebrews

The book of Hebrews is the bridge that connects the Old Testament and the New. These covenants are completely different and yet many Christians approach God on the basis of Old Testament Law instead of New Testament faith. The entire book is about Jesus and how He is the guarantee of a new and better covenant. It is essential for every Christian to understand.

Hebrews 1 - The Superiority of Christ

Hebrews 1 is about the supremacy of Christ Jesus. It paints a wonderful picture of how He is superior to the angels because of His redemptive work on the cross. Jesus is the exact representation of the Father and was sent to communicate to us the true nature of God. By understanding who Jesus is and what He said, we can know the fullness of God's nature and character.

Hebrews 2 - The Role of Christ in Salvation

Hebrews 2 talks about the role of Christ in salvation. Jesus was briefly humbled and took on human form so he could taste death for everyone. It was fitting that Jesus, through whom everything exists, was the author of salvation. He shared in humanity so that through His death he might destroy him who holds the power of death. We must pay close attention to this so we do not ignore such a great salvation.

Hebrews 3 - Jesus is Greater than Moses

Hebrews 3 conveys the fact that Jesus is our faithful high priest who eternally resides over the house of God as a son. It shows His superiority to Moses and the covenant of the law. This chapter also serves as a warning against hardness of heart and being lured away by sin and unbelief. We are to encourage each other daily and stand strong until the end with confidence in Christ.

Hebrews 4 - The Believer's Rest

Hebrews 4 offers true Sabbath rest for the people of God through faith in Christ. This rest for God's people is what was promised throughout the entire Old Testament. True Sabbath rest does not come from adhering to the law or taking a break from work one day of the week. The believer's rest comes to fulfillment in our lives by fellowshipping with Christ.

Hebrews 5 - Jesus is the Perfect High Priest

Hebrews 5 shows Jesus as God's appointed High priest who became the source of eternal salvation for everyone who believes. He was subjected to the weakness of the flesh yet without sin. He learned obedience through what he suffered so in the same way he is able to help those who will inherit salvation. Jesus was designed by God to be our high priest forever in the order of Melchizedek.

Hebrews 6 - Warning Against Falling Away

Hebrews 6 serves as a warning against walking away from the truth and becoming reprobate (damned). Falling away makes it impossible to come back to repentance because it subjects Christ once again to open shame. However, there are better things accompanying salvation for us who continue on with Christ. We can proceed toward that steadfast hope entering through the veil which Christ has opened to us.

Hebrews 7 - Melchizedek's Priesthood like Christ's

Hebrews 7 compares Jesus and Melchizedek, a priest forever without lineage. Abraham paid honor and tithes to Melchizedek and by doing so the Levitical priesthood was blessed by him as Levi was still inside of Abraham. In this fashion, Jesus is also a priest forever like Melchizedek. However He is not of the tribe of Levi; with a change in priesthood there must also be a change in the law. Jesus has proven His priesthood by his indestructible life. Because of this He is able to save completely those who draw near to God through Him since He always lives to intercede for them.

Hebrews 8 - Superiority of the New Covenant

Hebrews 8 shows that Jesus is the mediator of a new and better covenant which has been enacted on better promises. Jesus is ministering in the heavenly tabernacle at the right hand of God not in an earthly one (which was a copy and shadow of heavenly things). The New Covenant is written on our hearts and enables us to know the Lord in an intimate way. Jesus has promised to forgive our sins and remember them no more. The New Covenant has made the Old one obsolete.

Hebrews 9 - The Old and the New

Hebrews 9 shows how worship in the Old Testament could not perfect the worshipper because it related only to food, drink, various washings and regulations for the body. However, when Christ appeared He entered into the heavenly tabernacle and poured out His own blood on the mercy seat. The blood of bulls and goats were never able to cleanse the conscience of the worshipper, but the blood of Christ is able to save completely as it cleansed us thoroughly and we are now without blemish or accusation before God. Christ appeared at the consummation of the ages to put away sin by His sacrifice.

Hebrews 10 - Christ's Sacrifice Once for All

Hebrews 10 shows that the Law was never able to make perfect those who draw near because it was a shadow of the good things to come and not a reality in itself. Otherwise the sacrifices would have ceased to be offered. Instead they served as an annual reminder of sin. But when Jesus came He offered one sacrifice for sin for all time and then sat down at the right hand of the Father. Now we can draw near to God through the veil of Christ's body, having our hearts sprinkled clean and our conscience clear.

Hebrews 11 - The Faith Hall of Fame

Hebrews 11 paints a wonderful picture of the men and women who triumphed by faith; people who believed God and pursued His promises even though many didn't see them come to pass in their lifetime. This chapter defines faith and shows that it pleases God. This is a great reminder for us as we navigate this life, clinging to the promises of God and looking forward to Jesus' return.

Hebrews 12 - Jesus is Our Example

Hebrews 12 is a call to persevere looking to Christ as our example. He endured the shame of the cross to bring us into fellowship with God, in the same way we should keep our eyes on him as we run the race of life. We have received citizenship in an unshakable kingdom so let us show gratitude and offer our lives in acceptable service to Him.

Hebrews 13 - The Changeless Christ

Hebrews 13 is a mixture of warnings, requests and final exhortations. It is a reminder to the fellowship of Christ, to let love remain, show hospitality and honor each other. As well as remembering to pray for leaders in the church. This book ends on a wonderful note by reminding us that Jesus is the same yesterday, today and forever.

About Juli

Juli has been writing since a young age. The practice of journaling scriptural insights started during her sophomore year in high school as quiet time devotions. Since then, this habit of studying and writing on the scriptures has become a lifelong learning journey.

Juli currently blogs at JCBlog.net, a blog dedicated to *exploring God's Word and planting the seeds of life*. The internet has been a wonderful platform to share the good news of the gospel of Jesus Christ and her blog is well-read throughout the world.

Juli currently lives in Iowa with her husband. Read more about her at jcblog.net/juli-camarin.

This book, and others like it are available online at jcblog.net/books or by scanning the QR code.

Made in the USA
San Bernardino, CA
29 March 2014